experienced by meditators in this tradition, which includes insights that profoundly enrich the contemporary discourse on the nature of consciousness. But the book's original contribution is enhanced by Dennison's incorporation of EEG research—giving rise to his 'neurodhamma' perspective, which significantly furthers the dialogue between science and spirituality that is of such importance in our day."

—B. Les Lancaster, founding director of the Alef Trust and emeritus professor of transpersonal psychology, Liverpool John Moores University

"This is a remarkable book. Its depth of engagement, drawn on a lifetime's meditation experience in breathing mindfulness within the Theravāda tradition, as well as long exploration of some of the more esoteric practices almost lost in the reforms of the last century, is illuminated by contemporary neuroscience and psychoanalysis. There is no more compelling introduction to the richness of Theravāda meditation and its contemporary relevance."

—Professor Jaś Elsner, Oxford University

Jhāna Consciousness

Buddhist Meditation in the
Age of Neuroscience

Paul Dennison

SHAMBHALA

Shambhala Publications, Inc.
2129 13th Street
Boulder, Colorado 80302
www.shambhala.com

Cover art: The BU yantra, executed by the author and adapted by Will
Brown for Shambhala Publications
Cover design: Katrina Noble
Interior design: Lora Zorian

9 8 7 6 5 4 3 2 1

First Edition
Printed in the United States of America

Shambhala Publications makes every effort to print on acid-free, recycled paper.
Shambhala Publications is distributed worldwide
by Penguin Random House, Inc., and its subsidiaries.

LIBRARY OF CONGRESS CATALOGING-IN-PUBLICATION DATA
Names: Dennison, Paul (Consultant psychotherapist), author.
Title: Jhāna consciousness: Buddhist meditation in the age of
neuroscience / Paul Dennison.
Description: Boulder: Shambhala, 2022. | Includes bibliographical
references and index.
Identifiers: LCCN 2021049461 | ISBN 9781645470809 (trade paperback)
Subjects: LCSH: Meditation—Buddhism. | Neurosciences—Religious
aspects—Buddhism.
Classification: LCC BQ5620 .D45 2022 | DDC 294.3/4435—dc23/
eng/20220223
LC record available at https://lccn.loc.gov/2021049461

For my family first and foremost.
And for Nai Boonman, who planted a seed.

CONTENTS

PREFACE

From the time of the Buddha, across more than two and a half millennia, practical means of contemplation and meditation have been taught to understand the nature of self, perception, and consciousness. The underlying motivation has always been to understand suffering, its arising, its ending, and the Path to its ending. The Buddhist *Dhamma* is the body of teachings that comprise this Path, and it has been the role of the Buddhist *Saṅgha*, the communities of monks and nuns, to preserve the Dhamma. To this end monastics follow carefully protected ordination lines and rules of conduct that can be traced back directly to the time of the Buddha.

During his lifetime, the Buddha predicted that at some point in the future the Dhamma and its teachings would be progressively lost due to breakdowns in the functioning of the Saṅgha together with a devaluing of *samādhi*, which in the context of this book refers to samatha meditation and jhāna (see Chapter 14). Various estimations have since been made of the likely timescale of this deterioration, or decline, mostly in the range of three thousand to five thousand years after the Buddha's death. Although there have undoubtedly been many disruptions over the last two and a half millennia, the background to this book concerns the relatively recent so-called "modernization" reforms that swept across Thailand and Burma in particular, but then more extensively across Southeast Asia, from the early nineteenth century.

In Thailand, the first major event was the formation of a new ordination line in 1833, the Thammayuttikanikāya ("those who follow Dhamma," or Thammayut sect), by the monk Mongkut, who would later become King Rama IV of Thailand. Mongkut was the son of King Rama II and chose to ordain as a monk knowing his elder half-brother was more likely to succeed their father to become Rama III. Mongkut quickly became highly influential in the Saṅgha, as well as more widely as a future king, and was a leading figure in the reform movement that regarded the existing Saṅgha (from that point on referred to as the Mahānikāy, "the larger sect") as corrupt and unscientific in many of its practices. This reform movement believed the new order would more carefully follow the teachings of the Buddha.

Mongkut and others in the new movement believed that it was no longer possible to develop the complete Buddhist Path, and accordingly the new ordination ritual dispensed with the age-old formula to seek ordination to end suffering and to attain enlightenment, *nibbāna*, replacing it simply by an aspiration to "go forth" into the order of monks.

It might also have been a factor that the renowned meditation master Suk Kai Theun, spiritual mentor to Monkut's father and grandfather, the kings Rama II and Rama I, had died just one year before Mongkut ordained, leaving something of a leadership vacuum in the old practice traditions he represented.

The new Thammayut sect took a more austere line than the centuries-old Mahānikāy, eating only one meal a day and rejecting all practices they saw as superstitious or linked to older "magical" (Thai, *saiyasat*) roots. Those old practices are now commonly referred to as *boran kammaṭṭhāna*, traditional meditation practices, by Buddhist scholars and ethnologists. Many *samatha* practices related to the states of meditative concentration known as *jhāna*, particularly those that develop high-energy states of *pīti*—also popularly regarded as saiyasat—were treated with wariness or simply rejected.

Whatever good intentions may have been behind the early reforms, there is no doubt in retrospect that establishing a second ordination line weakened the ability of the Saṅgha to function with a unified voice to protect the Dhamma.[1] This came to a head from the 1950s onward when heavy political promotion of a "new" *vipassanā*, or insight meditation, method from Burma led to active suppression of jhāna traditions that had been central to the Path since the time of the Buddha. The reform movement claimed that jhāna meditation was in fact not necessary to develop the entire Buddhist Path.

Within a few years, temples across Thailand and Burma, and soon more widely with repercussions worldwide, were instructed to cease teaching and practicing jhāna meditation, and to instead train in and teach the "more scientific" vipassanā methods.

Such is the backdrop to this book: how the esoteric, beautifully creative, and sometimes magical traditions of the pre-reform era, reminiscent in some cases of tantric Mahāyāna practices, came to be lost in Southeast Asia apart from minor traces, to then re-emerge or be reborn in the United Kingdom from the early 1960s onward. The nature of this re-emergence has centered around jhāna meditation, both the form (*rūpa*) jhānas, and the formless (*arūpa*) jhānas, as well as a parallel development of insight, or vipassanā, alongside the jhānas—an interdependence rather than entirely separate modes.

As well as the centrality of the jhānas, a key feature of this re-emergence has also been recognition of an essential involvement of the body, including its energization during development of the second rūpa jhāna by the jhāna factor pīti. Taken together, these features are highly reminiscent of pre-reform practices of the Yogāvacara, once widespread across Southeast Asia. Yogāvacara is closely related to the broader designation boran kammaṭṭhāna, mentioned already, but is the preferred term in this book because of the way it captures the profound interrelationship between mind and body—that is, it is a yoga that develops (or should develop) as a natural outcome of jhāna meditation.

Since early seeds in the 1960s, which steadily developed over more than fifty years and in the quite different cultural context of the West, there now exists a complete teaching of the four rūpa (form) jhānas and the four arūpas, or formless practices, popularly referred to as the arūpa jhānas, as preparation for the Path.

These developments have taken place under the umbrella of the Samatha Trust established in 1973 as a charity (it is now a charitable incorporated organization, CIO) to foster practice and study in the samatha-vipassanā tradition, including pre-reform understandings of the jhānas. The Trust operates three centers—a national meditation center in Wales and two regional centers in Manchester and Milton Keynes—supported by a wide network of local groups that meet in many cities across the UK, as well as in the US. Courses are offered in various aspects of meditation practice (not only the jhānas) and related activities—details are available on the Trust's website, www.samatha.org.

Although much of the content of what follows includes detailed descriptions of how the jhānas are developed, the book is not intended as a definitive manual of meditation. Like all other descriptions of meditation, but particularly so for the jhānas, words need to be put aside at the moment of taking up practice, and what unfolds is specific to the individual. Also, of course, a good teacher helps!

While I hope the book reflects to some extent the wonderfully diverse and rich tradition that has developed under the umbrella of the Samatha Trust, much of what is described is based on personal experience; it reflects my own personal and specific interest in the Yogāvacara and is certainly not intended as an overall description of Samatha Trust activities, which include a wider range of interests and activities than I could ever hope to cover. As author I take full responsibility for any errors or mistakes, or ruffled feathers, that this book may contain or provoke.

Paul Dennison
London, 2021

JHĀNA CONSCIOUSNESS

Dhammachakra Mudra: The Principal Buddha Rūpa at the Samatha Trust National Meditation Centre, Powys, Wales, 2001.

INTRODUCTION

Yogāvacara refers to the meditation practices and traditions that existed for centuries across Southeast Asia until the 1950s "reforms" in Thailand and Burma. The term *Yogāvacara* literally means a practitioner "whose way is yoga," where *yoga* in Sanskrit means a yoking together of mind and body. At its heart is the teaching and practice of jhāna meditation, which requires meditators to progressively disengage their personal "I" from their habitual everyday sensory consciousness, lived in since birth, to develop states of deep absorption leading to insight into the nature of existence and identity.

Jhāna belongs within what is commonly described as the *samatha* division of Buddhist meditation, often translated as "tranquility" or "serenity," with the second division being *vipassanā*, translated as "insight" or "wisdom." *Mindfulness*, a much more familiar term in the West and well known in its own right as a recognized treatment for recurrent depression, is just one of several basic factors underpinning both samatha and vipassanā. Historically, over more than 2,500 years, Buddhist teachers have regarded both jhāna meditation and vipassanā as essential practices to complete the Path. Usually translated as "absorption," *jhāna* has a secondary root, *jhāpeti*, meaning "to burn up," which is a reflection that jhāna is a highly active and far from passive state, and that the translation of samatha as tranquility or serenity can be rather deceptive.

In core Buddhist meditation traditions, extending back to the time of the Buddha, samatha and vipassanā went hand in hand; they were twin aspects of the Path toward understanding the human condition and the arising and ending of suffering, leading ultimately to enlightenment, nibbāna. The reforms of the 1950s, however, attempted to remove this interdependence; samatha and jhāna practices were attacked as unscientific and were suppressed in favor of a "new" Burmese vipassanā tradition that claimed jhāna, and therefore samatha, was not necessary to develop insight and realization of Buddhist goals.

The Yogāvacara tradition describes samatha and vipassanā as the "twin kammaṭṭhāna," and this recognition of their interdependence and joint functioning underpins the approach of this book.

It has to be said that the reform movement was very successful, and by the mid-1960s any organized teaching of the old samatha practices had all but disappeared, certainly in Thailand and Burma, but soon across South and Southeast Asia and eventually worldwide. The new face of Buddhism had become vipassanā. In addition, many Buddhists in Thailand where the suppression had been most aggressive also believed it was not possible, in any case, to develop and practice jhāna in a lay context outside monastic and forest meditation traditions.

However, in the West the 1960s marked an explosion of interest in Eastern philosophy and meditation, popularly captured by The Beatles' fascination with the self-styled Yogi Maharishi and transcendental meditation, as well as by the plight of Tibetan Buddhists and the suppression of their practices by the Chinese. A few accomplished Tibetan meditation teachers settled in England in the early 1960s, at around the same time that other Buddhist practices were becoming more available, including the "new" vipassanā as taught by a number of Thai monks involved with preparing the ground for the first Thai temple in London. Little, if anything, though, was by then spoken about samatha practices.

In the vibrant year of 1962, a "refugee" of the reform movement arrived in England from India. A former Thai-Cambodian Buddhist monk, Nai Boonman (*Nai* is a more formal version of *Mr.*) had escaped the reforms affecting his home temple in southeast Thailand near the Cambodian border to spend three years studying Buddhist Abhidhamma (higher doctrine)[1] in India, but at the end of his studies chose to disrobe rather than return to Thailand, where he would have been expected to become part of the new vipassanā movement. In London he was quickly noticed by the English Saṅgha Trust and within weeks invited to teach meditation at their Hampstead *vihāra*.

He was also soon given a job by the Thai Embassy to help organize the establishing of the new Thai temple and moved into the basement apartment of the embassy, where he lived for the next ten years. Ironically, the job of organizing and smoothing the way for the new temple meant working closely with the monks who would be based there, whose role it would be to teach and promote the very same Burmese vipassanā method that he had sought to avoid. Surrounded by this new public face of Thai Buddhism, Boonman trod a delicate path in teaching meditation and chose to focus on *ānāpānasati*, mindfulness of breathing, which could not be criticized. Over the following years he kept a low profile, and although ānāpānasati in reality is closely aligned, historically, with samatha and jhāna meditation, overt use of the word *jhāna* was carefully avoided to avoid censure by the Thai hierarchy in London.

Nai Boonman's unusual skills in meditation—which indicated a different order of experience than those of the reform monks—were quickly recognized by those who joined his classes in London. This in turn led him to be noticed by members of the Cambridge University Buddhist Society, second only to the London Buddhist Society in actively promoting meditation and Buddhist studies in the UK at that time. Boonman was soon invited to teach a weekly class in Cambridge—of which I was one of the original members—which began in early 1964 and has continued with an unbroken succession of teachers up to the present day.

Members of Nai Boonman's classes in those early years knew little about the background of reforms in Thailand and Southeast Asia, or the suppression of samatha and jhāna practices, and it was only gradually realized that Nai Boonman's teachings completely bypassed the reforms. In fact, his teachings over the next ten years laid the seeds for the eventual re-emergence of the old practices in a completely different Western context.

Looking back over more than fifty years, as one of the original participants, I know of no other teacher from the pre-reform era who held to such a clean lineage to avoid colluding with or being overwhelmed by the reforms. Senior teachers who remained in Thailand, Burma, and elsewhere in the region, including some very highly regarded and influential meditation teachers, had little choice but to operate within the reform system that had become the new norm embraced by the Saṅgha hierarchy. Inevitably, over the years, their teachings were affected and colored by the environment and new orthodoxy they had to operate within.

The years 1964–67 in Cambridge and London were a particularly intense period, with a growing network of serious meditators. Links with the Tibetans developed quickly, particularly with Chime Rinpoche, who established a center near Cambridge in Saffron Walden, and Trungpa Rinpoche, who had moved from Oxford to settle at a center, Johnstone House, in Eskdalemuir, Scotland. Johnstone House was a rambling country house established as a meditation retreat center not long before by another important figure of those times, Anandabodhi, a Canadian monk who had ordained in Burma in the late 1950s. In one of those "chance" but undoubtedly fated encounters, Anandabodhi had met Boonman in India the year before Boonman disrobed, with both realizing they shared a deep interest in meditation. When Nai Boonman finally arrived in London they met again, and it was Anandabodhi who introduced Boonman to key figures in the UK Buddhist world, as well as acting as guarantor for Boonman to obtain a visa to allow him to settle and work in the UK.

Anandabodhi's first meditation training was in the new vipassanā method, first in Burma and then in Thailand during 1958–61. In Thailand, however, he became intrigued by the suppression of samatha and jhāna practices, which led him to make his own explorations, including practicing for a while the Dhammakāya (dhamma-body) samatha method at Wat Paknam, the home temple of Luang Por Sodh, who was renowned in Thailand for his ability in psychic power practices.

Luang Por Sodh died in 1959, and I do not know whether Anandabodhi gained his knowledge of samatha meditation by practicing with Luang Por Sodh himself or from Sodh's senior students, particularly some highly experienced nun practitioners whom Sodh favored to continue his teachings. Whatever the case, he developed an interest in the old traditions of the jhānas, including stories of monks reputed to have developed psychic powers, so that when he met Nai Boonman in India he quickly picked up on Boonman's reputation as a jhāna practitioner with knowledge of those esoteric methods.

When they met again in London, and during the first year of Nai Boonman teaching meditation at the Hampstead Buddhist vihāra, it was rumored that one evening Anandabodhi pressed Boonman for a demonstration of psychic power, which Boonman politely declined and soon after retired upstairs to bed. Some ten minutes later, the house began to vibrate and then shake violently as though struck by a minor earthquake. Perhaps there had indeed been a minor quake at the time, but no one present believed that, and this episode might be read in the context of the discussion of pīti, and the ability of some meditators to arouse states of very high energization, in Chapter 3.

Anandabodhi was a great facilitator, as well as a friend of the Cambridge University Buddhist Society, and he was instrumental in helping both the Tibetans and Nai Boonman establish themselves in England, introducing them to each other, which led to many years of fruitful interaction. Nai Boonman and the Tibetans clearly recognized great similarity in their practice experiences, despite the very different structures of Theravāda samatha and Tibetan *shamatha*—the common factor undoubtedly being the understanding of jhāna meditation. Yet they never encroached on each other's teaching territories, and they and their students interacted harmoniously over many years, all respecting their different traditions. A few of Boonman's students, myself included, benefitted greatly in those early years by taking part in retreats not only with Nai Boonman, but also with Trungpa Rinpoche and Anandabodhi at different times.

In 1966, in a wonderful act of *dāna*, generosity, Anandabodhi transferred ownership of Johnstone House to the Tibetans, and over the following years it steadily developed into the thriving and internationally known Samye Ling Tibetan Buddhist Center we are familiar with today. Anandabodhi returned to Canada soon after, where a large group of meditators developed around him, and several years later he was recognized as a Tibetan incarnate lama and took the name Namgyal Rinpoche. Not long after Anandabodhi left England, another major change took place when, in 1967 or 1968, Trungpa married and moved to the US, where he became famous in establishing Tibetan Buddhism and his own secular teachings, which he dubbed the Shambhala teachings.

By 1967, Nai Boonman and a few of his Cambridge students agreed on a long-term plan to work toward establishing a meditation center to develop the teachings and practice of samatha and jhāna meditation. A first step was to establish a charitable trust, but this had to be put on hold due to two of the key figures leaving Cambridge to take up their first academic appointments—Lance Cousins to teach Buddhism in Manchester University, and myself to establish a radio-astronomy research project and to teach astrophysics in Adelaide University, Australia. It was finally in mid-1973 when I returned to England that the process was completed, and the Samatha Trust was born.

The following year, after ten years in England working at the Thai Embassy in London while quietly developing and teaching the old samatha and jhāna practices, Nai Boonman returned to Thailand, entrusting his most experienced students to continue the teaching. His final instruction to myself and Lance was that we should jointly lead intensive retreats together, at least annually, a shrewd request on his part given our very different skills and temperaments, but also in retrospect establishing a pattern that to this day has avoided overfocus on any one individual teacher.

I was sitting with Boonman in the departure lounge at Heathrow airport, waiting for his flight to be called, when a monk from the Thai temple in London waiting for a different flight joined us. At one point the monk turned to me and reminded me of the Buddha's words, "this dhamma is beautiful in the beginning, beautiful in the middle, and beautiful at the end," adding "Nai Boonman has taught the beginning, now it is up to you [meaning Nai Boonman's students] to complete the middle." He didn't mention "the end," and soon after both their flights were called and they left.

As instructed, Lance and I led annual intensive meditation retreats, which took place at various retreat centers across England, and over the following years regional groups were established in many cities as well as in Ireland, Wales, and the US.

As meditators became more experienced, they in turn were invited to teach by myself and Lance, typically after five to ten years of practice, as one-step-ahead teachers, all the while with the growing body of meditators slowly gathering donations toward eventually purchasing a property to become a national meditation center. As those new teachers gained experience, they themselves would later invite others to teach, and so on over the years, leading to several generations of teachers. Not long after its foundation, the Samatha Trust made a decision that would have far-reaching implications, which was to adopt a principle of operating entirely through donations, with no charge made for the teachings, and with teachers taking no personal remuneration. This is the ancient Buddhist principle of dāna that has continued as a fundamental policy of the Samatha Trust up to the present day. Over the decades following, the Trust has avoided entirely the tendency in some organizations for teachers to become guru figures supported entirely by teaching meditation, which has inevitable and mostly negative consequences on the interchange and transmission between teachers and students.

In the late 1970s a regional samatha center was established in Manchester, but it was not until 1986 that sufficient funds had been accumulated to buy an eighty-acre hill farm in Powys, Wales, which would become the Samatha Trust's national meditation center. Over the following years, restoration works to the old farmhouse and a complete rebuilding and conversion of the original barn into a large shrine room and library were carried out entirely by meditators, who learned the necessary skills as required. This took ten years, until in 1996 an opening ceremony was held attended by over three hundred practitioners, together with representatives of Thai, Sinhalese, Burmese, and Western monastic Saṅghas. Nai Boonman also attended, his first visit to the UK since returning to Thailand twenty-two years earlier. Beginning the following year, it became Boonman's habit to visit annually to lead practice retreats at the national center over three- to four-week periods.

As the Trust's activities developed, recognition of the importance of the teachings being offered grew worldwide, and in May 2000 the Trust was honored by a gift of Buddha relics from Thailand. As the Trust's then chairman, and accompanied by Nai Boonman, I received the relics on behalf of the Trust in a royal-sponsored distribution hosted by Bangkok's Rama IX temple, of recently discovered Kusinaran relics. The Samatha Trust was the sole lay organization to receive relics among monastic groups worldwide, an unprecedented honor.

Around the same time, monastic and lay Buddhists in Thailand sponsored the casting of a magnificent bronze Buddha statue, approximately 2.4 meters high, designed by Thailand's leading artist and authority on Buddha images, Ajahn Professor Vichai of Silpakorn University, Bangkok, as a gift to become the main Buddha statue for the new shrine hall in the National Center. The Rama IX temple in Bangkok organized and coordinated events and the casting, which took place on the outskirts of Bangkok in mid-2000. Several representatives from the Samatha Trust attended as well as a large number of monks and Thai lay supporters who had sponsored the creation and casting of the new Buddha statue, which was also given the seal and blessing of the king of Thailand.

The inauguration and installation of the statue, Phra Buddha Dhammachakra, took place in June of the following year, 2001, at

Fig. 1. Nai Boonman, center, and the author, left, with the Thai king's secretary, right, waiting to receive relics of the Buddha.

the Samatha Trust's national meditation center. It was attended by senior Thai monks from both Thammayut and Mahānikāy sects, together with a large group of Thai laypeople who had sponsored the gift, as well as monks from both the UK's Chithurst and Amaravati monasteries, the Burmese, Sri Lankan, and Thai temples in the UK, several hundred of our own meditators, and, of course, Nai Boonman.

Such is the background to this book, which focuses on the Yogāvacara and a re-emergence of practices and understandings of the jhānas as they slowly took on new form and life in this Western context over the more than fifty years after Nai Boonman's sowing of the first seeds in the early 1960s.

In the early years, most practitioners had little understanding of any deeper significance of what was being taught, which to many was simply "meditation." There were, however, early glimpses of the more esoteric aspects of the teachings. For example, in the

Fig. 2. Casting ceremony for Phra Buddha Dhammachakra,
Bangkok, 2000.

early 1960s some of Nai Boonman's students became intrigued by
a small Pāli Text Society volume titled the *Yogāvacara's Manual*,
based on a palm-leaf manuscript discovered in Sri Lanka in the
late 1800s.[2] Its enigmatic and disguised descriptions of yoga-like
practices felt strangely familiar, particularly in its descriptions of
high-energy states causing the body to shake or jump in the air.

By that time, some of Nai Boonman's meditators were beginning to experience similar effects, particularly myself and two
American postgraduates. Just prior to coming to Cambridge, the
Americans had participated as volunteer students in Timothy
Leary's experiments with psychedelic drugs at Harvard—and one
or both of them had also volunteered in a government program to
test the effects of LSD. For both, the strong energization of pīti
reactivated "bad trips," causing them to pause their meditations
for several months to settle down. Nai Boonman described these
effects as "psychic power practice" or "jhāna play," but chose not to
elaborate further. In fact, a skilled teacher in core samatha traditions usually avoids too much explanation and uses conventional

Fig. 3. Phra Buddha Dhammachakra, National Samatha Centre,
Powys, Wales.

language only sparingly, choosing instead to teach by "form," by
the use of metaphor, and particularly by embodying the teaching
as a lived presence. When a meditator becomes familiar with this
level of "form," it is easy to recognize a fellow jhāna practitioner,
even if from a different tradition, as happened in the mutual recognition between Nai Boonman and the Tibetans in the mid-1960s.

Regarding this principle of minimal explanation, Nai Boonman was an exemplary teacher, and his return to Thailand in 1974 after ten years of teaching, and not returning for twenty-two years, well and truly left the onus on his meditators to find their own way and to develop "the middle," as the monk at Heathrow Airport had commented. In retrospect, it was also a matter of trust that the ages-old Yogāvacara tradition—in essence the Buddhist Path—would find its own expression in a different cultural context with Westerners of very different psychological types to those typical of Asian practitioners.

It is important to note that Boonman explicitly discussed very little of the historical background or details of the old Yogāvacara traditions—neither in the years before his return to Thailand, nor during his subsequent twenty-two years in Thailand, nor following his return visits after 1996. Also, the developing Samatha Trust tradition at first placed little emphasis on Buddhist rituals such as chanting or taking refuge, with the exception of main festivals such as Vesākha Pūjā, when members would often take part in joint events with other Buddhist traditions. In fact, many members did not feel a strong need to identify as "Buddhist" at all, although usually after some time it would become implicit as part of a slow realization of being part of an ancient Buddhist tradition.

Because of the different cultural context of lay meditators in the West, and undoubtedly due to Nai Boonman's minimal approach to teaching to avoid setting up preconceptions, many of the directive practices described in boran kammaṭṭhāna texts such as "embedding" syllables or the pītis at certain locations in the body, or visualizing Dhammakāya forms also at certain locations in the body, are absent in the Samatha Trust tradition. The purposes behind those ancient forms of practice are, however, mostly understood. In the Samatha Trust tradition, the effects of the ancient forms are achieved in different ways more intrinsic to the development of the jhānas and more suited to the new Western context. Some techniques are described in Chapter 7. The transmission of the qualities of the old traditions came not so much in the particulars of technique and ritual, but via Nai Boonman's embodied presence: a rare combination of deep stillness on the one hand with a tangible sense of latent power on the other. And despite these remarkable qualities, he still somehow managed to be "quite normal," as he would often encourage his students to strive to be. And so, over the years, various features of what some of his students came to recognize as related to the Yogāvacara emerged in a natural and gradual way.

One of the most significant of those features has been the development of strong energization, pīti, as a key factor in developing jhāna, which is largely absent from other, more Westernized post-reform, "new-samatha" traditions. This near disappearance of the central role of pīti may have been due to the sometimes-startling expressions of such states of high energization being confused with "possession" or pathological seizures, which were suppressed in the reforms as superstitious and unscientific.

Some meditators in the Samatha Trust tradition have also developed the practice of chanting as a parallel form of meditation, including in more recent years a growing understanding of the use of pitch and intonation to affect the nervous system energies in the body—which is also related to understanding pīti and its tranquilization, passaddhi, in developing jhāna.

Interest in the "roots" of language, such as the evocative power of syllables and yantras, also evolved naturally for some practitioners, as well as, for a significant number of meditators, an interest in body-related practices such as tai chi and some martial arts, which have been helpful in understanding the fine-material level of awareness necessary to develop the jhānas. Some members also over the years have followed the tradition common in some Buddhist countries to ordain for a limited period or spend time in Buddhist temples in Southeast Asia to deepen their awareness of the ancient lineages.

Nai Boonman, of course, has been aware of these developments over the years, either through direct reports from his meditators or by his own observations when visiting the UK since 1996. His responses have always been to show interest and happiness at the efforts of his meditators, with minimal comments or explanations yet with subtle encouragement and hints, which has allowed this tradition to develop naturally in its new Western context.

Yogāvacara, then, is a tradition with jhāna meditation at its heart, and since jhāna is a meditational state disengaged from sensory consciousness, conventional language is inadequate to lead meditators to its direct experience. In fact, as noted above, too much "explanation" or reading of texts carries the risk of causing meditators to rely on habitual cognitive processes, to try to "think themselves" into jhāna, which can lead to a kind of facsimile experience of what they imagine jhāna to be. This is one of the distortions of jhāna discussed later in this book.

The understandings described in the following chapters stem from direct experience, over many years, of lay Western meditators practicing within a natural re-emergence of an ancient lineage. No attempt is made to analyze in any great detail written expressions of the Yogāvacara as found for example in the two best-known publications, the *Yogāvacara's Manual* or *The Path of Lanka*, or more recent boran kammaṭṭhāna manuscripts currently being studied by academics and ethnologists, some of whom, increasingly, are practitioners themselves.[3] As noted above, commonalities between the modern tradition described here and the extant historical texts include recognition of the importance of pīti and the central role of jhāna meditation, but there are also significant differences.

The structure of the book reflects this. Part 1 begins with a description of "invocation" from a starting point of what is written in Yogāvacara texts, even though in this tradition a somewhat less formal mode has developed naturally. This is followed in Chapters 2 through 5 by descriptions of the four rūpa jhānas in some detail and in particular detail in Chapters 5 and 6, which deal with the fourth rūpa jhāna and the overall scheme of the four jhānas. A steadily developing understanding of the jhānas has been the central core of this reborn tradition, with some aspects only becoming clear in the last two decades, particularly as to how wisdom, or vipassanā, develops alongside and intricately intertwined with the jhānas rather than as a separate mode, as has been largely assumed within scholastic interpretations of Theravāda Buddhist practice.

Also, the descriptions of the jhānas in this book are unique in being informed by the first in-depth neuroscience study of jhāna meditation. The study was based on EEG (electroencephalogram) brain activity recordings of meditators practicing within the Samatha Trust tradition, carried out from 2014 to 2019 and published in the leading peer-reviewed academic journal *Frontiers in Human Neuroscience* in 2019.[4] The groundbreaking results confirm a progressive disengagement from our habitual sensory consciousness as meditators develop the jhānas. Chapters 2 through 6 include brief summaries of the key findings from this study for each of the rūpa jhānas, while more complete descriptions, including original brain recordings, are reserved for Part 2 of the book.

Chapter 7 extends the discussion into the peripheral world of the Yogāvacara, describing practices around the use of characters, mantras, and yantras that have sometimes achieved almost cult status in fringe groups around the periphery of serious meditational practice. Such fringe activities have included areas of saiyasat, or "gray" magic, including sacred tattoos or yantras for protection, mantras or "spells" to influence others, and forms of astrology informed not only by the planets but by states of high concentration, to name but a few. Yet in the core areas of the Yogāvacara these simply reflect an awareness of the "fine-material" level of experience of the jhānas; practitioners are not attached to these activities, but view them rather like a background of interesting and sometimes rare and beautiful flowers in the surrounding garden.

Chapters 8 through 11 return to the jhānas to describe the arūpa, or formless practices, often referred to as the four arūpa jhānas or as developments from the fourth rūpa jhāna. This completes Part 1 and the book's tour of the jhānas.

Part 2, Chapter 12, describes the EEG study of meditators and the resulting neuroscience understandings of the jhānas more fully than the brief descriptions in earlier chapters. Supplementary material in full color, including segments of the original EEG recordings, is provided at www.shambhala.com/jhana-eeg.

Chapter 13, "Consciousness," begins with a comparison of ancient Buddhist and modern neuroscience understandings of sensory consciousness, which in many areas show a remarkably close overlap of understanding. Disruption to sensory consciousness during the development of the jhānas is revisited, to describe insights into the frequency bands of sensory consciousness and their relation to the development of thought and consciousness, leading to a brief description of hierarchies of consciousness beyond sensory and jhāna consciousness. The final section considers the subjective experience of jhāna consciousness, and implications for the illusory sense of "I."

Chapter 14 concludes Part 2 and the book, and extends the discussion to consider the Buddhist Path to realization. It includes an analysis of its distortion and near destruction in the "reforms" of the early nineteenth century through the twentieth century, before extending the discussions in the book as a whole to elaborate on the interrelations between the jhānas and the stages of realization, the Path.

The lay context to this work is important to acknowledge. All of the practitioners involved in the EEG study have been and are fully involved in typical responsibilities of work and family life. Some have spent short periods as Buddhist monks, but overall, they are all committed to a lay path. Interestingly, as the decades have passed, the lay nature of this emerging tradition has been acknowledged and respected by different monastic Saṅghas with whom the Samatha Trust has developed mutually respectful relationships. This is a satisfying continuance of a pattern of parallel monastic and lay traditions existing alongside each other over the long history of the Yogāvacara. Also, as mentioned already, none of those teaching in the Samatha Trust tradition receive any monetary remuneration; teaching is an act of sharing and generosity, dāna.

The Yogāvacara is sometimes referred to as a gradual path, equally accessible to lay as well as monastic practitioners. However, it is also described as offering everything needed to complete the full Buddhist Path to realization in a single lifetime, as is also said of related practices in Tibetan yoga. This strange juxtaposition of qualities—the gradual combined with great depth and power—is one of the many fascinations of the jhānas and the Yogāvacara.

It is hoped that the insights described in this book will complement the emerging academic and ethnographic studies of ancient palm-leaf manuscripts that continue to be found in Cambodia and Thailand, particularly through the additional information that will be referred to throughout from the EEG study, which has opened a new window into understanding the mechanisms of jhāna and their profound effects on brain activity, with implications for understanding consciousness.

The decision to write this book has been largely a response to so much having been lost during the "reforms," and my goal has been to redress at least some of those losses. It is also my hope that the material and descriptions in the book might convey some of the magical creativity of pre-reform Yogāvacara practices as they have re-emerged in this new Western context.

Okāsa!

PART ONE
ANCIENT TRADITIONS:
JHĀNA AND YOGĀVACARA

The Saṅgha gathers to listen to the full-moon recitation of the
Pāṭimokkha, Wat Sai Ngam, Suphanburi, Thailand, 1992.

1. Invocation

The picture opposite shows a full-moon monthly recitation of the monks' Pāṭimokkha, which for southern schools of the Theravāda is the code of 227 rules that monks live by, as enumerated in the Vinaya Piṭaka,[1] one of the three divisions of Buddhist texts that deals with matters for the Saṅgha, alongside the two other divisions of the Sutta and Abhidhamma Piṭakas.

After shaving their heads in the morning and following a ritual confession to a fellow monk, as witness, of any infractions during the previous month, the monks listen attentively as one of their members from a raised seat recites the whole of the Pāṭimokkha from memory. The recitation has to be perfect, since anything less would make the Pāṭimokkha ritual invalid. The assembly is attentive in order to notice the slightest error, which must then be corrected immediately, with the flawed section repeated until the gathering is clear and agrees that the recitation is perfect. The entire ritual typically takes around an hour.

At the end of the recitation, the lineage is regarded as restored, and the Saṅgha purified. Lineage means not only the ordination lineage that might apply to this particular assembly of monks, such as the Mahānikāy or Thammayut sects in Thailand, but the entire lineage of the Buddha's teaching that can be traced back over 2,500 years. Recitation of the Pāṭimokkha is the first example, and perhaps the most important, of invocation, the subject of this chapter.

The Pāṭimokkha ritual is also a reminder, in microcosm, of the ancient practice from the time of the Buddha, and probably earlier, of memorizing long discourses and their precise ritual recitation. Tradition records that this was the procedure at the First Council following the Buddha's death, which allowed his teachings to

be passed on in complete detail to successive Saṅghas and to the
world, first by oral transmission and then in the written forms of
the Pāli Canon of the Theravāda.

INVOCATION IN YOGĀVACARA TEXTS

Although Yogāvacara is predominantly an oral tradition, some
material dealing with its practices has been written in the form of
palm-leaf manuscripts, and two books based on these have already
been mentioned: the *Yogāvacara's Manual*, from manuscripts
written in Sinhala and discovered in Sri Lanka, and *The Path of
Lanka*, translated by François Bizot from Cambodian manuscripts
in 1992. New manuscripts or fragments continue to be found in
Cambodia and in Thailand, which has led to a resurgence of interest in the pre-reform practices.

The often cryptic and enigmatic style of these texts makes them
difficult to interpret unless supported by direct meditation experience on the part of those researching them, which may be why they
were composed in such a manner. This is reminiscent of Tibetan
tantras, equally cryptic and difficult to interpret, and in both cases
it is likely such texts were originally aimed at regional traditions
under a specific teacher. Care is therefore needed not to overint-
erpret or generalize from one text to another, although repeated
themes such as invocation do arise.

Invocation has the same roots in Latin as *evocation—vocare* or
vox, meaning related to voice. The different prefixes impart important differences in meaning: evocation (where *e-* denotes a release
outward) is to give voice to, or bring into being something already
known, whereas invocation (*in-* as in inward) means to give voice to
or bring into being something from outside, not previously known,
something new. There are parallels in most religions in using invocation as part of esoteric and ritual practices—for example, in
ancient Egyptian practices such as the rituals and invocations in
their *Book of the Dead*, or in the rituals of the *Tibetan Book of the
Dead*, or in Indian and Tibetan tantras and mantras.

The question of how something new, never experienced before, can come to be experienced for the first time is a profound question, and relates to the nature of jhāna. Because jhāna lies outside the conditioned timeline of sensory consciousness, where each moment of consciousness is conditioned by the previous, and in turn conditions the next, it is not possible to think oneself into jhāna and so a different approach is needed. This is the role of invocation.

Invocation in the Yogāvacara's Manual

In this text, the invocation begins with sections in Pāli commonly found in Theravāda pūjās, or rituals. First is the familiar *Namo tassa* . . . ("homage to the Buddha") chant, followed by taking refuge in the Buddha, the Dhamma, and the Saṅgha. Then follows recollection of the Buddha's qualities (*iti pi so* . . .), the Dhamma (*svākkhāto* . . .), and the Saṅgha (*supatipanno* . . .). These are then followed by chanting the *Mettā Sutta* on loving kindness.[2] The invocation ends with a dedication of any merit resulting from undertaking these practices to teachers, supporters, mother and father, and all beings, followed, finally, by an aspiration toward nibbāna.

Next follows a meditation practice based on ānāpānasati, or mindfulness of in- and out-breathing. This leads eventually to development of the *nimitta* (mental image), the five levels of pīti (energization), and the jhānas, all of which will be dealt with in some detail in the chapters that follow. When these stages have been mastered, all the other objects of samatha, such as *kasinas* (an external object representing earth, air, fire, water, or a color) or the *brahmavihāras* (loving kindness, compassion, sympathetic joy, and equanimity), are described in turn before turning to development of insight, wisdom, and the Path.

Invocation in The Path of Lanka

The Path of Lanka invocation is a Khmer version of the same homage as above, entailing the recollection of the qualities of the Buddha, Dhamma, and Saṅgha, but extended to include the noble persons—the *sotāpanna* (stream-enterer), *sakadāgāmin* (once-returner), *anāgāmin* (non-returner), and *arahat* (fully realized, or enlightened)—who have attained the four stages of the Path. This is then followed by a request for the twin kammaṭṭhāna, which are the two divisions of Buddhist meditation practice mentioned earlier: samatha and vipassanā. Although often described as two divisions, in the Yogāvacara they are regarded as interlinked and inseparable, unlike during the reforms when they were treated separately with the claim that vipassanā could be developed without jhāna.

Then, departing from the *Yogāvacara's Manual* version, a section taken from the Mahānikāy ordination ritual follows, beginning with the word *Okāsa*. Uttered at the start of many rituals in the Yogāvacara, Okāsa is related to *ākāsa*, space, and has the meaning "let it be made manifest." It is therefore the epitome of invocation and is the first example in this book of the use of syllables or mantras as an alternative to conventional language. The rationale is that in the moment when the final syllable of Okāsa ends, in that moment of emptiness or space, whatever is invoked to become manifest will become manifest.

Okāsa!
namo tassa bhagavato arahato sammāsambuddhassa

ukāsa vandāmi bhante sabbaṃ aparādhaṃ khamatha me bhante mayā katampuññaṃ sāminā anumoditab-baṃ sāminā kataṃ puññaṃ mayhaṃ dātabbaṃ sādhu sādhu anumodāmi

sabbaṃ aparādhaṃ khamatha me bhante ukāsa dvāra-
taye kataṃ sabbaṃ aparādhaṃ khamatha me bhante

Homage to the Blessed One, the perfected one, the fully
enlightened one

May I salute you, Venerable Sir. May you forgive me all
of my faults, Venerable Sir. May the master rejoice in the
merits I have acquired. May the master transfer to me
the merits [he has acquired]. Sādhu, Sādhu. I rejoice.

May you forgive me all my faults, Venerable Sir, [com-
mitted] through the doors (of the senses—namely,
body, mouth, and the mind); may you forgive me all my
faults, Venerable Sir.[3]

This is similar to the ritual confession by monks every full
moon before recitation of the Pāṭimokkha and highlights the
reciprocal relationship between teacher and aspirant in sharing
merit. (Equivalent practices may well exist for bhikkhunis and
ten-precept nuns.) The invocation ends here for the Yogāvacara
aspirant, whereas in a Mahānikāy monk's ordination it is followed
by a request for robes, and initiation for the sake of ending suffering and for the attainment of nibbāna. The aspiration for nibbāna
is repeated at other points in Yogāvacara texts and is in any case
implicit from the moment the lineage is brought to mind. This is
in contrast to the Thammayut ordination ritual where the aspiration for nibbāna was dispensed with as part of the 1830s reform
movement in Thailand.

As in the *Manual*, invocation is followed by meditation practice,
again based on ānāpānasati, with detailed development of the nim-
ittas and the stages of pīti. The rest of *The Path of Lanka* focuses on
enigmatic and cloaked interchanges between master and aspirant,
and sections detailing the use of syllables, in particular the formula

A RA HAM (see Chapter 7). Mastery of other subjects of samatha is implied, but not described in detail as in the *Manual*.

Overall, invocation calls on the continuity of lineage from the Buddha to the noble disciples who have attained the four Paths through to the aspirant's current teacher. This has two aspects: first it establishes a direction forward, but second and most importantly, it is coupled with the will to do (Pali, *adhiṭṭhāna*), which describes resolute determination to commit to seeing something through to completion and is expressed in the invocation, *Okasa*! It is also recognized in samatha meditation generally, and the Yogāvacara in particular, that strong faith in the lineage and in one's current teacher is a necessary supporting factor.

INVOCATION AND THE BOJJHAṄGAS

There are several different systems of classification within Buddhist theory to conceptualize the Path to enlightenment or realization. The main ones are the stages of the Eightfold Path itself; the classification of the four rūpa jhānas and the four arūpas; and the *bojjhaṅgas*, or factors of enlightenment, which are, in Pāli and English, as follows:[4]

- *sati*, mindfulness
- *dhamma-vicaya*, investigation
- *viriya*, vigor
- *pīti*, energization or joy
- *passaddhi*, tranquilization
- *samādhi*, concentration or absorption
- *upekkhā*, equanimity

The seven bojjhaṅgas are particularly relevant to understanding the Yogāvacara and will be referred to in different ways throughout this book. They are mentioned many times in Buddhist suttas alongside other parallel classifications, as for example in this extract from the *Ānāpānasati Sutta* translated from the Pāli by Ñāṇamoli Thera:

The four foundations of mindfulness, when developed and much practiced, perfect the seven enlightenment factors. The seven enlightenment factors, when developed and much practiced, perfect clear vision and deliverance.[5]

The first factor, sati, carries essentially the same significance as invocation does in the Yogāvacara. Both sati and invocation establish a point of reference in time and space to begin to develop the further bojjhaṅgas, the Yogāvacara path, or both in parallel.

Although we might talk about invocation and sati as starting points, it is a mistake to think of either the bojjhaṅgas or the Yogāvacara path as following a linear, A-to-B course. The factors and stages are developed interactively. For example, sati alone would be rather static without a degree of interest and discrimination, or dhamma-vicaya, the second bojjhaṅga. And with the further addition of viriya, vigor, sati is transformed into a dynamic vector, to borrow a term from physics, which leads one forward in practice.

Likewise, if invocation is to be grasped correctly, it will be imbued with these same factors of sati, dhamma-vicaya, and viriya—sati because it has to be a new moment or mental act in time and space, dhamma-vicaya to add a direction toward understanding or truth beyond conventional language, and viriya to add the quality of willpower.

Perhaps the most direct example of invocation, for many meditators, is their first contact with a tradition through meeting a teacher who has direct experience, ideally of the Path—that is, the Buddhist Path to realization or awakening, or nibbāna. Given the right time, right person, and right place, a meditator may catch a glimpse of something at first only vaguely understood and outside conventional experience—a contact that establishes a moment in time and space and leads the meditator onward.

This was certainly the case in the early years of Nai Boonman's teaching, when his quality of embodied stillness inspired students to develop their own practices. For experienced meditators, contact with this stillness remains a primary method of invocation, but now it is the recollection of the meditative stillness they themselves have developed that allows for quick reconnection to a continuity of practice when appropriate. During more formal events such as intensive retreats or group practices within the Samatha Trust tradition, simplified versions of invocation do take place, though they are not necessarily described formally as such.

Finally, there are two points that will recur throughout this book. The first is the idea of a "mental act." The verbal formula in invocation is a starting point, which quickly becomes a mental act and no longer a crudely verbal procedure. Once familiar with invocation, the aspirant can advert to the lineage in a moment, which encompasses past, present, and a possible future outside the linguistically based habitual processes of this-that, or A-to-B.

Second, the notion of invocation anticipates a loosening of the role of conventional language, a theme that will reappear in the chapters on the jhānas, which require disengagement from sensory consciousness and its dependence on language. This theme can also be found in the almost magical use of syllables, mantras, and yantras described in Chapter 7.

2. The First Rūpa Jhāna:
Attention, Vitakka, and Vicāra

Invocation establishes a direction and a setting for meditation, which is kammaṭṭhāna, literally "place of work" in Pāli. In the Yogāvacara, the kammaṭṭhāna is the twin kammaṭṭhāna of samatha and vipassanā together, listed as part of the invocation. In practice it is simply not possible to establish even the first rūpa jhāna, on which all the higher jhānas depend, without a parallel development of insight into the processes that bind a person to sensory consciousness. In this chapter we begin with the first of the form, or rūpa, jhānas.

The first rūpa jhāna requires meditators to work through the delicate stages of temporarily disengaging from their habitual sensory consciousness, usually for the first time in their lives, and if this stage is rushed and disengagement incomplete, distortions of understanding are likely to occur, including overestimations of what is believed to have been attained.

When asked, "What do you teach?" by a group of monks in the 1960s, Nai Boonman answered, "I teach the first jhāna." Behind this apparently modest statement lies an understanding that if someone can be at least helped toward experiencing the first rūpa jhāna, the experience will never be forgotten and will eventually lead them to develop further.

In Pāli, rūpa is "form" and denotes something that can be perceived by the senses. It is the first of the five aggregates (*khandhās*) of Buddhism that constitute a human being and sensory experience: *rūpa* (form), *vedanā* (feeling), *saññā* (perception), *saṅkhāra*

Temple bells, Bodh Gaya, India.

(mental formations or fabrications), and *viññāṇa* (consciousness). In sensory consciousness, rūpa takes the object position in relation to *nāma*, mind, with nāma as the "subject" in the ongoing flux of moments of consciousness.

The four rūpa, or form, jhānas are referred to as the "fine-material" realm, *rūpa-loka*, as distinct from the sensory realm, *kāma-loka*. The objects of jhāna consciousness become progressively more subtle than any outer sensory object and are sometimes referred to as mind-made. This fine-material realm may seem unfamiliar to us, since much of the time we function in a more concrete world of "this" or "that" in which objects and experiences are underpinned by language. However, it is not entirely absent in everyday consciousness and comes to the fore in moments of intuition and creativity when the rigidity of language is relaxed.

THE JHĀNAS IN BUDDHIST SUTTAS

The oldest descriptions of the jhānas as described by the Buddha are found in suttas dating back more than two millennia, particularly in the Dīgha and Aṅguttara Nikāya collections, where they appear as succinct formulas. Despite the problems in using conventional language to describe the jhānas, these original descriptions in Pāli are nevertheless very helpful and will be referred to for each of the jhānas in the chapters that follow. Below is the formula for the first of four rūpa jhānas[1] in the original Pāli with an English translation from *The Path of Purification: Visuddhimagga* (Vism.).[2] I include the *Visuddhimagga* translations as typical and fairly representative attempts to translate the Pāli jhāna factors, which I will examine in detail and, in several instances, suggest what I believe are better translations in the light of subjective experience as well as the findings of the EEG study.

In Pāli,

> **vivicc' eva kāmehi vivicca akusalehi dhammehi**
> **savitakkaṃ savicāraṃ vivekajaṃ pīti-sukhaṃ**
> **paṭhamaṃ jhānaṃ upasampajja viharati.** (Dīgha
> Nikāya 2)

> *Quite secluded from sense desires, secluded from*
> *unprofitable things [the meditator] enters upon and*
> *dwells in the first jhāna, which is accompanied by*
> *applied and sustained thought with happiness and bliss*
> *born of seclusion.* (Vism. IV, p. 133)

One of the main themes of this book is that to develop the jhānas requires disengagement from the human default sensory consciousness, and the opening phrase in the Pāli formula above is immediately relevant to this. The process of disengagement in terms of meditators' subjective experiences, as well as real and measureable changes in brain activity, will become clearer when the EEG study of brain activity during the development of jhāna is described later.

The phrase "Quite secluded from sense desires" (*vivicc' eva kāmehi*) has often been interpreted as a requirement to suppress or withdraw from sensory attraction and to adopt a more moderate and even celibate life, which for young adults interested in meditation yet wishing to lead a normal lay life could be rather off-putting, to say the least. Also, the Pāli word *viharati*, "dwells," corresponds to the word *vihāra*, used to refer to a monastery or dwelling place for monks. Taken together, it might be assumed that jhāna meditation is the province of monastics, monks, or nuns, and it has sometimes been assumed that it is not possible to develop the jhānas while living a perfectly normal household life.

In the Yogāvacara, however, there have always been parallel traditions of practice—one for monks and nuns, another for householders, with recognition that the full Path is possible for either. From this perspective, the more important significance of the phrase "quite secluded from sense desires" is that it refers to a transition to another *dwelling* (in jhāna) quite distinct from our habitual sensory consciousness. The problem is not so much with the sensory world; it has more to do with a dependence or craving for sensory stimulation. The early teachers in the 1960s and 1970s, Nai Boonman and the Tibetans in particular, were good models for striking a healthy balance in developing the jhānas while still enjoying normal everyday lives within the sensory world.

The first rūpa jhāna is characterized by five "factors": *vitakka, vicāra, pīti, sukha,* and *ekaggatā citta,* often translated as applied attention, sustained attention, joy, happiness or bliss, and one-pointedness or unification of mind. The first two factors, vitakka and vicāra, are the dominant factors for the first jhāna, and their crucial role is confirmed by the EEG study, as will become clear later.

Although not the predominant factors, the third and fourth jhāna factors, pīti and sukha, also develop significantly in the first rūpa jhāna as a result of disengaging from sensory consciousness. In the *Visuddhimagga* translation, *pīti-sukhaṃ* is rendered as "happiness and bliss," with variations such as "joy and bliss" or "rapture and bliss" offered by other translators. I do not believe these are the best translations for *pīti* and *sukha*, and the meanings of these Pāli terms will be explored more fully beginning in the next chapter.

The phrase *vivekajaṃ pīti-sukhaṃ* is translated in the *Visuddhimagga* as "with happiness and bliss born of seclusion," where "seclusion" refers to separation from sense desire. Looking ahead, this contrasts with the second jhāna formula, in which these same two factors develop as "born of concentration." The significance of this difference will also become clear as this and subsequent chapters unfold.

The fifth jhāna factor, ekaggatā citta, is common to all the jhānas and describes a depth of concentration in which the mind is absorbed in the object. There have been some disagreements as to whether this factor applies to the first rūpa jhāna, since it does not appear in the Sutta formula above, but it has been pointed out that the phrase "born of concentration" for the second jhāna directly implies such a depth of concentration for the preceding first jhāna.[3] In this book I prefer to use "unification of mind" rather than "one-pointedness," as I believe it better captures the experience of an all-encompassing absorption.

THE KAMMAṬṬHĀNA OF SAMATHA: *BU DDHO* AND ĀNĀPĀNASATI

The *Visuddhimagga* lists forty traditional samatha meditation objects. Of these, only the simplest techniques—including ānāpānasati and the ten kasina meditations—are said to lead to all four rūpa jhānas.

The first three brahmavihāras, or divine abodes—loving kindness (mettā), compassion (*karuṇā*) and sympathetic joy (*muditā*)—can lead to the first three rūpa jhānas but not the fourth, due to the remainder of pleasant feeling. The fourth brahmavihāra, equanimity (upekkhā), transcends any dependence on happiness or bliss and is the object of the fourth rūpa jhāna, so this practice therefore can lead to the fourth rūpa jhāna. The ten objects of repulsion (*asubhas*) or stages of decay of a corpse, as well as mindfulness of the body, depend on applied thought, vitakka, and so can lead only to the first rūpa jhāna, but not beyond.

Of the remaining objects of meditation, the eight recollections—of Buddha, Dhamma, Saṅgha, morality, liberality, qualities of *devas* (celestial beings), death, and peace—as well as the analysis of the four elements (earth, water, fire, air) and disgust toward food, lead to access concentration (upacāra samādhi), but they are too complex in their mental maneuvering to lead to jhāna. Finally there are the four formless states—infinite space, infinite consciousness, nothingness, and neither-perception-nor-nonperception—referred to as the four formless, or arūpa, jhānas.

In practice, ānāpānasati, the method favored by the Buddha, tends to be regarded as the preeminent route, although the ancient Bu Ddho method described below also focuses on the breath and is often practiced as a preliminary before taking up ānāpānasati. The kasina meditations involving physical objects were historically quite popular, particularly the earth kasina meditation in which a meditator initially gazes at an external disk of earth before closing the eyes to internalize the image. These meditations are described in detail in two important commentarial texts: the fifth-century *Visuddhimagga* of Buddhaghosa and the third-century *Vimuttimagga* of Upatissa Thera.

Nowadays, however, these are mostly regarded as "special" practices suitable to particular meditators at particular stages in their development. Similarly, other objects from the list of forty are also more likely to be suggested by a teacher to a specific pupil to correct imbalances of temperament before taking up ānāpānasati.

Bu Ddho

The form of breath control known as Bu Ddho is ancient, well known in pre-reform Buddhism, and is one method of samatha that to some extent survived the reforms.[4] The word *Buddho* in Pāli is literally "one who knows," and the practice involves silently intoning the syllables BU on the in-breath and DDHO on the outbreath; it is a good example of the use of syllables in Yogāvacara practices. Like all samatha practices used to develop jhāna, the guidance of a teacher is important, which should be born in mind as a limitation to the descriptions that follow in this and subsequent chapters. This is particularly the case for Bu Ddho.

During inhalation, while intoning BU, the meditator holds the intention to arouse energy, from the diaphragm and navel area upward through the chest and throat to the crown of the head. Exhalation is gradual while intoning DDHO, letting go of thinking, distractions, or "doing" and relaxing into simple peace and stillness. As a meditator becomes familiar with the technique, intonations become more subtle, and movement of energy upward leads to the development, usually, of a bright mental image, or nimitta, which the meditator is increasingly able to hold as a stable object while slow exhalation continues in the background. After a while, the sequence may be repeated, with the duration of the DDHO syllable typically lengthening each time, and attention on the nimitta leads to an approach toward the first rūpa jhāna.

The Yogāvacara is replete with the use of yantras to integrate form with syllables; the syllables are derived from Pāli roots but written mostly using the old Cambodian Khom script, sometimes interspersed with occasional other characters such as Thai or Lao. Yantras offer an alternative to conventional language, and when drawn correctly they can act as a focus for meditation as well as being a form of invocation. Figure 4 shows the syllable BU written in the Khom script, while Figure 5 shows two related yantras.

The left-hand yantra (Thai, *yan*) in Figure 5 shows the character BU enclosed by the character DDHO, symbolizing the energy aroused by BU "contained" by the stillness of the body during the outbreath, DDHO. This presages the role of energization, pīti, and its tranquilization, passaddhi, in developing the second rūpa jhāna.

The right-hand yantra, "layers of Buddha," is made up entirely of successive layers of the syllable BU, which rather beautifully encapsulates the subjective experience of arousing energy, pīti, during repeated in-breaths while intoning BU.

The Bu Ddho technique has been popular over the ages as a relatively straightforward method to gain a first experience of the first rūpa jhāna, and particularly for arousing pīti, which plays a key role in the Yogāvacara. In the pre-reform era (that is, before the mid-1960s), this method was prevalent in many meditation temples in Thailand, Cambodia, and Laos. Also, if someone is able to develop jhāna with this method, even without full mastery, then turning attention to the question of "who is it that knows" (the implicit question that lies behind the word Buddho, "one who knows") can be an effective method to develop strong insight into the nature of self.

However, by itself BU DDHO does not allow the meditator to develop a detailed understanding of what disengaging from sensory consciousness entails, compared to the gradual path of ānāpānasati. As a result, while it may lead a practitioner quite quickly to a momentary experience of jhāna, for a novice the experience may immediately lead to excitement and a rebound back into sensory consciousness. Even in those cases where a meditator is able to sustain jhāna to some degree, they mostly realize quite quickly that the better long-term strategy for developing mastery is to turn to ānāpānasati.

Ānāpānasati

In the *Ānāpānasati Sutta*, the Buddha describes sixteen stages of developing mindfulness of in- and out-breathing, one of the key features of which is to "discern" when the breath is long or short

Fig. 4. The Khom character BU.

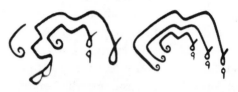

Fig. 5. *Left*: Yan, BU DDHO; *right*: yan, "Layers of Buddha."

(or quick). The significance of this is not as a passive acknowledgment of the length of breath; instead it is a detailed development of bringing the length of breath into conscious awareness, rather than breath unconsciously changing with mood as normally happens in sensory consciousness. The sixteen stages progressively develop mindfulness of body, of feelings, of mind, and of mental processes.

In a different context within the Tibetan tradition, Chögyam Trungpa wrote in his book *The Path Is the Goal*:

> [Your] breathing is the closest you can come to a picture of your mind. It is the portrait of your mind in some sense . . . The traditional recommendation in the lineage of meditators that developed in the Kagyu-Nyingma tradition is based on the idea of mixing mind and breath.[5]

The tradition taught by Nai Boonman, summarized in Figure 6, is closely related to the more familiar sixteen stages of ānāpānasati, with one key difference: four lengths of breath are used, two longer than normal (relative durations 9 and 6) and two shorter (relative durations 3 and 1), with a clear emphasis that in developing jhāna the "normal" or habitual length of breath is not used (in the diagram this is marked by the central horizontal gray line).

This technique has sometimes been misunderstood by teachers in post-reform ("new samatha") traditions as exerting too much control over the breath, whereas in practice once the lengths become familiar, they are maintained effortlessly as part of overall mindfulness. The true significance of using different lengths of breath is that it marks the beginning of disengaging from habitual sensory consciousness. The four lengths create a mandala-like space within which jhāna can be safely developed, and from which meditators can withdraw back to normal breathing and default sensory consciousness with no disturbance.

Meditation begins with the stage of "counting" (Figure 6), by establishing mindfulness, sati, on the breath by mentally counting one to nine on the in-breath and nine to one on the out-breath for the longest length; one to six and six to one for the longer length; one to three and three to one for the shorter length; and counting simply one, one for the shortest length. This is a very simple mental act of placing attention on each number sequentially while breathing in and out. It is, in other words, vitakka, the first jhāna factor, placing attention. It restricts the habits of sensory consciousness to a simple focus on the breath and number, but in these beginning stages a practitioner is still well within sensory consciousness. Counting corresponds to an early stage of mindfulness of the body in the traditional *Ānāpānasati Sutta* description.

The next stage, "following," is to follow the breath via the felt sensations in the body as it moves in and out between nose-tip and lower diaphragm, to establish the second jhāna factor, vicāra, sustained attention. This requires an awareness of sensation and feeling, a degree of subtle investigation or curiosity as to meaning, therefore adding dhamma-vicaya, investigation—the second bojjhaṅga—to the already established sati. The stage of following

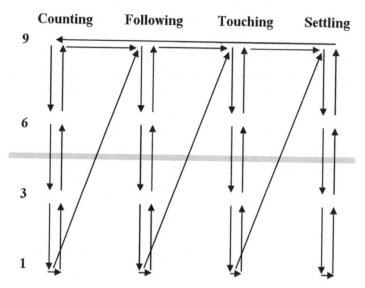

Fig. 6. Sixteen stages of ānāpānasati.

falls within the stage of mindfulness of feeling in the *Ānāpānasati Sutta* description.

THE NIMITTA (MENTAL IMAGE) AND ACCESS TO JHĀNA

The stages of counting and following are the basis for developing vitakka and vicāra. As attention stabilizes, the habits of thinking, labeling, and naming ease, interest in the practice deepens, and moments of peace and happiness begin to arise, often with more available energy (pīti and sukha). At first these developments may be subtle and easily missed, or taken for granted, and if they do become stronger then the tendency is to be drawn back into thinking about this new development, or "commentating" on it—the habits of sensory consciousness.

By this time the meditator will have progressed to the third stage of "touching" (Figure 6), resting attention on the sensation of the touch of the breath at the nose-tip. The task is now to settle deeper into a growing sense of contentment—resisting any desire to think discursively, or any thoughts of "getting anywhere" or wishing to be or do anything other than settle into deeper stillness. This also requires a meditator to better understand the deep habits of liking or disliking, wanting or not-wanting, that lie at the roots of attachment and craving. In other words, vipassanā necessarily develops naturally alongside samatha—the twin kammaṭṭhāna.

This is now the central ground for disengaging from sensory consciousness. The practice becomes increasingly mind-based, and the sensation of the breath at the nose-tip is gradually replaced by the nimitta, or mental image, which represents a meditator's growing awareness or "sign" of their own consciousness—or to borrow a term from consciousness studies, its *qualia*. Compared to a more distinct meditation object such as one of the kasinas mentioned earlier, the object in ānāpānasati, the breath and its nimitta, is much more subtle; patience, as well as guidance by a competent teacher, is required in allowing the nimitta to develop. For some meditators the nimitta may be experienced as visual—a clear or diffuse light just ahead, or progressively permeating the body. For others it may be a sense of touching something with the mind, or it might be an auditory phenomenon, as though listening to silence, among other possibilities. The association with one or another sensory mode is an internalized reflection or remnant of the habits of sensory consciousness, and as absorption deepens such distinctions fade.

The meditator allows this process to take its course toward deeper stillness without interfering or "commentating," while fully aware of whatever form the nimitta takes by a kind of peripheral vision.[6] Eventually, the nimitta becomes more stable, at which point the meditator can transfer attention directly onto it in the stage of "settling" (Figure 6). This is now the threshold of jhāna, and all that is required is to allow absorption to deepen into unification of mind, ekaggatā citta, where the subtle breath, the nimitta, and consciousness with its associated jhāna factors become one in jhāna consciousness.

The description of the sixteen stages above may seem daunting, and there is no doubt that they present a challenge to the patience of a new meditator and require confidence in the teacher and the tradition in order to persist. To become familiar with all sixteen stages might typically take six to twelve months before they become familiar as part of overall mindfulness. From that point on practice becomes more a letting-go—of the habits of thinking, labeling, liking, and disliking that underpin sensory consciousness—and a general movement from complexity to a simpler and deepening sense of peace and stillness, while remaining fully aware.

In the first rūpa jhāna, the factors of vitakka and vicāra are central, while the further jhāna factors—pīti, sukha, and ekaggatā—are secondary. The meditator who experiences the first rūpa jhāna gradually comes to understand the interrelationships between the nimitta and stages of development of pīti, and that understanding in turn is the basis for developing the second jhāna, in which pīti takes center stage.

THE HINDRANCES: SUPPRESSION OR DISENGAGEMENT?

In analyzing the phrase *vivicc' eva kāmehi* in the formula for the first jhāna, translated as "apart from sense desires," the *Visuddhimagga* adds a parallel interpretation of *viveka* to mean apart from, or separate from, the hindrances. The hindrances are mentioned in many places in the Suttas as obstacles to attaining jhāna, and are listed as sense desire, ill will, sloth and torpor, restlessness and remorse, and doubt. Most approaches to dealing with the hindrances stress the need for patient understanding of why they arise, what they mean in terms of attachment and craving, and then how to minimize their impact.

In Yogāvacara texts they are acknowledged, sometimes in an invocation "may I be free of the hindrances," but generally they are not made a primary focus as something to be worked on separately or prior to the kammaṭṭhāna of actual practice. This is in contrast to a possible overfocus in some traditions in which they are regarded as "obstacles" placed in one's path that must be overcome. Such an overfocus risks either feeding the underlying problem or trying to suppress it, with consequences of incomplete withdrawal from sensory consciousness and distorted experiences of jhāna as described in Chapter 6.

If a meditator is impatient, suppression becomes a likely result, in which case it will be difficult to achieve jhāna other than as a brief momentary experience before an almost immediate and reactive regression back to sensory consciousness. Such is the nature of repression, recognized by Freud over a century ago as a strategy doomed to failure; whatever is repressed remains ever-present in the unconscious, needing only a slight trigger to resurface.

For some temperaments, and in the absence of an experienced teacher, there is also the potential trap of assuming a price must be paid to justify relief from the hindrances, leading to asceticism or what are historically known as *tapas* in some yoga traditions (*tapas* derives from the Sanskrit root *tap*, to burn, and refers to disciplined practices to consume or burn off impurities or obstacles). The *dhutaṅgas*, or ascetic practices, of the Buddhist forest meditation traditions[7] are similarly regarded as means of purification to weaken or shake off the hindrances, and when practiced with faith and equanimity can enhance a person's practice. However, teachers are usually careful to suggest them according to a person's character type, as they can be misunderstood or even hazardous practices in some circumstances.

The same principle applies to some traditions' overemphasis on long sittings, sometimes several hours in the early stages of developing an approach to the jhānas. While this might be appropriate for some temperaments at the right time, for others and sometimes particularly for Western temperaments, it can also lead to suppression of the hindrances with the accompanying problems described above. It is important to recall the Buddha's own experience as a young boy recollecting an experience of the first rūpa jhāna while in a pleasant and relaxed mode, and his later rejection of ascetic practices as an adult before returning to the route of the jhānas.

The Yogāvacara as a gradual path seems largely free from the trap of suppression, and the additional perspective from the EEG study described throughout this book is very helpful in clarifying more clearly what the hindrances actually represent when viewed through the lens of neuroscience. Put briefly, rather than the simplistic and discouraging assumption that they are obstacles, or a meditator's problem, they can equally be regarded as signs of slow but steadily developing success in affecting changes in brain networks while disengaging from sensory consciousness. This will be discussed more fully in Chapter 6 after all four rūpa jhānas have been described.

SIMILE OF THE BELL

It is the task of a meditator developing the first rūpa jhāna to master attention in its two aspects, vitakka and vicāra, and this is well-illustrated in the *Vimuttimagga* and *Visuddhimagga* by the simile of the bell. The first strike of the bell is vitakka, establishing mindfulness, sati, as a moment in time and space. Reverberation is vicāra. If attention rests without wavering on the reverberation as it slowly fades, savoring the feeling with an attitude of interested attention (dhamma-vicaya), even reverence, then as the reverberation fades to silence the meditator is taken to a still point in a similar manner as develops in the approach to the first rūpa jhāna.

In the section dealing with ānāpānasati, the *Visuddhimagga* develops the simile further as follows:

> . . . just as when a gong is struck. At first gross sounds occur and consciousness [occurs] because the sign of the gross sounds is well apprehended, well attended to, well observed; and when the gross sounds have ceased, then afterwards faint sounds occur and [consciousness occurs] because the sign of the faint sounds is well

apprehended, well attended to, well observed; and when the faint sounds have ceased, then afterwards consciousness occurs because it has the sign of the faint sounds as its object

—so too, at first gross in-breaths and out-breaths occur and [consciousness does not become distracted] because the sign of the gross in-breaths and out-breaths is well apprehended, well attended to, well observed; and when the gross in-breaths and out-breaths have ceased, then afterwards faint in-breaths and out-breaths occur and [consciousness does not become distracted] because the sign of the faint in-breaths and out-breaths is well apprehended, well attended to, well observed; and when the faint in-breaths and out-breaths have ceased, then afterwards consciousness does not become distracted because it has the sign of the faint in-breaths and out-breaths as its object.[8]

This describes the process of attention becoming progressively less prone to distraction, while simultaneously the breaths become increasingly subtle, eventually to the point of (apparently) ceasing, at which point consciousness remains undistracted, taking as its object the sign of the previous most subtle breaths. The sign, here, is the nimitta as described earlier.

Some early academic studies of the jhānas speculated whether the centrality of vitakka and vicāra to the first rūpa jhāna implied a continuation of thinking not dissimilar to that in everyday consciousness. The simile clarifies that vitakka and vicāra are aspects of a form of attention that disengages from the discursive thinking typical of ordinary sensory experience.

THE NEUROSCIENCE OF THE FIRST RŪPA JHĀNA: KEY FINDINGS

From 2014 to 2019, thirty practitioners of ānāpānasati meditation with an interest in developing the jhānas volunteered to have their electrical brain activity (EEG; electroencephalogram) recorded while meditating. These were lay practitioners actively involved in ordinary life, following a wide range of occupations, many with families and children, and with meditation experience ranging from four to fifty-plus years.

The results of the study were remarkable and unprecedented in neuroscience terms, but from a Buddhist perspective they have provided a previously unexplored window into understanding the detailed mechanisms of jhāna meditation, as well as the nature of consciousness, and have been a primary motivation for deciding to write this book.

In this chapter and the remainder of Part 1, summaries of key findings from the EEG study for each of the jhānas will be presented, with more detailed presentations including examples of real-time raw EEG recordings reserved for Part 2. The intention is to develop an overview of the jhānas as a whole before offering the opportunity to delve deeper into the more complex neuroscience in Part 2. In addition, supplementary explanatory material is available at www.shambhala.com/jhana-eeg.

The *Frontiers* report dealt entirely with ānāpānasati meditation, the principal modality taught by the Samatha Trust, and the most important insights have come from that study. However, it is said that if a person develops a degree of mastery in ānāpānasati they will be able to practice to the same level of development in any of the other samatha modalities of meditation with comparative ease, and this neuroscience discussion for the first rūpa jhāna also includes insights from the Bu Ddho technique based on a recording of one member of a small group of meditators within the Samatha Trust to have explored that modality out of personal curiosity. Part of the motivation to explore the Bu Ddho method is that it is a fascinating example of the role of syllables in the Yogāvacara, to be described in Chapter 7.

The comparison between the Bu Ddho technique and ānāpāna-sati is intriguing. While ānāpānasati is a carefully staged gradual progression through increasingly subtle processes of mindfulness and increasingly strong concentration, Bu Ddho is a strongly focused willed practice from the outset using the syllables BU and DDHO to embody both meaning and intention. In the case of BU the intention is to arouse energy, followed by tranquilization of that energy toward jhāna during intonation of DDHO on the out-breath.

The gradual nature of ānāpānasati, on the other hand, might be expected to have advantages in identifying characteristics of the jhānas as they are developed, but in practice this was not straightforward. A simplistic view that each jhāna might have a clear "signature" proved unrealistic, and it was only after almost two years of detailed analysis that it was recognized that the very complex recordings showed certain *themes* of activity that began to make sense when viewed as stages of withdrawal from sensory consciousness.

Overall, taking the two modes of practice together, the key findings can be summarized as follows.

From Bu Ddho meditation

- Very fast response of the brain's electrical activity (within two to three seconds) following a meditator's willed intention to begin practice.
- Initial suppression of front-of-brain (cognitive processing) activity alongside enhanced activity of the temporal lobe auditory cortex areas of the brain during intonation of BU.
- This then progresses to powerful slow waves developing at frontal sites, in some cases showing a power increase

of more than 5,000:1, unprecedented in neuroscience as a response to a person's willed intention. Slow waves are unusual in neuroscience, and when they do occur are usually associated with states of unconsciousness, unlike in meditation where the subject is fully aware.

· At the same time, faster rhythms typical of everyday cognitive processing were observed to fade in comparison.

· As a meditator transfers to intonation of DDHO on the out-breath, all activity fades into a relatively quiet EEG, until the process repeats on the next BU DDHO cycle.

· Overall, the Bu Ddho technique demonstrates powerful excitation coupled with a slowing down of brain activity characterized by intense slow waves, followed by increasingly deep relaxation.

From Ānāpānasati: Spindles

The most common EEG theme by far across the whole group of meditators was the occurrence of spindles in their EEGs as they worked toward developing jhāna, specifically the first rūpa jhāna. Spindles are disruptions of the brain's normal and rather random alpha rhythm (fluctuations in electrical activity at around 10 Hz) into brief wave-packet bursts known to be related to disruptions of attention, such as in the approach to sleep or anesthesia or in situations of conflicted attention, such as distracted driving.[9] The spindles during meditation, however, differed radically from those more familiar occurrences, particularly in the deeper brain networks driving them, which were found to correspond to the mechanisms of attention known as the dorsal and ventral attention/perception streams of neuroscience.

The dorsal attention network connects the occipital (posterior) visual cortex at the back of the head to frontal sites related to cognitive processing via upper (dorsal) parietal regions of the brain. This network is known to be fast and short-term, rather like the RAM in a computer, and establishes a position in time, therefore corresponding well to the basic moment-to-moment function of placing attention in sati and the jhāna factor vitakka.

The ventral attention network also links occipital areas to frontal sites, but via core (limbic) and side (temporal) areas of the brain related to long-term memory, feelings, and emotions. Taken together, these additional networks add meaning and salience to attention, linking information in both time and space, with a correspondingly longer timescale, which corresponds well to the functions of dhamma-vicaya, investigation, and the second jhāna factor, vicāra, both of which require development of salience.

Bu Ddho meditation is an exercise in willpower, using the syllables BU and DDHO to channel intention. The dictionary definition of *intend* is to fix the mind on something to be accomplished, which has all to do with directing and sustaining attention. Similarly, analysis of spindles in ānāpānasati reveals disruption of attention as the primary mechanism responsible. The dorsal and ventral attention networks of neuroscience are central to everyday sensory consciousness, and the significance of spindles is that they are a sign of disruption of those networks as meditators transfer their habitual everyday attention away from the outer sensory world, first to the breath and eventually to the inner meditation object (nimitta) that is mind based, as described earlier in this chapter.

In the published EEG study, spindles were interpreted as the first signs of success for meditators developing vitakka and vicāra (and therefore the first two bojjhaṅgas, sati and dhamma-vicaya) in approaching the first rūpa jhāna. The fact that all the subjects recorded showed spindle activity at some time and to some degree confirms the key role of mastering attention as a first step in attempting to develop the first rūpa jhāna, and therefore by extension as a basis to go further to develop the higher jhānas.

These results also suggest that attention is the main supporting factor for sensory consciousness, since it is the attention networks in the brain that are the first to be disrupted as a meditator begins to disengage from sensory consciousness.

3. The Second Rūpa Jhāna: Pīti, Energization

In Buddhist Suttas the development of the second rūpa jhāna is described by the following formula:

> *In Pāli,*
>
> **vitakka-vicārānaṃ vūpasamā ajjhattaṃ
> sampasādanaṃ cetaso ekodi-bhāvaṃ avitakkaṃ
> avicāraṃ samādhijaṃ pīti-sukhaṃ dutiyaṃ jhānaṃ
> upasampajja viharati.** (Dīgha Nikāya 2)
>
> *With the stilling of applied and sustained thought [the
> meditator] enters upon and dwells in the second jhāna,
> which has internal confidence and singleness of mind
> without applied thought, without sustained thought,
> with happiness and bliss born of concentration.*
> (Vism. IV, p. 148)

The phrase *vitakka-vicārānaṃ vūpasamā*, "with the calming of applied and sustained thought," confirms the statement of the previous chapter that vitakka and vicāra are the key factors for the first rūpa jhāna, and that understanding those factors and the nature of attention is central to developing the first rūpa jhāna and in disengaging from sensory consciousness. That disengagement or "seclusion" from sense desire is the foundation of pīti and sukha in the first rūpa jhāna; recall that in the formula for the first rūpa jhāna, pīti and sukha are described as "born of seclusion."

In the second rūpa jhāna, however, a meditator consolidates separation from sensory consciousness by developing ever-stronger concentration, leading to an increase of pīti and sukha now described above as *samādhijaṃ*, "born of concentration."

As pīti is the dominant jhāna factor of the second rūpa jhāna, this chapter will examine pīti in some depth, particularly in light of the additional insights from the EEG study of brain activity which suggests energization may be the primary characteristic of pīti, not adequately captured in the translation above of pīti-sukhaṃ as "happiness and bliss." First, however, I need to say more about the preparation stages in developing the jhānas, leading eventually to their mastery.

PREPARATION AND MASTERY

There are two common views expressed in many meditation texts, including the *Visuddhimagga* and commentaries, that might appear to differ from the oral traditions in terms of how the successive jhānas are developed. Taking the example of the first two rūpa jhānas, it is typically taught that to develop the next higher jhāna a meditator should first emerge from the previous jhāna, reflect on its coarseness, and then reflect on the fact that the next higher jhāna is finer. To develop the second rūpa jhāna, one would abandon vitakka and vicāra as coarse and then re-enter into the more subtle second rūpa jhāna.

Taken at face value, this might suggest a degree of cognitive analysis as preparation for the next higher jhāna, which might be understood as a return to sensory cognitive processing, albeit briefly, which in turn risks undoing the gains established in the first rūpa jhāna. Those gains are precisely the degree of disengagement from sensory consciousness needed to develop the first rūpa jhāna. What is probably intended by "emerge" and "reflect," however, is something similar to the process described below as the fifth and final stage of mastery of jhāna, "reviewing," which is more a matter of direct understanding with qualities of insight, even wisdom, rather than crude cognitive processing.

The oral tradition of the jhānas also offers an alternative but closely related approach, where, before practice, a meditator who has attained proficiency in the first rūpa jhāna "determines" (Pāli, adhiṭṭhāna) an intent to practice beyond it. When that point is reached, the intent is recalled automatically, without discursive thinking, taking the meditator to the immediate threshold of, in this case, the first jhāna (not a regress to sensory consciousness) where there is an automatic reflection, again without discursive thinking, to know directly that vitakka and vicāra are now implicit and no longer need any conscious effort, at which point the meditator adverts back into unification of mind and establishes the second rūpa jhāna directly, without active vitakka and vicāra.

The second difference of understanding in the textual tradition is the view that a meditator should master each jhāna fully before attempting to develop the next. The reality, though, is that in becoming familiar with the first rūpa jhāna, the ground is already being actively prepared for the second; all the jhāna factors are being developed to some extent, and it is simplistic thinking rooted in the habits of linguistic sensory consciousness that leads to the assumption of a linear A-to-B process and a correspondingly rigid separation between stages.

The experience within pre-reform oral traditions and the Samatha Trust tradition is that when a meditator has a sufficient or good-enough understanding of the first jhāna, they may start to work toward the second jhāna. It is as though the jhāna factors and the potential for all the jhānas is present from the moment a meditator determines to disengage from sensory consciousness— the moment of invocation and establishing mindfulness on the meditation object. Rather than a linear process, it might be better described as a matter of depth—or even more subtly, as a superposed hierarchy that functions in a way similar to how the bojjhaṅgas or the Noble Eightfold Path unfold interactively and do not follow a rigid linear path.

Describing the classical Buddhist scheme of cause-and-effect known as dependent origination in 1980, the eminent American Theravādin scholar-monk Bhikkhu Bodhi states rather eloquently that "each link thus performs a double function: while rewarding the efforts expended in the accomplishment of the antecedent stage, it provides the incentive for the commencement of the consequent stage. In this way the graduated training unfolds organically in a fluid progression in which, as the Buddha says, 'stage flows over into stage, stage fulfills stage, for crossing over from the hither shore to the beyond.'"[1] I am suggesting a similar process applies in developing and understanding the jhānas.

So long as a meditator is not driven by impatience, or craving, starting to work on the next higher level while consolidating the previous can clarify the preceding level and be of great help, a principle that applies in many areas of life. It is certainly clear in the sixteen stages of ānāpānasati (Figure 6), in which each successive stage of the sequence of counting, following, touching, and settling both clarifies and deepens a meditator's experience of the preceding stage. It is also the principle behind the Samatha Trust tradition of one-step-ahead teachers, as an opportunity for teachers to deepen their own understanding by, in effect, learning from their students.

This area of interlinked yet progressive development of the jhānas is also related to the concept of mastery. The Buddhist Suttas and commentaries refer to three levels of experience of jhāna and five aspects of its mastery. The levels of experience are listed as lower, middling, and higher, and are related to the ability of a meditator to extend the duration of the jhāna.

The stages of mastery described in the *Visuddhimagga* are fivefold—mastery of adverting, attaining, duration, emerging, and reviewing—but in the context of the discussion so far I choose to first consider all the stages leading to attainment as "preparation." This includes the initial invocation, and then involves becoming familiar with the hindrances mentioned briefly in the previous chapter, which I prefer to interpret as symptoms of disengaging from sensory consciousness (see also Chapter 6). At first this is part of working with attention, vitakka, and vicāra. When the hindrances become sufficiently stabilized and the meditator is able to resist the habitual pulls toward thinking, "wanting," or "not-wanting," then it becomes possible to touch and experience jhāna, at first usually only momentarily. In fact the first experience may be so fleeting as to be not reflected on, but with patient practice it becomes possible to become aware of the moment of touch as "adverting," followed by the moment of unification of mind or absorption, as "attaining."

Mastery of duration develops alongside a deeper understanding of vitakka, vicāra, and feeling states. As vitakka and vicāra become effectively automatic, feelings of contentment take the foreground with even less urge to be anywhere other than the direct experience that is deepening in meditation. This corresponds to a further weakening of attachment to the habits of sensory consciousness, and the growing contentment allows a meditator to extend the duration of the jhāna experience.

Managing the duration also implies a growing awareness of when and how the experience comes to an end. At first this may depend on the preparation stages, the initial invocation, and the meditator's determination and willpower, which eventually weaken to a natural ending of the jhāna experience. Eventually, however, it becomes possible by a mental act of adhiṭṭhāna to "determine" the duration at the moment of adverting and emerge at a predetermined time. At this point the first four stages of mastery become complete, accompanied by a degree of tranquility and freedom appropriate to the particular jhāna.

The fifth stage of mastery, reviewing, closely related to recollection, is sometimes glossed over without full appreciation of its importance, and so it is described separately below, together with recollection.

Reviewing and Recollection

The fifth mastery in Pāli is *paccavekkhanā*, a combination of *pati* and *vekkhanā*. The prefix *pati* denotes "against"; the two together describe the experience of having turned toward what immediately preceded this moment of reflection or reviewing, in this case the just-experienced jhāna. Because the immediately preceding jhāna state is free from the hindrances and from the habitual attachment processes of sensory consciousness—including liking/disliking, or wanting/not-wanting—this is a moment of clear comprehension close to wisdom or direct knowledge. It might also be considered a development of mindfulness, sati, to sati-*sampajañña*, "knowing together with." Following this direct understanding and knowledge of what has been experienced, recollection at a future time becomes possible, which completes the five aspects of mastery.

At first, the subtlety of the stage of emerging may be unclear before reverting to sensory consciousness, and it is therefore of great benefit if a meditator introduces recollection as a regular exercise at the end of a practice even from the early stages of ānāpānasati. In fact without beginning to practice recollection, meditators may not even realize they have touched jhāna at all in their initial experiences. The procedure is simply to stay with the stillness a little longer at the end of a practice before moving—either mentally or physically—and without being drawn back to *thinking about* what has been experienced. The quality of the stillness itself will be the quality of the jhāna that has been experienced, without thinking about it. In the case of the first rūpa jhāna, this will include feelings of stability and steadiness due to the stability of vitakka and vicāra, with some degree also of peace and happiness. After a while the state loosens back to ordinary sensory consciousness, reflection, and thinking. This process will be elaborated further as we move on to describe the higher jhānas.

This is different from (for example) ending a practice to examine what can be remembered using conventional language, no matter whether spoken or not. Since jhāna lies outside normal language, any conclusions made about what is believed to have been experienced are likely to be cognitive constructions, missing the point or misinterpreting direct experience. So the forms of recollection or reviewing described above do not involve a return to coarse everyday cognitive "thinking about."

The capacity to formulate cognitive constructions as a kind of facsimile experience of jhāna should not be underestimated, particularly for those who rely on strongly developed thinking and intellectual capacities, including what might have been read about jhāna. In fact, it will become clear in Chapters 12 and 13 that brain networks habitually operate in feedback patterns, recognized in both modern neuroscience as well as in Buddhist dependent origination, that make such reinforcement of cognitive constructions rather easy. It is one of the aims and benefits of jhāna meditation to disengage from such processes.

THE NIMITTA AND PĪTI

Recollection of, familiarity with, and confidence in the processes of vitakka and vicāra allows attention to become stable and largely automatic as part of sati, mindfulness, and strengthening concentration.

Subjectively, the experience of pīti and sukha "born of concentration" has two aspects: a sense of more available energy, which equates to viriya, vigor, the third bojjhaṅga; and feelings of contentment, happiness, or even bliss, affecting both body and mind. At this stage, or even earlier for some meditators, there develops a clear relationship between pīti as energization and the nimitta (or mental image, mentioned in the previous chapter as the visual, tactile, auditory, or other sensory phenomena that meditators experience initially) as a growing awareness of their own minds.

The role of pīti and its interrelationship with the nimitta is central to the Yogāvacara. In both the *Yogāvacara's Manual* and *The*

Path of Lanka, invocation is immediately followed by ānāpānasati and an aspiration for the three forms of the nimitta and the five pītis.

The first level of development of the nimitta is the transition from the physical sensation of the touch of the breath at the nose-tip to the growing awareness of the consciousness of that touch. This is the preliminary work, or *parikamma* nimitta, the first of the three forms of the nimitta aspired to in the Yogāvacara invocations, and is said to be apprehended by the "door of the eye."[2] This first form is changeable and elusive, and the meditator needs to resist any pull to examine it as a primary object, continuing to develop ever more subtle attention to the breath, and the associated feelings and sensations, while concentration steadily increases.

As the level of mind-experience becomes more familiar (also referred to as the "fine-material" level of experience), the nimitta becomes more stable and becomes held entirely in the mind in its second form, the *uggaha* nimitta, or acquired sign, which in the Yogāvacara is said to be apprehended by the "door of the mind."

As the breath becomes finer and more subtle, everything comes together toward absorption, or ekaggatā citta: unification of mind, the fifth jhāna factor, as in the first rūpa jhāna. The nimitta, the breath, and consciousness of the whole come together as the *patibhāga* nimitta, the third form of the nimitta, or counterpart sign, apprehended now by the "door of touch." This leads to the embodied experience of jhāna and is the basis referring to this practice as Yogāvacara, for it is a means of yoking body and mind.

The term *samādhijaṃ*, "born of concentration," in the formula for the second rūpa jhāna reflects the higher level of concentration required to develop the second jhāna. The term *samādhi*, used here, is itself usually translated as "concentration," but derived from the Sanskrit root *sam*, meaning "together," "unite," or "complete," it conveys something more akin to yoga, a unification or complete state, in this case of body-mind, where nothing feels left out. Although not named as a jhāna factor, *samādhi* conveys much more clearly than the term *ekaggatā citta* the subjective experience of "embodied presence," and from this point can be said to become a feature of the second and higher jhānas.

Interestingly, during the early years of his teaching in London and Cambridge, Nai Boonman almost exclusively described meditation in terms of concentration and mindfulness, with no mention for many years of the jhāna factors and their meanings until a significant practical experience of the jhānas had developed. In many respects, concentration and mindfulness stand for samatha and vipassanā, and both begin in very simple ways to eventually become the final two stages of the Eightfold Path: *samma sati*, right mindfulness, and *samma samādhi*, right concentration. Although neither sati nor samādhi are named as jhāna factors, they are both present all the way through.

Pīti develops in parallel with the nimitta, usually beginning in the touching and settling stages of ānāpānasati, and at the stage of the uggaha nimitta it is experienced as bodily sensations of varying intensity as listed in Table 1. Subjectively, it is as though the body is increasingly coming to life, or waking up, which also becomes part of the experience of samādhi.

When the nimitta develops to the stage of the patibhāga nimitta, pīti is mostly experienced as light, while at the same time the physical sensations become increasingly tranquilized and part of the developing samādhi and eventual absorption of jhāna. The Pāli terms for the stages of pīti are listed in the left-hand column of Table 1, with the descriptions of each from *The Path of Lanka* and the *Yogāvacara's Manual* in columns 2 and 3, and associations to the five elements in column 4.

The five pītis are also sometimes linked in the same order to the five jhāna factors, which at face value might seem to suggest the full range of the pītis becomes available only to a person who has experience of all four rūpa jhānas, which does not quite fit subjective experience. The more likely point might be that it is the all-pervading suffusion of the fifth pharanā pīti that marks the point

Table 1: Stages of Development of Pīti

Pīti	The Path of Lanka	Yogāvacara's Manual	Element
1. *khuddikā pīti*	Cool shivers across the body	Lesser thrill	Earth
2. *khanikā pīti*	Cool envelops the body	Momentary flash	Fire
3. *okkantikā pīti*	Carried by waves that flood the body	Flooding rapture	Water
4. *ubbegā pīti*	Raised and glides	Transporting rapture	Air
5. *pharanā pīti*	The body empties and inflates	All-pervading rapture	Space

where all bodily disturbance fades to be replaced by a degree of equanimity present to some degree in the absorptions of each of the second and higher jhānas.

There are also references in the *Manual* and *Path* to qualities of the nimitta, including color for the different levels of pīti, as well as "placing" the pītis (or syllables) in order at different locations in the body. One such group of locations includes the head, throat, sternum, navel, and the whole body.

The Path of Lanka descriptions of the pītis are as bodily sensations, physical movements, and effects, closer to my preference for "energization" rather than "joy" as a translation of pīti. Bu Ddho practice also suggests an arousing of energy, as does the EEG evidence to be described below. On the other hand, the translations from the *Yogāvacara's Manual* use the ambiguous word "rapture" for the three strongest forms of pīti, which superficially suggests a mental feeling. However, the Pāli words *okkantikā*, *ubbegā*, and *pharanā* are better translated as "wave-like," "transports," and "suffuses," as in *The Path of Lanka* descriptions, with no implication of joy or happiness, or any other feeling. Rapture is therefore not a good rendering, although this is not to say that a mental feeling tone such as joy or happiness might not arise as a secondary reaction to pīti. This secondary reaction might have been assumed to be the chief characteristic of pīti itself by authors of these Yogāvacara texts. Although there is an implicit understanding in the Yogāvacara that certain areas in the body have particular significance during the processes of developing the pītis, this is not explicitly described in terms of chakras, as in yoga traditions. In fact, any descriptions of the body in Yogāvacara texts tend to be enigmatically cloaked— and probably deliberately so. In the tradition taught by Nai Boonman, there is also no reference made to chakras, and the only example of "placing" in the early teachings was to suggest gazing "ahead" (with eyes closed) in the initial stages of developing the nimitta. When asked about chakras, Boonman replied that it was better to let the practice unfold without expectations that it would develop in a particular way.

On the other hand, the nature of the practice using four lengths of breath implicitly develops an awareness of different areas of the body, particularly when following the course of the breath and the subtly different sensations at nose-tip, throat, chest, and diaphragm. Meditators also become more mindful of any tensions and other sensations in the body, including awareness that deeply held memories can sometimes affect certain areas of the body. Usually, if not interfered with (and after the meditator has gained familiarity with pīti), such tensions dissolve or become integrated into deeper levels of samādhi.

Also, when becoming familiar with the higher jhānas, meditators realize that the nimitta does not "belong" anywhere and can be placed by a simple act of will anywhere in the body. This is often coupled with mettā or loving kindness practice, first to oneself and gradually suffusing the whole body with the *mettā-nimitta*, and then expanding it outward beyond the body to others and to all beings.

In the long run, meditators come to understand that the subtleties of the nimitta and pīti are far removed from rigid distinctions or positions. As experience develops, the nimitta can not only be placed anywhere, but also its brightness and color can be changed by an act of will, and it can be used skillfully to restore balance in the nervous system, sometimes for purposes of healing.

Pīti and Passaddhi

The arousal of high energy states observed in the EEG at this stage of a person's progress in developing the jhānas strongly suggested that such energization is the counterpart of the jhāna factor pīti, related to a freeing and increased availability of energy due to less being required to maintain the complex cortical networks supporting our everyday sensory consciousness and "I" self-representation.

As the second most prevalent theme following spindles, this release of energy also corresponds to ancient understanding of the jhānas, that, following the mastery of attention (vitakka and vicāra) in the first rūpa jhāna, the second rūpa jhāna involves mastering pīti. Normally pīti develops naturally, its strength varying for different meditators—for some it is quite mild, while in others it is strong enough to make the body shake or even jump in the air. Some meditators describe it as a sense of the body waking up, and the task in the second rūpa jhāna is to experience this process and to learn how to tranquilize the energy (passaddhi, the fifth bojjhaṅga) into deeper absorption or samādhi.

In the mostly oral traditions of the Yogāvacara, methods are sometimes taught to deliberately arouse especially intense pīti, which some meditators find helpful in deepening their understanding of the subtle nature of its arousal and then tranquilization. The Bu Ddho technique already described in the previous chapter is one method, and can be practiced even without using the syllables, simply with the intention to "collect" energy during each in-breath, progressively strengthening and brightening the nimitta during successive in-breaths. This is best practiced under the guidance of an experienced teacher and is not dissimilar to the Tibetan yoga practice of *tummo*, or "vase breathing."[3] In both cases the breath-energy is initially concentrated in the stomach/ diaphragm area, then led upward toward the crown of the head.

Some EEG recordings of what happens in the brain during such practices are described in Part 2. Much more dramatic than the rhythmic high-energy slow waves described in the normal development of ānāpānasati, the recordings have many similarities to EEG activity during epileptic seizures. These include brief "spike-wave" bursts in posterior regions of the brain as well as brief "ictal" bursts—a term used in epilepsy to describe bursts of EEG activity associated with physical movement, such as a jerk or spasm, which are usually followed by the main clonic seizure (see Part 2, Chapter 12). *Clonic* refers to the familiar outward signs of grand-mal epilepsy such as strong shaking or spasms, during which in epilepsy the subject is unconscious.

In several of the meditation examples, underlying cortical sources included temporal locations, which is a familiar finding also in temporal lobe epilepsy. Unlike in epilepsy, however, the meditator is fully conscious and with practice is able to arouse such states at will and with no discomfort, and equally to return to normal everyday functioning with no discomfort.

As a former consultant psychotherapist in a large London hospital, I remember showing a senior epilepsy consultant some early recordings. When he had finally convinced himself the recordings were genuine, he was stunned to realize such high-energy states, in many respects similar to grand-mal seizures, could be evoked at will, with no discomfort, entered for a duration, and left at will. Over the years, discussions have been held intermittently to explore whether elements of the techniques might be transferable and taught to epilepsy sufferers to try to mitigate the strength and frequency of their seizures, but to date this has not progressed any further.

One of the benefits of exploring pīti with these very active techniques parallels the stages of mastery of jhāna described earlier. First is mastery of its arousal, then managing its duration, and then the ability to tranquilize the energization and return to normal functioning with no problems or after-effects. Gradually the nature of pīti becomes clear, and rather than any false pride in being able to arouse strong pīti, the meditator realizes the more valuable skill is to manage the subtle processes of its incorporation into deeper samādhi by the application of passaddhi, tranquilization. They also realize how this reflects an increasingly important role of bodily integration into samādhi.

During the reform period, practices known for centuries as means to develop very strong pīti were effectively suppressed (perhaps due to outer appearances being confused with superstitious fears of possession) and are now no longer widely known or practiced. In the early years of the developing Samatha Trust tradition in the UK, a small number of Nai Boonman's students began to experience strong pīti, much to the surprise of Nai Boonman, who had not actively taught specific techniques. Some years later he commented to me that he found it remarkable that this could happen in a natural way for Westerners outside a monastic environment.

With the encouragement of Nai Boonman and following his return to Thailand in 1974, his more experienced students continued to develop their interest, on occasion teaching the techniques over the years, but generally in a low-key way, partly still as a reaction to the reform suppressions and a wish to protect the old techniques. However, by the mid-1990s it became clear how important such practices can be in deepening understandings of jhāna, and how rare it is to have the opportunity to develop this area. Subsequently it has become a regular practice on longer retreats, initially with Nai Boonman, to ask different meditators to demonstrate how powerful pīti can become in front of the larger group. These were, and are, powerful and moving occasions, often arousing strong pīti in some of those watching, helping to consolidate their own understanding of the processes.

SIMILE OF A TRANQUIL POOL

The simile of a tranquil pool for the second rūpa jhāna appears frequently in Buddhist texts, and this description is based on the *Visuddhimagga* version. It describes a still and clear pool of water, fed from a spring where the water (the symbol for "joy and bliss born of concentration") wells up cool and pure from within, saturating the entire pool (that is, suffusing every part of the meditator), and overflowing to spread afar.

This describes the culmination of the second rūpa jhāna when pīti, even the strongest development of flooding rapture, has been fully tranquilized by passaddhi into an all-encompassing body-mind samādhi. The still surface reflects reality like a mirror, with no ripples or disturbance. Still and clear.

In the Yogāvacara, which is replete with maternal and birth symbolism, this is sometimes likened to the safety and self-sufficiency of returning to the womb, but with more discrimination and possibilities than the original scene.

THE NEUROSCIENCE OF THE SECOND RŪPA JHĀNA: KEY FINDINGS

For the first rūpa jhāna, the EEG study highlighted the role of attention in the early stages of disengaging from sensory consciousness, with intriguing correspondences between modern neuroscience understandings of the brain's attention/perception networks and ancient jhāna models of attention described by the first two jhāna factors, vitakka and vicāra—directing or placing attention and sustaining attention, respectively. Disruptions of the "normal" attention networks of sensory consciousness were evidenced by spindles in the EEG, and in this section I describe the next most common theme of EEG activity as a meditator progresses toward the higher jhānas, which was the development of slow rhythmic activity that occurred to some degree for roughly two-thirds of the subjects, in some cases reaching very high intensity levels. Such slow rhythmic activity is unusual in neuroscience, except in some states of unconsciousness such as deep sleep or coma, yet meditators are still highly alert and fully conscious.

The EEG recordings of Bu Ddho practitioners described in the previous chapter also showed high intensity slow waves, but those were isolated single slow waves at frontal sites whereas the slow waves in ānāpānasati were sustained continuously over different areas of the head, sometimes for most of the duration of a recording up to forty minutes or more. The difference, I believe, relates to the Bu Ddho method being an exercise in willpower focused on the short-term use of the syllables BU and DDHO, whereas ānāpānasati is a continuous, gradual practice that develops through successively subtler stages.

At first glance, the meditation slow waves have some similarities to slow waves in the deepest stages of sleep or in some stages of anesthesia or coma, but on closer inspection they were found to be significantly slower, with time periods around eight seconds on average compared to around one second for the other modalities (related to the heart rate). In fact evidence was found of even slower rhythms with timescales of twenty to fifty seconds, rare in neuroscience and certainly never with such regular and consistent rhythmicity as observed during meditation. Such very slow activity is termed infraslow waves (ISWs) and was an early indicator of a likely slow metabolic factor during jhāna meditation, much slower than the faster electrical rhythms seen in the brain during sensory consciousness.

In some cases, these meditational ISWs reached extraordinarily high levels of intensity rarely if ever seen in neuroscience research, and it was eventually realized this could be the counterpart of the energization of pīti, the third jhāna factor, which is the dominant factor in developing the second rūpa jhāna as the gateway to the third and fourth rūpa jhānas.

Some meditators also showed high responsiveness to cued intentions to begin to develop the second rūpa jhāna, with rapid onset of strong ISWs. Once established, the ISWs typically followed a rhythmic cycle of alternating excitation/inhibition, therefore balancing overall energy over extended periods of time in this mode. Also, once established, the previously faster and weaker rhythms typical of everyday sensory consciousness gradually fade in comparison.

Alongside these major differences to slow waves in sleep, anesthesia, and coma, the most striking feature is of course that meditators are fully conscious—most would say vividly so.

Once these ISWs were identified, my study turned to analyzing the cortical regions responsible for this brain activity. This analysis—of over 2,500 seconds of data from seven independent recordings of the strongest and most clearly defined ISWs—revealed major and unexpected changes in brain networks as jhāna becomes more deeply established. The results are described in some detail in Part 2 of this book, but for now the key regions of interest can be summarized as follows:

· Frontal activity amounting to around 24% of the total activity
· Strong activity around the crown of the head amounting to around 44% of the total activity
· Activity at the rear of the head (occipital cortex) amounting to around 20% of the total activity
· Activity in the temporal/occipital cortex (left- or right-rear of head) amounting to around 12% of the total activity

Increasingly strong energization near the vertex, or crown of head area, accounted for almost half of the total brain activity. This indicates a developing vertical axis of brain network activity, which is so different from any previously recorded EEG activity during everyday consciousness that it was tentatively interpreted as a sign of a developing vertical axis of jhāna consciousness. This vertical axis appears to develop in the second rūpa jhāna, eventually dominating the overall brain activity in the higher jhānas as will become clear in the next two chapters. This crown-of-head energization was an unexpected and key finding of the study, as far as I am aware never previously seen in neuroscience studies of any other forms of meditation. It is tempting to speculate whether this kind of activation is related to ancient descriptions of a "crown chakra" in some yoga traditions.

In the *Frontiers in Human Neuroscience* paper, the frontal (~24%) and posterior/temporal (~12%) regions in the bulleted list above were hypothesized to represent activity around the subject-object poles of normal sensory consciousness—the posterior visual cortex as the "I/eye" subject position, and the frontal cortex normally specialized in executive/cognitive functions representing the object position.

4. THE THIRD RŪPA JHĀNA: SUKHA, "FULLY CONSCIOUS"

The development of the third rūpa jhāna is described as follows:

> *In Pāli,*
>
> pītiyā ca virāgā upekhako ca viharati sato ca
> sampajāno sukhañ ca kāyena paṭisaṃvedeti yaṃ
> taṃ ariyā ācikkhanti: "upekhako satimā sukha
> vihārīti tatiyaṃ jhānaṃ
> upasampajja viharati." (Dīgha Nikāya 2)
>
> *With the fading away of happiness as well [the
> meditator] dwells in equanimity, and mindful and fully
> aware feels bliss with his body; enters upon and dwells
> in the third jhāna, on account of which the Noble Ones
> announce: "[The meditator] dwells in bliss who has
> equanimity and is mindful." (Vism. IV, p. 151)*

Despite the above translation of pīti as "happiness," and in other translations as "joy," I shall retain the Pāli *pīti* or use "energization" as an alternative translation from here on, following the discussion in the previous chapter. Thus, *pītiyā ca virāgā*, "with the fading of pīti," is the starting point for the third rūpa jhāna.

COMPLETELY CONSCIOUS

The phrase *upekhako ca viharati sato ca sampajāno* is translated above as "dwells in equanimity, and mindful and fully aware." In other translations, *sampajāno* is rendered as "completely conscious," and this is the first occurrence in descriptions of the jhānas of an experience in which a meditator becomes fully conscious, or fully aware, which is an important concept given that we might superficially assume we are always fully conscious when awake. Its implication is that we are mostly not as fully conscious as we would like to think we are.

In the formula above, it is the fading of pīti in the second rūpa jhāna that leads to the quality of being "fully conscious" in the third. And recalling that Yogāvacara descriptions of pīti clearly describe bodily based energization, as does the EEG study, then it follows that it is the total calming of all bodily disturbance that leads to a purely mental experience of equanimity, *upekhako*, which is mindful and fully conscious, *sampajāno*.

This is in contrast to sensory consciousness, during which a person lives within an unbroken stream of being conscious of "this" or "that." In the first rūpa jhāna, even though the two aspects of attention, vitakka and vicāra, have become stabilized at the point of absorption, sensory consciousness is still nearby in potential, sometimes referred to as the "close enemy" of the first jhāna. And since vitakka and vicāra themselves perform a key role in the sensory consciousness of "this" or "that," a meditator in the first rūpa jhāna is still far from the perfectly undisturbed equanimity that develops in the higher jhānas, which is the quality being pointed to as underlying the "fully conscious" quality of the third rūpa jhāna.

Similarly, in the second rūpa jhāna, so long as any vestige of bodily disturbance remains, then a meditator is prone to bodily sensations, including those of pīti, becoming an object of consciousness, making perfect equanimity impossible. This is the case until the most developed stage of "all-pervading" pīti, when the whole body becomes suffused, leaving no part to be discriminated against any other part, corresponding to the stage of tranquilization of pīti that both completes the second rūpa jhāna and presages the equanimity, upekkhā, of the third rūpa jhāna, and later the fourth.

In the third rūpa jhāna, then, the meditator rests in equanimity. Consciousness simply consists in equanimity itself, experienced as sukha, translated above as "bliss." To help clarify the Pāli terms for the jhāna factors, including sukha, the Buddhist model of a person and mental functioning, the khandhās, or aggregates, provides a helpful background.

The Buddhist Khandhās

The five khandhās describe the processes that make up a person's engagement with the world; in other words they deal with sensory consciousness and what might be called associated thought processes. The factors are rūpa, vedanā, saññā, saṅkhārā, and viññāṇa, and the first stage in the sensory thought process is when attention is drawn to an object, rūpa, via sensory input.

The first reaction to such an input is affective—a very basic response in which the object is "felt." This is vedanā, feeling, experienced as pleasant, unpleasant, or neutral, with no emotional or higher-level cognitive processing at this stage. "Cognitive processing," here, refers to discriminative thinking or labeling of "this" or "that." If the impression is strong enough, saññā, perception, performs the function of recognition, usually in relation to memory, and then further processing and mental activities follow, described as saṅkhārā, usually translated as mental formations but which could equally be described as various levels of cognitive processing. Finally, the whole group of processes come together in consciousness, viññāṇa.[1]

In terms of the jhāna factors, the first factor, vitakka, the most basic aspect of attention, belongs to the earliest stage in the thought process where attention is drawn to the object, rūpa, with the second jhāna factor, vicāra, sustained attention, following closely. The next stage in the thought process related to vedanā, feelings, is paralleled in the jhāna sequence by the third and fourth jhāna factors, pīti and sukha.

Pīti and Sukha

As the extracts at the start of this and previous chapters show, *pīti* and *sukha* are commonly translated as "joy" and "happiness," which at face value appear to be feelings. However, in the analysis of mental processes in the Buddhist Abhidhamma, pīti falls within the saṅkhārā group of the khandhās, while sukha falls within the feelings group, viññāṇa.[2] So pīti is not regarded as a feeling, in which case "joy" is not an appropriate translation for *pīti*. As a member of the saṅkhārā group, pīti in the Abhidhamma is considered a conative factor, one of several factors that are active following perception and feeling that complete the thought process culminating in consciousness and action. The subjective experience during meditation while developing the second rūpa jhāna is of bodily energization, also confirmed in the EEG study, so the choice of "energization" as a preferred translation seems justified.

Sukha, on the other hand, commonly translated as "happiness" or "bliss," is a member of the feelings group, viññāṇa. The Abhidhamma describes feelings as arising in either the mind, the body, or both, but describes the sukha that arises as a jhāna factor as entirely a mental feeling. Bodily pleasant feeling, on the other hand, is described in the Abhidhamma as that which accompanies wholesome body consciousness. Certainly the subjective experience in samatha and jhāna meditation appears to be both pleasant bodily and mental feeling, difficult to discriminate separately and seemingly highly interdependent—that is, until the stage of the third rūpa jhāna, which we can now consider more carefully.

In the formulas for the first and second rūpa jhānas, the phrase *pīti-sukhaṃ* reflects the closely interrelated development of the two jhāna factors pīti and sukha together. Rather than translating these as "joy" and "bliss," I prefer "energization" for pīti, or perhaps even better would be to simply retain the Pāli, pīti. For sukha, in the case of the first two jhānas, "joy" or "happiness" seems more appropriate, while "bliss" conveys a more fully suffused quality I feel to be more appropriate for the third rūpa jhāna. The undeniable subjective sense of bodily happiness does not appear to be described as a jhāna factor, and we are left wondering whether modern understandings of interoception as the route by which we sense visceral and nervous system processes in the body might be relevant here.[3]

In the third jhāna formula, the relationship between pīti and sukha changes. Pīti now appears separately, as calmed, *pītiyā ca virāgā*, while sukha appears in the phrase *sukhañ ca kāyena paṭisaṃvedeti*, translated as "experiencing in the body bliss," which raises two questions. First, what is the actual nature of this sukha, given that the Abhidhamma clearly describes sukha as entirely a mental feeling in the third rūpa jhāna? Second and related, what is the meaning of the phrase "in the body"?

A clarification may lie with the Pāli term *kāyena*, which is a more complex term than its translation "in the body" conveys. While often used to refer to the physical body, both in the Suttas and Abhidhamma kāya can also be used in a different sense to mean any "group," such as the "mind-group" (nāma-kāya) or "body-group" (rūpa-kāya), or indeed the two combined in the nāma-rūpa of the whole sentient body.[4] In the description of the third rūpa jhāna, then, the phrase *sukhañ ca kāyena paṭisaṃvedeti* might more accurately refer to nāma-kāya, the mind-group, and not the physical body.

This is confirmed by Buddhaghosa in the *Visuddhimagga* in which, following the standard translation I am questioning, he elaborates as follows: the meditator "feel[s] the bliss associated with his mental body, and after emerging from the jhāna he would also feel bliss since his material body would have been affected by the exceedingly superior matter originated by that bliss associated with the mental body." He elaborates further that the bliss of the third rūpa jhāna is inseparable from equanimity (upekkhā) and quite different from any sense of euphoric happiness that common usage of the term "bliss" might suggest: "[he] has reached the perfection of bliss ... is not drawn toward it by a liking for the bliss ... is mindful with the mindfulness established in order to prevent the arising of happiness, and feels with his mental body the undefiled bliss beloved of Noble Ones ... 'He dwells in bliss who has equanimity and is mindful.'"[5] This supports the choice from here on to use "bliss" for the quality of sukha in the third rūpa jhāna, while using happiness for the sukha of the first and second rūpa jhānas.

THE CROWN CHAKRA

In the previous chapter, EEG recordings of increasingly strong energization near the vertex, or crown of head area, while developing the second rūpa jhāna were interpreted as being related to the jhāna factor pīti. It was also suggested that a developing vertical axis of brain network activity might be a sign of a developing vertical axis of jhāna consciousness, with intriguing similarities to the notion of a crown chakra in some branches of yoga.

In Hatha Yoga, the crown chakra, or Sahasrara, is regarded as the seat of pure consciousness and is visualized as a thousand-petaled lotus. In some Chinese Buddhist traditions it is visualized as a thirty-two-petaled lotus, and in Tibetan Buddhist yoga the crown chakra is referred to as the chakra of divine bliss. It is almost certainly related to the uṣṇīṣa in Theravāda Buddhism, which is the thirty-second of the "thirty-two marks of the Great Man," of which the Buddha is the exemplar.[6] The uṣṇīṣa is shown as a protuberance or sometimes flame at the crown of the head on Buddha statues, and it also occurs as an upward-spiraling stroke at the top of many yantras (see Chapter 7).

Overall, then, the growing dominance of this intense crown-of-head (vertex) EEG activity appears to fit well with the Abhidhamma and Sutta descriptions of a progression from the second to the third and fourth rūpa jhānas, toward "complete consciousness" characterized by equanimity and bliss.

SIMILE OF THE LOTUS POND

The simile for the third rūpa jhāna is a lotus emerging above the surface of a lotus pond:

> Just as in a pond ... lotuses are born, grow and stand in the water and are immersed in the cold water from root to neck, so this body is filled and saturated with bliss that is free from joy ... so he abides in the third meditation, jhāna, with body and mind filled and saturated with bliss that is free from joy.[7]

Related to this might be the experience of embodied presence often reported by meditators describing their subjective experiences in the second and higher jhānas, together with the sense when attaining the third rūpa jhāna of emerging from, and rising

Fig. 7. At a lotus farm in northern Thailand.

above, all distraction into a completely undisturbed, onlooking equanimity. Which probably explains the preference that many meditators find for images of lotuses rising above the surface of a pond, in preference to the varieties that remain on the surface.

THE NEUROSCIENCE OF THE THIRD AND FOURTH RŪPA JHĀNAS: KEY FINDINGS

The third and fourth rūpa jhānas share the quality of being "completely conscious," the only difference being the letting go of sukha and attachment to feeling in the fourth jhāna. Based on this common feature, we might expect the EEG evidence to be closely similar for the third and fourth jhānas, and this appears to be so from the EEG study. In the previous chapter, results across a group of experienced meditators showed a strong crown-of-head focus of activity developing, and this result was augmented by following two of those subjects as they were re-recorded after intervals of one to three years to examine how the higher jhānas develop as experience deepens. Here we simply summarize the main findings, with more details in Part 2 of this book and in the published study.

The group average figures described in the previous chapter, for meditators showing strong and rhythmic ISWs, displayed an approximately 44% dominance of activity around the vertex, with the remaining frontal and posterior activity interpreted as residual sensory consciousness activity. My hypothesis based on these observations was that, as a whole, that group was at various stages gaining experience in developing the second rūpa jhāna, perhaps with brief periods touching on the higher jhānas, characterized by high intensity pīti/ISW activity in the vertex source, indicating a developing vertical axis of jhāna consciousness.

Two subjects re-recorded after one- to three-year intervals showed progressive development of the crown-of-head source as experience grew, with the vertex dominance increasing dramatically to exceed 90% for varying durations. In both cases activity across the rest of the head was reduced in comparison to the crown-of-head activity, at times almost to the point of disappearing.

For one of the subjects, vertex dominance was sustained for over twenty minutes at the astonishing level of more than 99%, while at the same time the ISW activity showed evidence of an even slower rhythm of between twenty to fifty seconds, indicating a likely deeper metabolic component to the integration or absorption of samādhi. This might be an indication that this even slower rhythm is related to progressing from the third to the fourth rūpa jhāna, which would be consistent with the theory of hierarchies described in Chapter 13 where the timescale is predicted to increase each time one moves up a level in a hierarchy. More recordings will be needed to explore this hypothesis.

Following the pattern of relating modern neuroscience to ancient understandings of the jhānas, it is my hypothesis that such overwhelming crown-of-head dominance likely corresponds to the "complete consciousness" of the third and/or fourth rūpa jhānas. Further analysis of frequency structure showed the vertex source to be overwhelmingly made up of very slow (ISW) activity against a far weaker and almost insignificant residual background of high-frequency gamma-band activity. Such gamma activity in neuroscience is not well understood, but what is clear is that the intermediate frequency bands typical of default sensory consciousness had effectively disappeared.

5. THE FOURTH RŪPA JHĀNA: UPEKKHĀ, EQUANIMITY

The development of the fourth rūpa jhāna is somewhat different from the earlier jhānas, in which the jhāna factors are transcended in sequence. In contrast, the fourth rūpa jhāna emerges naturally from the third rūpa jhāna, in a sense marking completion of the third jhāna.

SUTTA DESCRIPTION OF THE FOURTH RŪPA JHĀNA

The fourth rūpa jhāna is the culmination of the series of four rūpa jhānas, and the Pāli formula reflects this by listing what has been let go in the previous jhānas:

In Pāli,

> sukhassa ca pahānā dukkhassa ca pahānā pubb'eva
> somanassa-domanassānaṃ atthagamā adukkhaṃ
> asukhaṃ upekkhā-sati-pārisuddhiṃ catutthaṃ
> jhanaṃ upasampajja viharati.
> (Dīgha Nikāya 2)

With the abandoning of pleasure and pain and with the previous disappearance of joy and grief [the meditator] enters upon and dwells in the fourth jhāna, which has neither pain nor pleasure, and has purity of mindfulness due to equanimity. (Vism. IV, p. 156)

The phrase *pubb'eva somanass-domanassānam atthagamā*, "with the previous disappearance of joy and grief," refers to what has been let go in the first and second rūpa jhānas, while *sukhassa ca pahānā dukkhassa ca pahānā*, "with the abandoning of pleasure [sukha] and pain [dukkha]," refers to the abandoning of all vestiges of pleasure and pain and their replacement by upekkhā, equanimity, which is achieved in the culmination, or completion, of the third rūpa jhāna, and at the moment of access to the fourth rūpa jhāna.

Unlike the progression from the first to the second or the second to the third rūpa jhānas, in which the jhāna factors vitakka, vicāra, and pīti are progressively mastered, the third and fourth rūpa jhānas are almost identical in sharing the quality of upekkhā, equanimity; and progression from the third to the fourth is subtler than for the preceding jhānas. In the third rūpa jhāna, the fourth jhāna factor sukha, as bliss, is experienced with near-perfect mindfulness and equanimity; and although this bliss is described as "exceedingly sweet" in the *Visuddhimagga*, it is experienced without greed, and the meditator is not moved by its experience.[1]

The *Vimuttimagga* describes a progressive development of equanimity in the jhānas, beginning in the first and second jhānas with equanimity experienced as non-action, neither hasty nor slow, as concentration develops toward ekaggatā citta, unification of mind. The specific term *upekkhā*, however, is reserved for the further development of equanimity in the third and fourth rūpa jhānas. In the third jhāna the quality of upekkhā is that the mind and body are unperturbed by the experience of bliss, while in the fourth jhāna upekkhā reaches perfection as both pleasure and pain are transcended (equivalent to no more wanting or not-wanting—that is, a temporary cessation of craving)—*adukkhaṃ asukhaṃ upekhā-sati-pārisuddhiṃ*, "neither painful nor pleasant, with purity of mindfulness by equanimity."

When a practitioner achieves adukkhaṃ asukhaṃ, the *Vimuttimagga* states:

equanimity removes the defilements immediately and entirely . . . the mind does not receive and thought does not reject. This is called the attaining to the "painless" and "pleasureless" [adukkhamasukhaṃ]. Middleness is the salient characteristic. Dwelling in a middle position is the function.[2]

Whether a meditator develops the fourth rūpa jhāna depends on the individual and on supporting conditions. To some extent this applies to all the jhānas, but particularly so for our modern lay context in which meditators juggle a complex mix of family and work responsibilities alongside meditation. In fact there is no urgent injunction to master any or all of the jhānas; if it happens it will require the right person, right place, and right time.

If those conditions apply, then the transition from the third to the fourth rūpa jhāna can develop in a natural manner as upekkhā, experienced as freedom, gradually takes over as the primary factor of the third rūpa jhāna while the subtle attachment to sukha fades. At that point, all that is needed to progress to the fourth rūpa jhāna is a recognition, or advertence to *adukkhaṃ asukhaṃ upekhā-sati-pārisuddhiṃ*, "neither painful nor pleasant, with purity of mindfulness by equanimity."

For some meditators, the process may be accompanied by discernment that even happiness is a subtle disturbance to the stillness and peace of upekkhā in the third rūpa jhāna. This is most likely to arise at the end of a practice, in the recollection or reviewing phase, while staying in the stillness to fully experience its qualities before returning to sensory consciousness. There may then arise a direct understanding of the subtle attachment to that happiness in the third rūpa jhāna, and a corresponding impulse to let go of any dependence, opening the way toward the fourth jhāna. This is an example of the interplay between the peace and stillness of samatha and the parallel development of vipassanā.

The fourth jhāna is the perfection of equanimity, upekkhā;

craving and attachment have been completely let go, at least for the duration of the jhāna, experienced with "mindfulness and full awareness like that of a man on a razor's edge."[3] Some meditators with an interest in quantum physics may be reminded in this comment of the concept of a "singularity"—a moment in space-time when normal laws of physics break down, yet with unimaginable potential. In Buddhist traditions this potential would include the Path and experience of enlightenment, nibbāna. And in esoteric traditions the potential also includes access to supernormal powers (*abhiññā*).

An Observer Effect?

The EEG study suggests another aspect of quantum physics may be relevant. During recordings, several meditators commented they were not able to go as far as they might normally in their individual practices at home, or on retreats, due to a subtle self-consciousness while being recorded. This self-consciousness relates partly to the technicalities and sensations of wearing a head-cap, as well as the presence of a technician observing and managing the recording.

My impression overseeing the study was that two key factors allowed participants to do as well as they did under such recording conditions: (1) the qualities that develop naturally in samatha meditation—calmness and patience; and (2) an increasing understanding of what it means to "dwell in a middle position." Their comments regarding a subtle self-consciousness were reminiscent of the "observer effect" in quantum physics, where as soon as anything is observed, it is changed or disrupted to some degree. This makes it difficult to imagine developing to completion the extremely fine balance of the fourth rūpa jhāna while being recorded, to say nothing of the difficulty of recording the arūpa (or formless) jhānas that will be considered in Chapters 8 through 11. It may have been our great good fortune that some subjects were in fact able to demonstrate some of the characteristics of the higher jhānas.

THE LIMINAL QUALITY OF THE FOURTH RŪPA JHĀNA

The fourth rūpa jhāna is described by the words *adukkhaṃ* and *asukhaṃ* in the Sutta formula quoted above, which are examples of the use of the initial letter "a" in the Pāli language to negate the meaning of the word that follows. This will be described in more detail in Chapter 7 as part of the Yogāvacara use of syllables, characters, and yantras to convey or point toward deeper meaning. In this case, *adukkhaṃ* and *asukhaṃ* mean "absence of pain" and "absence of pleasure," respectively, rather than "not pain" or "not pleasure."

In other words, *adukkhaṃ asukhaṃ*, translated as "neither painful nor pleasant," describes a neither-nor feeling state rather than a complete absence of feeling. This is once again reminiscent of quantum ideas, in this case of superposed states that only resolve into one or other form when intruded upon by an observer, or in the case of a subject in meditation by the intrusion of any form of discernment. Such nuances of meaning are not familiar in most Western languages, and the significance of this example will become clear when we discuss the formless states, or arūpa jhānas, in later chapters.

This "neither-painful-nor-pleasant" feeling also relates to the earlier comment that the third rūpa jhāna leads on to the fourth in a rather different manner than for the earlier jhānas. While sukha and dukkha are interrelated, each in a sense not existing without the other in comparison, the situation for "neither-painful-nor pleasant" is different; there is no single quality of feeling to be let go in order to access the fourth jhāna; the fourth jhāna is not conditioned by the third in the same manner as the earlier jhānas. It is quite simply through the perfection of upekkhā as the third jhāna comes to completion that the fourth jhāna is revealed.

The neither-nor, liminal quality of the fourth jhāna is related to loss of the usual anchors in time and space, as separation from sensory consciousness is completed. This is not only a remarkable achievement, but it is also a considerable challenge to the stability and deeper sense of self of a meditator. This is one of the reasons that there should be no hurry to develop the jhānas too quickly, and also a reason for the security of the mandala-like structure of four different lengths of breath used in this tradition in the approach stages—they provide a safe space to develop and enter jhāna and to safely withdraw back to sensory consciousness. It is also a reason why in modern times it is important to explore the mental health stability of a new meditator before too quickly agreeing to teach jhāna meditation at all.

THE SIMILE OF THE WHITE CLOTH

The simile of the white cloth for the fourth jhāna also captures its liminal quality. This description is from the *Vimuttimagga*:

> As a man might sit down and cover his body with a
> white cloth from head to foot, in such a way that no
> part of his body is left uncovered, so a bhikkhu covers
> his body and limbs with purified mindfulness, in such
> a way that no part of him is not covered with purified
> mindfulness.[4]

While the *Vimuttimagga* refers to a monastic context, this description is equally applicable to the lay situation, male or female. It is significant that purified mindfulness is highlighted as the all-encompassing (white cloth) quality of the fourth rūpa jhāna. The descriptions in both the *Vimuttimagga* and the *Visuddhimagga* go on to clarify this as "purified by equanimity" and relate that this depth and purity of mindfulness is specific to the fourth jhāna and does not develop in the lower jhānas.

For a meditator developing the fourth rūpa jhāna, it is sometimes interesting to experience this in practice. For this exercise, a fine white cotton cloth that retains some translucency is preferred. It is draped over the entire body, touching the ground around the meditator with no gaps, and sometimes a wide-brimmed straw cap may be used to stop the material directly touching the face. The focus is not on the white cloth, but nevertheless the initial sense at the beginning of a practice is of some subliminal awareness of the meditator's surroundings, with an experience of being neither within the world nor fully separate from it. It is as though the white cloth used in this way acts as a subtle invocation of some of the qualities of the fourth jhāna described above, and for some this practice has been of help in deepening their understanding of the fourth rūpa jhāna.

THE EEG EVIDENCE: KEY FINDINGS

The third and fourth jhānas were not clearly discriminated as to EEG brain activity in the previous chapter, since there are (as yet) no clear differences to distinguish the two, apart from the intriguing suggestion in a few cases of two different rhythms of infraslow waves. There are also subjective reports that do describe different qualities of equanimity with or without bliss as discussed above, but as previously stated, subjective reports can be difficult to rely on in a quantitative scientific study.

Given the great similarity between the third and fourth jhānas as depicted in Buddhist texts, the similarity between EEG recordings is not surprising, and the results given in the previous chapter appear to correspond to the description of meditators in both jhānas as "completely conscious" in the sense of undisturbed equanimity and separation from sensory consciousness, with highly focused EEG activity around the crown of the head replacing previously widely distributed activity typical of everyday sensory consciousness.

A Vertical Axis of Jhāna Consciousness

The intense focus of brain activity near the vertex encompasses areas of the brain that are highly connected deeper into core regions such as the thalamus, and further to the upper brain stem and then to the spinal cord. This vertical axis suggests that quite different networks of connectivity develop during jhāna meditation compared to the suggested front-back axis of our default sensory consciousness. It is also highly likely that those networks include what is known in neuroscience as the ascending reticular activating system (ARAS), which connects just such areas of the brain and is involved in processes not just of attention but specifically arousal and consciousness. This network is also known to be disrupted in situations of unconsciousness and coma, whereas in the forms of meditation we are describing, meditators are highly aware and fully conscious.

Such a brain-body axis via the intermediate regions of the upper brain stem, coupled with the extremely slow EEG rhythms revealed in the EEG study as jhāna deepens, also suggests that metabolic processes become involved that have timescale factors considerably slower than the much faster neuronal processes in the brain, which in turn suggests involvement of the extensive tree-like networks of the vagus nerves in the body that regulate the major organs and control the autonomic nervous system balance between sympathetic and parasympathetic activity. It was therefore of interest to test whether autonomic nervous system balance is affected during jhāna meditation, and monitoring heart-rate variability (HRV) before and during meditation is one means of doing so. Preliminary results of a pilot study, described in Part 2, Chapter 12, confirmed a significant increase in HRV and therefore in parasympathetic activity as part of the deeply peaceful state of jhāna.

It is an intriguing feature of the manner in which jhāna practice has developed in the Samatha Trust tradition that meditators become increasingly aware of the importance of the body and its role in meditation, which appears to contradict descriptions in some "new samatha" traditions that claim the body "disappears" during jhāna. The evidence of a vertical brain-body axis from the

EEG study, as well as the increases in HRV noted above, strongly suggest that the experience of embodied presence described by many meditators in this tradition is indeed an experience of deep peace in the body as much as in the mind.

6. Summary of the Four Rūpa Jhānas

An intriguing overview of the rūpa jhānas, as described in Yogāvacara texts such as *The Path of Lanka*, is as follows:

- The first rūpa jhāna is said to be experienced through the physical eye, rooted in the coarse and subtle human body.
- The second rūpa jhāna is said to be experienced through the Deva eye, rooted in the coarse and subtle Deva body.
- The third rūpa jhāna is said to be experienced through the eye of wisdom, rooted in the Brahmā body in the rūpa-loka form realm.
- The fourth rūpa jhāna is said to be experienced through the eye of omniscience, rooted in the Brahmā body in the arūpa-loka formless realm.[1]

This progression through the jhānas involves all three "realms": the kāma-loka of the sensory world, the fine-material rūpa-loka, and the formless arūpa-loka presaged in the fourth rūpa jhāna. Completion of the four rūpa jhānas is therefore wide-ranging and a major achievement for a meditator. More often, though, progression through the jhānas is a work in progress for much if not all of a meditator's life, and in this chapter I summarize some of the main points of working on this lifelong project.

A "Neurodhamma" Interpretation of the Hindrances

The "hindrances" to developing jhāna in Buddhist meditation are often assumed, at least in part, to be a meditator's problem, and therefore experienced as discouraging. "I need to work on my hindrances"; "What is the antidote to doubt? Or ill-will?"; and so on. A "neurodhamma" view, on the other hand, might see them as normal reactions to a meditator's attempts to disengage from default consciousness—symptoms of disruption to the brain's default networks, and in other words signs of slow but steady progress in affecting changes in those brain networks.

Since each of us has lived within our default consciousness since birth, it is a big challenge to withdraw from it, and meditators should not be surprised at experiencing resistance to doing so. Because of its all-pervasive nature in our lives as our habitual consciousness that supports our sense of "I am" and "I do," this default consciousness possesses considerable momentum, rather like a massive flywheel that once set spinning, as in the cycle of dependent origination, is difficult to slow down. From this point of view, the hindrances reflect subjective experiences of withdrawing from ever more subtle components of this default consciousness, as reflected by the jhāna factors and the EEG evidence as follows:

- Vitakka, or redirecting attention, represents the first stage of disruption to the dorsal attention network of sensory consciousness and is the first challenge to the momentum of our default consciousness. The hindrance of *sloth and torpor* is the subjective experience of struggling against that momentum.
- Vicāra represents the next stage of disruption to the ventral attention network of sensory consciousness, as a meditator develops the salience aspects of refined attention to the touch of the breath at the nose-tip, to "feel" the experience and to minimize doubt as to where attention is placed. Vicāra therefore relates to overcoming the second hindrance of *doubt*.
- Pīti reflects the emergence of energy freed once attention has been stabilized by the work of vitakka and vicāra, and the next layers of sensory consciousness that meditators work with concern liking and disliking. The hindrance of

disliking, or *ill will*, closely related to fear, is the dominant hindrance of this pair at this stage and is related to the underlying fear of loss of self that lies latent in default consciousness, against which ill will is the defensive coping strategy (compare this to the "fight-flight" reactions in the oldest parts of brain functioning). Passaddhi or tranquilization of pīti overcomes fear and ill will.

· Sukha, or happiness, begins with quite subtle feelings of contentment that gradually suffuse the body with satisfaction and confidence, reflecting freedom from fear and ill will, or the need to "defend." As sukha develops, the hindrance of *restlessness* (and *remorse* for any underlying past actions linked to fear and ill will) subsides.

· Ekagattā citta, unification of mind, is the culmination of withdrawal from sensory consciousness; it therefore corresponds to overcoming the overall hindrance of attachment to the entirety of our default consciousness— that is, *sense desire.*

This interpretation of the hindrances also highlights the crucial need for meditators to be patient in allowing sufficient time to fully understand attention in its twin aspects of vitakka and vicāra, as the threshold to developing the first rūpa jhāna. Without mastering attention, withdrawal from sensory consciousness will be incomplete, easily leading to misunderstandings (including overestimation) of what is being experienced.

THE NIMITTA, VITAKKA, AND VICĀRA

Developing vitakka and vicāra is also closely aligned with development of the nimitta:

· Vitakka corresponds to the basic cognitive process of attending to the touch of the breath at the nose-tip, or development of the preliminary-work (parikamma) nimitta. In the Yogāvacara, this is said to be apprehended via the "door of the eye" (similar to attending to an external kasina with the eyes open).

- Vicāra signals the meditator starting to discern the "feel" and salience of the sensation of the breath and is a step toward apprehending the qualia of consciousness itself. This parallels development of the acquired sign, or uggaha nimitta, which is mind-made rather than fixed at the nose-tip. In the Yogāvacara the uggaha nimitta is apprehended via the "door of the mind." This is also the stage at which pīti develops, as energization experienced as physical sensations.

- The work of vitakka and vicāra culminates in a stability where the breath and nimitta become, in a sense, insepa-rable, signifying the fully developed counterpart sign, or patibhāga nimitta, which is now steady enough to lead the meditator deeper into jhānic absorption. In the Yogāvacara this is apprehended via the "door of touch," reflecting the deep integration of body and mind in samādhi.

RECOLLECTION REVISITED

The importance of recollection was mentioned briefly in Chap-ter 3, and having now described all four rūpa jhānas, we can say a little more. As a meditator becomes familiar with the higher jhānas, it is necessary to find another way of conceptualizing the processes beyond the crude naming and comparison of conven-tional language. At the end of a meditation practice, then, it is recommended to remain with the experience of stillness without moving or opening the eyes, resisting any reliance on language or any inner dialogue with oneself as an attempt to recollect what has been experienced and how it was accomplished.

For example, if the meditator had been deeply absorbed in the upekkhā of the fourth rūpa jhāna, the stillness at the end of prac-tice would have a deep sense of freedom and spaciousness, with absolutely no urge to move mentally or physically from a perfectly balanced presence, which might very well last for a considerable time if the meditator has no other responsibilities to attend to. After a while, an awareness of sukha, mental bliss, will arise, and in that moment the meditator will understand directly that the practice just left was the fourth rūpa jhāna and that this arising of sukha marks the third rūpa jhāna. This is direct knowledge on a par with opening the eyes and simply seeing and understanding, with no need for discursive, language-based cognitive processing. It is also an expression of *reviewing*, the fifth stage of mastery.

The deeply blissful and satisfying quality related to the third rūpa jhāna might also last for a considerable time, eventually to fade and be replaced by a still deeply satisfying peace, but one where the body in particular is experienced as being totally at peace, as in the second rūpa jhāna, when pīti has been tranquilized by the activity of passaddhi.

Again after some time, the meditator will become aware of a pull to "attend"—not yet to fall back into verbal conceptualization, but nevertheless a pull back toward the processes of vitakka and vicāra of the first rūpa jhāna. The meditator will still feel deeply peaceful and happy but is now only one remove from sensory conscious-ness. Finally, sooner or later, the driving force behind developing the series of jhānas will no longer be sufficient to maintain the fine-material access awareness and qualities of the jhānas, and the meditator will return quite naturally to full sensory consciousness.

In this way meditators come to know "where they have been" and gradually develop a deeper understanding of the jhāna factors based on direct experience rather than words. This then makes it possible to recollect the qualities of any particular jhāna and even-tually to become able to simply "go there," which expresses a highly developed mastery of the jhānas and completion of the fifth stage of mastery of reviewing described in Chapter 3.

A deeper benefit of this practice is that it allows a meditator to witness the operation of both modes, samatha and vipassanā as the twin kammaṭṭhāna, and the reality of their inseparable operation.

It becomes understood, by repetition: first that jhāna cannot be developed at all without a significant development of insight or vipassanā to resist the habitual processes of sensory consciousness, and second that the moment of emerging from jhāna is immediately followed by a reviewing moment of consciousness that knows directly, with deep insight, the qualities of the preceding jhāna. The meditator learns directly—akin to seeing—the intricate and reciprocal relationship between samatha and vipassanā, or jhāna and *paññā* (wisdom), and that in some mysterious manner they become united in the experience and deep stillness of jhāna.

"STAGES," MASTERY, AND THE ILLUSION OF SPACE-TIME

Recollection is of great help in developing awareness of the fine-material sphere as distinct from ordinary sensory consciousness. Other practices, particularly involving the body, are also very helpful, such as tai chi and some other martial arts practices like aikido, which develop sensitivity to fine-motor movements and the subtle interoceptive awareness that can allow a person to feel the most subtle movements of their limbs as well as the tensions and connections within the body. Eventually it becomes possible to develop a peripheral fine-material awareness that can be ever-present to some degree as part of overall mindfulness, sati.

Associated to this fine-material awareness, when coupled with a growing experience of the higher jhānas, will be less dependence on the habits of sensory consciousness such as recognition, naming, or comparison, which ultimately means less dependence on conventional language. And since it is language that underpins an ordering of sensory experience in time and space, a new quality to everyday experience begins to open up, one less dependent on such ordering. Since these same processes underpin our sense of "I am" and "I do," our overreliance on the I-construct fades with continued practice, which is in accord with the parallel development of vipassanā alongside samatha in the twin-kammaṭṭhāna model of the Yogāvacara.

As our reliance on conventional language begins to fade, the notion of developing the jhānas in stages, of "getting somewhere," of second to third to fourth, becomes far too crude. Once a meditator has sufficient experience of the second and third rūpa jhānas, even if not yet perfect, it is possible to let go entirely of the idea of stages and simply allow the stillness of jhāna to deepen, and then deepen more. The all-encompassing peace, stillness, and clarity constitute the sense of presence, and the stillness alone as the "signature" of jhāna is sufficient to lead the meditator into complete absorption. However, this requires a sophisticated understanding of mindfulness and discrimination, where sati informed by dhamma-vicaya becomes sati-sampajañña, mindfulness that discriminates directly without any trace of discursive comparison. Sampajañña derives from the same root as paññā, wisdom, and sati now approaches the right mindfulness of the Eightfold Path.

The kind of sati required needs to be increasingly subtle to match the stillness, and in fact both go together. If the breath is allowed to follow a natural process of becoming increasingly fine, so as not to disturb the stillness, then eventually in the fourth rūpa jhāna everything comes to a still point of what might be called "un-breath," rather than in- and out-breath. In the Yogāvacara tradition, this is likened to the breath of the fetus in the womb.

With an experienced teacher, and especially with regular practice of recollection, a meditator can develop very significant mastery and understanding of the more subtle meanings of the stages of ānāpānasati and the jhānas. In the tradition that has developed in the Samatha Trust, an experienced meditator who has practiced in full all sixteen stages of ānāpānasati might be encouraged to explore different routes through this matrix-like structure of stages. Some examples are shown in Figure 8, with different ordering and sequences across the four lengths of breath and the four stages of counting, following, touching, and settling.

Plot 1, the first path shown in Figure 8, reproduces the overall structure of the earlier Figure 6, showing the sixteen stages that result from four lengths of breath counted as nine, six, three, and one (with the "normal" length indicated by the horizontal gray bar), and the stages of counting, following, touching, and settling. This is the starting point for a meditator in this tradition to become familiar with all the different lengths of breath, mostly taking the long routes shown in plot 1.

Plots 2–9 show examples of different routes, each to be practiced in forward and reverse order. After repetition (usually many repetitions over an extended period) of different paths through the stages, the real significance of counting, following, touching, and settling gradually becomes clear, particularly in how those stages relate to the jhāna factors. They become understood by feel rather than verbal conceptualization, and in the same manner as learning a complex piece of music or a Buddhist chant, perhaps in Pāli, the meditator becomes able to simply go to the different stages directly with fluency. And, somewhat differently, the significance of the different lengths of breath also becomes clear in the manner in which different areas of the body respond, without the need for further conceptualization, such as the idea of chakras. This is all about becoming familiar with form, without needing to analyze constituent components.

This same approach can then be applied to the four rūpa jhānas once a meditator has sufficient familiarity with them all, even if not fully mastered. As with the stages of ānāpānasati, the four jhānas may be practiced in forward order, reverse order, or in alternate order until they are so familiar by feel that they can be accessed simply by a direct mental act of advertence.

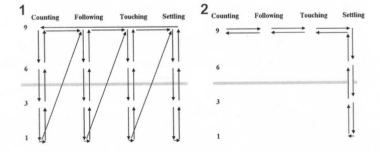

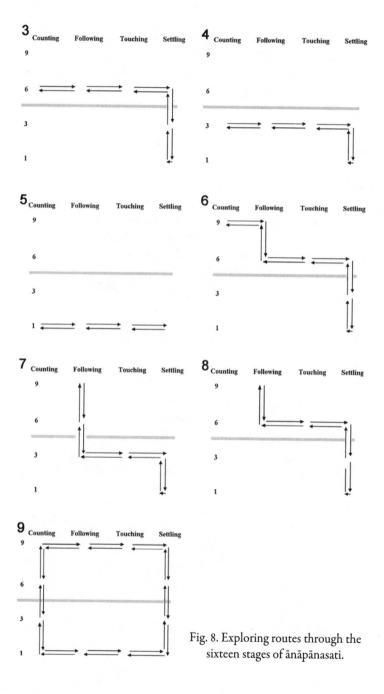

Fig. 8. Exploring routes through the sixteen stages of ānāpānasati.

If we label the four jhānas RJ1, RJ2, RJ3, and RJ4, for example, the basic order would be RJ1 to RJ2 to RJ3 to RJ4, and then back to RJ3 to RJ2 to RJ1. A meditator might then explore different orders such as RJ1 to RJ3 and back to RJ1, or RJ2 to RJ4 and back to RJ2, then RJ1, among other possibilities. This may seem unrealistic to those who hold to a strict separation of the jhānas, and the idea of going directly to different jhānas might be dismissed as impossible. The only way to test this is to put aside what may have been read and to explore what happens directly without prejudgment.

The aim, initially, is not to "perfect" any particular jhāna, but to gradually recognize a level of subtle perception that allows a "determination" (adhiṭṭhāna) to be made at the threshold of jhāna to move between the jhānas directly. This approach will become clearer to meditators if they move on to develop the arūpa jhānas as described in Chapters 8 through 11.

Order and Mastery in the Yogāvacara

There are equivalents to the above in some Yogāvacara texts, albeit heavily disguised and mostly concerned with working with the five pītis (Table 1, Chapter 3), although the procedures can also be applied to a fivefold reckoning of the jhānas. This alternative model of five rather than the four rūpa jhānas described in the Suttas is a product of the Abhidhamma. In the fivefold model, mastery of vitakka and vicāra is developed separately in the first and second jhānas, so that the second jhana of the fourfold model becomes the third in the fivefold model; the third in the fourfold model becomes the fourth in the fivefold model; and so on.

The Path of Lanka describes practicing to "enter" in six modes: to enter in succession, for control, for duration, in a group, in a circle, and to be fixed. Thus:

1. To enter in succession, one at a time until each becomes familiar, is the basic mode of developing the five pītis listed in Table 1, Chapter 3.

2. To enter for control is to practice alternate pītis such as 1 to 3, 2 to 5, etc., as well as in reverse order.

3. To enter for duration is to practice pīti 1 to 4, 2 to 5, etc., and then in reverse order. Such a large jump is very difficult unless a degree of mastery of duration for each stage has been developed, and for each of the pītis (see discussion on mastery in Chapter 3).

4. To enter in a group is to develop each of the pītis 1, 2, 3, 4, and 5 in sequence and to hold them in mind together; and then repeat the sequence in reverse order.

5. To enter in a circle is to practice each in turn, 1, 2, 3, 4, and 5, while at the same time positioning them into a circular form, visualized at the five points of the component parts of the Khom character "A." (This use of characters will be described further in the next chapter.)

6. And finally, to enter "to be fixed." This rather enigmatic phrase probably refers to ekaggatā citta, the absorption of jhāna, as the culmination of developing the pītis, in particular pharanā pīti or all-pervading rapture (Table 1).

The similarity between the rather enigmatic descriptions in *The Path of Lanka* and the methods outlined in Figure 8 that have emerged independently in a quite different Western context is fascinating, and taken as a whole the two approaches help to clarify how mastery of the jhānas is developed. Recollection and reviewing have been described already as one key method, and the repeated practicing of different routes through the stages of ānāpānasati, or the pītis, and finally the jhānas is a related form of recollection where it is the feel and form of the stages, or jhānas, that becomes not only "re-collected," but deeply imprinted in the meditator's mind-body. This is what is meant by *The Path of Lanka* stage-6 description, "to be fixed."

It is striking that in both Yogāvacara texts, the *Manual* and the *Path*, the stages of pīti take center stage rather than a more familiar description of the jhānas. It is as though the jhānas are being described in terms of the pītis, making the point that the stages of the jhānas might better be regarded as a progressive integration of bodily energies into a unified embodied experience of complete awareness, rather than the sometimes-assumed idea in some forms of post-reform samatha that the jhānas are deep concentrated states far removed from any activity of insight or wisdom, paññā, as well as being completely cut off from bodily awareness.

The description "to be fixed" also corresponds to the stage of settling in the ānāpānasati model described in Figure 6 and in Chapter 2. When fully developed and accompanied by pīti, a deep integration of the meditator's mind-body system develops, culminating in the fifth jhāna factor, ekaggatā citta, in the first and second rūpa jhānas, and then upekkhā in the third and fourth. The "wax-taper practice," which will be described later (in Chapter 11), is another method to "fix" the jhānas into the mind-body of the meditator.

Fourfold and Fivefold Models of the Jhānas

Some final comments on the fivefold model of the jhānas are germane to this discussion. Table 2 lists the features of both the fourfold and fivefold models side by side, where the dominant factors for each jhāna are marked bold, with the other factors not yet fully developed listed below. The factors in parentheses have been mastered or incorporated and are no longer an active focus.

In the fourfold model, vitakka and vicāra are considered to be sufficiently closely interrelated (as the two aspects of attention revealed by the EEG study) to be mastered together in the first jhāna, while in the fivefold model they are dealt with separately, therefore adding an extra jhāna. Ekagattā is deliberately not listed in Table 2 as a factor for the first jhāna in the fivefold model due to a controversy in Buddhist academia as to whether unification of mind occurs in the first rūpa jhāna.

In an article entitled "Jhāna and Buddhist Scholasticism," Martin Stuart-Fox (1989) suggested that ekagattā was added into the

Table 2: The Fourfold and Fivefold Models of the Jhānas

Fourfold Model of the Rūpa Jhānas (RJ) and the Jhāna Factors

RJ1	RJ2	RJ3	RJ4
Vicāra Vitakka	Pīti	Sukha	Upekkhā
Pīti	Sukha	Ekagattā	
Sukha	Ekagattā		
Ekagattā			
	(Vicāra)	(Pīti)	(Sukha)
	(Vitakka)	(Vicāra)	(Pīti)
		(Vitakka)	(Vicāra)
			(Vitakka)

Fivefold Model of the Rūpa Jhānas (RJ) and the Jhāna Factors

RJ1	RJ2	RJ3	RJ4	RJ5
Vitakka	Vicāra Vitakka	Pīti	Sukha	Upekkhā
Vicāra	Pīti	Sukha	Ekagattā	
Pīti	Sukha	Ekagattā		
Sukha	Ekagattā			
		(Vicāra)	(Pīti)	(Sukha)
		(Vitakka)	(Vicāra)	(Pīti)
			(Vitakka)	(Vicāra)
				(Vitakka)

first jhāna of the fivefold Abhidhamma model simply for consistency, in order to have five jhāna factors for all the jhānas, and that there is no clear justification for claiming that the first rūpa jhāna in a fivefold model could develop unification of mind, ekaggatā citta.

We can go further by noting that in the EEG study, both of the neuroscience attention networks—the dorsal stream related to vitakka and the ventral stream related to vicāra—are disrupted together in the approach to the first rūpa jhana in the fourfold model.

Also, vitakka is only short-term. It establishes a moment in time—that is, a moment of mindfulness at the points of repeatedly placing attention—while vicāra on the other hand adds discrimination to establish salience in order to sustain attention. Therefore the development of vicāra necessarily follows vitakka to establish salience, which implicitly requires awareness of past moments, the present moment, and a projected time course—that is, temporal depth. Without a degree of temporal depth, unification of mind is meaningless, and it is therefore an error to formulate a first jhāna based only on the first stage of attention, vitakka. In fact, what is labeled as a separate first jhāna in the fivefold model is rightly simply the first stage in developing the first jhāna in the fourfold model. This also corresponds to the subjective experience; the initial stage of repeatedly placing attention, by itself, cannot fully grasp the meditation object until supported by vicāra.

It is tempting to conclude that those who composed the *Yogāvacara's Manual* and *The Path of Lanka* were more influenced by the Abhidhamma's fivefold model of the jhānas than by the older Sutta descriptions, but this may not be so. Both works avoid naming the jhānas explicitly, whether in a fivefold or fourfold structure, preferring to describe the subjective experience of a meditator's practice in terms of five stages: five pītis, five jhāna factors, five hindrances. The authors might well have taken the same view outlined above, where the fourfold model of the Suttas corresponds to the overall experience of a meditator developing the jhānas, while acknowledging that mastery of attention in the first jhāna involves discrimination of two factors together, vitakka and vicāra—hence five jhāna factors overall.

DIFFICULTIES ESTABLISHING JHĀNA AND DISTORTIONS OF JHĀNA

The first rūpa jhāna is the gateway to further progress in developing the jhānas. And since the core factor in the Pāli formula for the first jhāna is the phrase *vivicc' eva kāmehi*, translated as "apart from sense desires," then it follows, in different terminology, that disengaging from everyday sensory consciousness is the crucial factor, confirmed by the EEG study.

It cannot be overemphasized, though, what a major undertaking such a disengagement is, as recognized above in the section describing the hindrances as a reaction to such attempts. It is the task of a teacher to help a meditator negotiate this process, to learn to neither rush it nor to attempt a suppression of the hindrances, either of which can lead to misunderstandings or distortions of the jhāna experience.

Having experienced these difficulties first-hand, as well as having witnessed others' struggles to find a right path forward over more than fifty years, it seems to me that two features of the Samatha Trust tradition are particularly important and helpful. The first is the use of non-normal lengths of breath in ānāpānasati, and the second is the development of pīti; both of these were devalued or suppressed in the "reforms" of the 1950s–1960s in Southeast Asia, particularly Thailand and Burma, a situation that persisted in the post-reform aftermath that spread worldwide from the 1970s onward.

Length of Breath

Regarding length of breath, the heavy promotion of "new" vipassanā during the reforms, replacing samatha and jhāna practices, emphasized watching the breath and not controlling it. This avoidance of breath control continued into the post-reform era, including from the 1980s onward when there was a resurgence of interest in jhāna meditation.

The reason for choosing different lengths of breath, as noted earlier, is to mark a new kammaṭṭhāna, place of work, as a conscious choice in beginning to disengage from sensory consciousness. Quite apart from meditation, this should make sense through observation of how the breath mirrors a person's emotional state living in a sensory world. This is always so to some degree, but particularly evident in mental illness—the breath patterns for persons suffering from acute depression, bipolar disorder, schizophrenia, or panic attacks, to name a few, are so floridly different to each other as to almost enable diagnosis simply from observing patterns of breathing. Although maybe not so obvious in everyday life, such patterns are ever-present to some degree.

Hence, even from the earliest stages of introducing this pre-reform tradition to the UK, it was emphasized how using different lengths of breath was a deliberate choice to mark a departure from the habits of everyday consciousness, with the added benefit of allowing safe development of sometimes intense states of pīti, and then a return to normal breathing and sensory consciousness with no difficulty, especially important for lay practitioners.

There is also an important related factor in how awareness of the length of breath becomes part of a deepening consolidation of mindfulness, sati. It has already been noted that once the stages and lengths of breath are familiar, a meditator no longer needs to keep awareness of the length of breath at the forefront of awareness, since it becomes part of overall mindfulness. In fact, for many years Nai Boonman described the tradition as one of a balance between mindfulness and concentration, and he repeatedly advised meditators not to let either mindfulness or concentration lapse compared to the other, particularly in the closest stages of approach to jhāna.

The importance of balancing concentration with mindfulness right up to the point of absorption is not unlike the statement quoted in Chapter 5, from the *Vimuttimagga*, that "middleness is the salient characteristic. Dwelling in a middle position is the function." Although this quotation refers to the fourth rūpa jhāna, it could be applied to all the jhānas in terms of the balance between concentration and mindfulness.

Pīti

The reforms in Southeast Asia, even those developing from the early nineteenth century in Thailand and Burma as precursors to the later 1950s–1960s reforms, attacked anything that could be labeled as superstitious, dangerous, or verging on black magic (Thai, *saiyasat*). This would certainly have included manifestations of pīti characterized by high energy and the bodily effects described in Table 1 of Chapter 3, which in their most powerful forms might easily be confused with seizures, madness, or possession.

As a result, such practices, which had mostly been protected within monastic communities, became even less visible, and then in the second-phase reforms from the mid-1950s were actively suppressed. When Nai Boonman began teaching ānāpānasati in the UK from early 1964, great care was taken not to openly teach practices that involved strong developments of pīti, such was the rigidity of views of the new orthodoxy. Nevertheless, a natural development of strong pīti did take place, but it is fair to say that the Samatha Trust kept a low profile for many years while quietly helping meditators develop their understanding.

The importance of pīti is crucial in developing the second rūpa jhāna. Although a momentary experience is possible with only a limited development of pīti, to fully master the second jhāna and then beyond that the third and fourth rūpa jhānas, a much more thorough understanding and development of pīti is necessary if the body is to become integrated fully into the experience of samādhi.

Facsimile Jhāna

When a meditator touches jhāna for the first time, how the experience develops depends on the approach stages. If the approach has been gradual via ānāpānasati, particularly if a protected space of different lengths of breaths has been established, then a meditator may be aware without too much excitement that something different has happened, and with the aid of recollection and guidance from a teacher will become able to extend the duration of the jhāna, gradually coming to understand the jhāna factors and develop further.

In other instances, however, the situation may not be so straightforward. If the approach stages are rushed, and particularly if the significance of lengths of breath is not understood as a means to allow a progressive disengagement from sensory consciousness, then disengagement is likely to be incomplete, in which case the only way a person can develop even a first brief experience of the first rūpa jhāna will be through some form of suppression of the hindrances. This is typically by long sittings, intense cognitive exercises to counter each hindrance by its opposite, or by "paying a price" in the form of ascetic practices of one form or another.

Suppression of the hindrances is the most common problem, since anything suppressed is always nearby ready to resurface, as Freud realized in the early years of psychoanalysis. Suppression cannot sustain a first experience of jhāna, as it will quickly lead to a rebound, either to sensory consciousness or to the near threshold of jhāna. If to sensory consciousness, then repeated practice may enable the meditator to at least sustain the threshold stage longer.

The threshold position is an interesting state in its own right and is in fact a significant first achievement for a meditator. Even though the hindrances may be in abeyance only through suppression, the mind will be less cluttered, more joyful, and actually quite responsive compared to everyday sensory consciousness, which sets the stage for a meditator to believe they have experienced jhāna and are sustaining it. Particularly for a temperament that relies heavily on thinking, any previous readings or intellectual knowledge about the jhānas can lead to a process of formulating and constructing an experience to correspond to what is expected, has been read about, or has been heard.

In addition, a too-rapid approach to jhāna will almost certainly lack adequate understanding of craving and attachment, or wanting and not-wanting, leaving meditators prone to believing what they want to believe, including that jhāna is now understood, which easily extends into thinking that the higher jhānas, too, in subsequent practices, have also been mastered. This results in a kind of facsimile jhāna, a superficially convincing version of jhāna, which might be sincerely believed by the practitioner, but to an experienced teacher does not quite ring true, as though the meditator is not fully part of the experience being described.

Once this mode develops, it can become very entrenched. In fact, since the normal functioning of brain networks in everyday sensory consciousness involves modes of feedback reinforcement (see Chapter 13), then the facsimile mode may be repeatedly "confirmed" as valid to the person experiencing this mode. However, despite its facsimile nature, it is still a better basis than what might be the alternative without meditation, and with help from a competent teacher the process of separating from sensory consciousness might be revisited and completed.

Deep States of Concentration

There seems no doubt that some practitioners in post-reform developments of samatha meditation enter deep states of concentration where they feel all contact with the body and the sensory world disappears or ends completely for a while. This has even led to controversies as to what is "correct" jhāna, and whether anything other than such an experience is jhāna at all, or at best a form of jhāna-lite.

In earlier years when some students of Nai Boonman also showed a tendency to be drawn into overconcentrated states, Boonman was quick to re-emphasize the need to maintain mindfulness alongside concentration as long as possible, certainly beyond any expectations or point of letting go or "dropping into" jhāna, to avoid what he on some occasions referred to as wrong concentration. The form of mindfulness required at this stage is rather subtle, far removed from any form of discursive process, and similar to the dilemma when the breath appears to disappear in deeper jhāna, the stage of "un-breath" alluded to earlier in this chapter, the task for a meditator is to nevertheless maintain a middle position, which is essentially the balance between mindfulness and concentration.

In fact, if development has been gradual and progressive through the stages of ānāpānasati, then as a meditator approaches the threshold of jhāna, sati will have developed to the stage of sati-sampajañña, which allows a form of direct awareness, knowing, and fine perception to continue right up to the experience of jhāna. Many jhāna practitioners in this reborn pre-reform tradition would also claim that a degree of fine perception persists through all four rūpa jhānas and the first three arūpa jhānas. However, to maintain the balance between concentration and mindfulness right up to the threshold of jhāna, of unification of mind (and body), needs strong saddhā, faith, and a teacher who understands the process to help the meditator resist the impulse to let go too soon. To use the quantum physics analogy, this is also something like approaching a singularity, such as a black hole, where all conceptions of space-time break down. Until experienced, it is not possible to conceptualize how—as the "singularity" is approached—the immense power of concentration can transform into the immense peace and stillness of jhāna.

In this balanced state, the sensory world or body does not disappear completely, but since the meditator no longer has attachment to that mode and is not moved to reflect or connect to external sensory channels, it does not intrude into the jhāna experience. This is clear in the EEG of someone in the third or fourth jhānas in this tradition, to be more fully described in Part 2, when all network activity in the brain typical of sensory consciousness ceases. However, without taking any part of the body as object, it is nevertheless "known" and experienced by the meditator as a unified mind-body state of deep integration and clear awareness. This is a knowing quite different from discursive cognitive knowing, however, and is associated with a level of fine perception not typical of sensory consciousness. That such fine perception can exist in jhāna does not appear to be recognized in most post-reform traditions.

The deep concentrative states that can develop when mindfulness lapses can be extremely alluring, and in some cases quite addictive, frequently leading to a rigidity of view that this is the true and only way to practice jhāna. It is in development of the arūpa formless states, however, that the real importance of maintaining mindfulness in tandem with concentration becomes apparent: it is difficult to imagine that, without the insight or wisdom quality of sati-sampajañña alongside samādhi and upekkhā in the rūpa jhānas, the arūpas could be developed at all other than as cognitive constructions, no matter how subtle, overlaid on the mode of the deep concentrative states.

However, from a neuroscience perspective there is something intriguing and suggestive in how the deep concentrative states are sometimes described as "dropping into" jhāna, or into bliss, which is reminiscent of the wake-sleep transition, or of the equally switch-like transition from wakefulness into anesthesia, or, thinking back to the Burmese vipassanā practices of the 1950s–1970s, the tendency for some meditators at that time to drop into *bhavaṅga* (a state of unconsciousness similar to deep nREM sleep).[2] Although still not fully mapped by neuroscience, areas of the midbrain and upper brain stem are known to be involved in the wake-sleep switch, and as noted earlier, the upper brain stem probably also plays an important role as the interface between brain and body in jhāna consciousness. Also, given that the second and higher jhānas develop slow-wave EEG activity, and that deep sleep and anesthesia also develop slow-wave activity, albeit somewhat different from the much slower rhythms in jhāna, it is likely that these very different modes of sleep, anesthesia, and jhāna share in common some of those networks in the brain.

It may be, then, that in some circumstances, components of the wake-sleep networks might become activated, triggering the mode experienced as "dropping into" deep concentration. A question then arises as to why this does not happen for someone who has developed through the tradition that informs this book. The answer to this might be twofold. First, there is the centrally important role of pīti in the Samatha Trust and other Yogāvacara traditions, effectively "waking" the body to become part of a mind-body samādhi that perhaps makes the body no longer vulnerable to the wake-sleep networks. And secondly, the Yogāvacara and the tradition taught by Nai Boonman emphasize a balance between mindfulness and concentration right up to the most subtle point of establishing a final mind-body samādhi, which, if let go too quickly, might result in overconcentration and the experienced deep concentrated states. It would be interesting to examine the EEG of someone in the deeply concentrated mode.

Not wishing to fall into the unproductive argument over true or false jhāna, I would speculate that deep concentrative modes may well have validity for some practitioners, perhaps as a form of "bhavaṅga jhāna" where the body is not yet fully incorporated in a complete mind-body samādhi, but as a prelude to further development. If the practitioner is not attached to such modes too strongly, such deep concentrative states may eventually lead to a course similar to that described in this book, particularly if meditators are moved to develop further toward the arūpa jhānas.

A related comment concerns the characteristic "embodied" nature of the jhāna experiences described throughout this book, in contrast to some descriptions in post-reform modalities of jhāna in which the body "disappears." This embodied experience has been described by meditators as "nothing left out" of the samādhi experienced in the higher jhānas, which corresponds to the EEG evidence that all the intermediate-frequency-band structures typical of sensory consciousness fade to be replaced by much slower rhythms indicative of a metabolic, bodily component to the jhāna experience, along a vertical axis in the higher jhānas.

So far there is no detailed EEG evidence from new-samatha, post-reform jhāna traditions to compare, but if it transpires that frequency-band structures typical of sensory consciousness persist in those modes, it would raise interesting questions as to whether the second and higher jhānas can be fully developed in those modalities, since the brain and its networks would still be interacting with the sensory world, even if unconsciously so, as in deep sleep or bhavaṅga.

Phra Bo Khem figures, Laos. Stages of development of Buddha nature.

7. TWILIGHT LANGUAGE, SYLLABLES, AND YANTRAS

It may be no coincidence that on the one hand language is a defining feature of sensory consciousness, while on the other hand the more symbolic and form-based aspects of language have been a central feature of esoteric Buddhism since the time of the Buddha. This chapter will explore the curious and fascinating world of syllables and yantras, and what has been referred to by some as "twilight language," but first I offer some brief background on the nature of conventional language, which implicitly raises the question as to the nature of the "unconventional."

CONVENTIONAL AND OTHER UNDERSTANDINGS OF LANGUAGE

The role of language in sensory consciousness underpins our sense of "I" as subject, in relation to objects or ideas, with verbs representing actions and a time course. This is well-described by grammar and provides a reliable structure to our everyday engagement with others and life, and it can be said that we live most of our lives immersed in conventional language. This changes radically in developing jhāna meditation, however, when the habits of naming and labeling have to be resisted to disengage from sensory consciousness, and we begin to sense that there are other aspects to how meaning is conveyed and how knowledge arises.

Over the ages philosophers and others from quite different disciplines than esoteric Buddhism have also mused over these questions. The German philosopher Gottfried Wilhelm Leibnitz, for example, from an early age explored the idea of a "primal language of thought," later writing in his *New Essays Concerning Human Understanding*, "I truly think that languages are the best mirrors of the human mind, and that an exact analysis of the signification of words would show us better than anything else the workings of the understanding."[1]

Some three hundred years later, Freud, the father of psychoanalysis, who was strongly influenced by Leibnitz, wrote, "Words which we use in our everyday speech are nothing other than watered-down magic. But we shall have to follow a roundabout path in order to explain how science sets about restoring to words a part at least of their former magical power."[2] Freud was particularly interested in how speech conveys latent meaning that the speaker is often unaware of consciously, which is a key part of a psychoanalyst's skill in seeking to understand the deeper meaning of a patient's symptoms. Freud also realized that in extreme cases words can become "things," detached from interrelational meaning, which he saw as one of the defining characteristics of psychosis. The awareness of latent meaning in speech also underpins the use of syllables, mantras, and yantras to convey otherwise unconscious meaning in the Yogāvacara.

The Structure and Neuroscience of Language

Phonemes are the units of speech in all languages that include vowels, consonants, and syllables; they are outer representations of the thought and feeling processes we express in conventional speech. A vowel is a sound produced with an open vocal tract such that the tongue does not touch the lips, teeth, or roof of the mouth, and vowels can be shorter or longer according to the feeling and meaning needing to be expressed. Consonants are speech sounds articulated with either complete or partial closure of the vocal tract, and they articulate boundaries between different segments of speech creating rhythms that convey important information to the listener. A syllable is a unit of organization for a sequence of speech sounds and is typically made up of a nucleus (usually a vowel) with initial or final margins (usually consonants). Syllables are building blocks of words—they establish the rhythm of a language, its prosody, its poetic meter, and its stress patterns.

Since we have already been considering how the EEG relates to activity in the brain during silent meditation, it is also interesting to consider how it is affected by speech—in other words, during sensory consciousness. And it turns out that there is a remarkable correspondence between average durations of speech units and the frequency bands that characterize everyday consciousness. Phonetic features such as vowels and consonants with short durations of ~20–50 milliseconds are associated with fast gamma (>50 Hz) and beta (15–30 Hz) oscillations in the brain's electrical (EEG) activity; syllables and words with somewhat longer average durations of ~250 milliseconds are associated with slower theta (4.5–7.5 Hz) oscillations; and even longer sequences of syllables and words embedded within a prosodic phrase and with durations of ~500–2000 milliseconds are associated with even slower delta oscillations (1–4 Hz).

In other words, the brain's electrical EEG activity during sensory consciousness is intimately related to conventional language. It is then no surprise to find those networks of brain activity profoundly disrupted when meditators disengage from the inner dialogue of "this" or "that" toward an inner awareness not based on conventional language.

Correlation between the acoustics of spoken language and EEG recordings has also demonstrated that temporal cortical responses in the brain's theta and beta bands contain enough information to discriminate single words,[3] and the growing understanding of the relationships between speech and brain activity confirms the links between speech and the involvement of various brain networks related to emotion, memory, and somatic activation.

The relation of these brain networks to language lends further confirmation that language is a central characteristic of sensory consciousness, and in the following sections we will be looking at the intermediate realm between sensory and jhāna consciousness where the use of language takes on more subtle and sometimes unexpected dimensions.

The Language of the Dhamma

The Buddha taught in Northeast India where the spoken language is believed to have been a version of Maghadan Prakrit, and as a former prince he would also have known Sanskrit. Initially his teachings were passed on orally, before being written down after his death in Gandhāri, and then they were recorded in Pāli, which became the Pāli Canon of Theravāda Buddhist texts. These earliest texts were written with reverence and appreciation of the forms of the characters, first on birch leaves and later palm leaves. Some birch-leaf fragments found in sealed clay jars and dating from the early first century B.C.E. can be seen in the British Museum collection.

It is not difficult to understand how these early written records became revered as sacred texts, in that they embodied the teachings of the Buddha, and how for the largely illiterate people hearing them read, the characters themselves and their forms became almost magical in carrying the meanings spoken. From this developed a reverence for the magical properties of language and script, rather than the sometimes too rigidly cognitive understanding of language that we tend to assume in the West.

This same attitude to texts is still very apparent today in Buddhist countries—certainly in Southeast Asia, where most laypeople do not have much knowledge of the Pāli language yet listen with reverence to monks chanting extracts or entire Suttas in Pāli at ceremonies to make merit, at funerals, blessings, and festivals, and so on. In fact, many monks also have only a rudimentary knowledge of Pāli, having been taught the chants by repetition, with some basic explanation of the meaning through translations into their own languages, such as Thai. The result is that certain key phrases become remembered and take on special significance. Take *Karaṇīyam attha-kusalena*, for example. These opening words of the *Mettā Sutta* on loving kindness, which translate as "this is what should be done, by one skilled in good," are capable of evoking the feel of the entire Sutta, even if it has not been memorized as a whole.

Another example is *Iti pi so*, "thus indeed is he . . . ," which forms the beginning of the recollection of the Buddha, also mentioned previously as part of invocation:

Iti pi so Bhagavā arahaṃ sammā-sambuddho vijjā-caraṇa-sampanno sugato loka-vidū anuttaro purisa-damma-sārathi satthā deva-manussānaṃ Buddho Bhagavā ti.

Thus indeed is he, the Blessed One: an arahat, fully enlightened, endowed with clear vision and virtuous conduct, sublime, knower of worlds, incomparable leader of men to be tamed, the teacher of gods and humans, enlightened and blessed.

The *Iti pi so* chant is regarded as especially auspicious and is chanted multiple times—for example, in preparing holy water (Thai, *nam mon*, literally "mantra water") for blessings. A monk leading the ritual holds a lit beeswax candle horizontally over a monk's bowl partially filled with water, while the group of monks and laypeople chant the *Iti pi so*, usually nine times. The dripping wax symbolizes fertilization in the womb that the monk's bowl represents, and the birth of all good qualities. Some readers who have taken part in blessing ceremonies in Buddhist countries may have fond memories of being liberally sprayed with such water by a monk using a bunch of birch stems dipped in nam mon.

Figure 9 is a yantra formed around a Buddha footprint, of the

Fig. 9. *Iti pi so* chant in Khom script with Buddha footprint.

complete *Iti pi so* chant written in the ancient Cambodian Khom script, starting at the bottom of the left-hand inner arc, continuing from the bottom of the left-hand outer arc, and ending at the bottom of the right-hand inner arc.

For someone, like myself, who finds it hard to remember or learn chants, the words *evaṃ me suttaṃ* are especially useful! Usually translated as "thus have I heard," these are the words that introduce *all* the Suttas that are believed to be discourses of the Buddha himself, transmitted in an oral tradition before being written down. In this way, recollection of *evaṃ me suttaṃ* may be used to invoke qualities of all the Suttas, together, that a person may have heard over the years, or know parts of, without concerning too much to remember any of them in their entirety.

TWILIGHT LANGUAGE

It is from this context of the oral Buddhist tradition that there developed "cults," or tantras, which, in the case of esoteric Buddhism and the Yogāvacara, made use of syllables, mantras, and yantras. *Tantra*, from the root *tan*, "to extend," means an elaboration—for example of a meditation technique. *Mantra*, derived from the root *man*, has the sense of guiding or binding the mind. *Yantra* (Thai, *yan*), from the root *yam*, "to support," is a supporting device or structure with a quality of precision. Southeast Asian yantra are generally much simpler than northern-Buddhist mandalas and usually incorporate syllables or characters.

In the Buddhist *Patisambhidāmagga*, the Path of Discrimination, believed to date from the mid-third century B.C.E., it is stated that one of the attainments of the arahat is mastery of four discriminations (*patisambhidā*)—of meaning, dhamma, language, and perspicacity. This is another way of formulating wisdom and insight, but the discrimination of language in this list suggests that the arahat penetrates to the roots and meanings of language itself, meaning beyond words, irrespective of specific linguistic structures, reminiscent of Leibnitz's "primal language." Related to this is the comment in the later *Vimuttimagga* that "knowledge of others' minds is called the knowledge of discrimination," implying a discrimination that does not rely on conventional language.

In 1986, Roderick Bucknell and Martin Stuart-Fox published a book titled *The Twilight Language*, based on Bucknell's efforts while spending time as a monk in Thailand to unravel the symbolic meanings behind early Buddhist descriptions of meditation and the development of wisdom and meaning embodied in ritual and forms. He was strongly moved by Tibetan examples, and in fact the term "twilight language" (*saṃdhyā-bhāṣā*) comes from descriptions of the cloaked nature of Tibetan tantra texts.

Yogavacāra texts also show a fascination with symbolic meaning, and the examples that follow illustrate an understanding of the elusiveness and multiple levels of meaning in language, and the importance of form. It is this use of syllables, characters, and magical diagrams that Bucknell and Stuart-Fox refer to as twilight language.

SYLLABLES AND YANTRAS

In this section I describe some of the main combinations of syllables found in the Yogāvacara, and how they are combined with drawn visual forms in yantras.

NA MO BU DDHA YA ꧁ ꧂ ꧃ ꧄

This group of syllables forms a mantra that appears frequently in Yogāvacara texts but is also well known across all Buddhist schools. In the Tibetan Dzogchen lineage, for example, it is regarded as the "essence of all mantra." Although in Pāli Buddhism it is usually translated as "I take refuge in the Buddha," in Dzogchen and Yogāvacara the literal meaning is considerably less important than the qualities and feelings it invokes in a person who uses it as a mantra or invocation to connect to the qualities of the Buddha and the Buddha's Path to enlightenment. In these esoteric traditions, the characters symbolize the following, in different contexts:

- the embryo in the womb with five branches: head, arms, and legs;
- the five elements earth: water, fire, air, and space;
- mother, father, king, family, and teacher; or
- the five aggregates, or khandhās, that make up a person: rūpa (form), vedanā (feelings), saññā (perceptions), saṅkhārā (mental formations or fabrications), and viññāṇa (consciousness).

The last group of khandhās is the subject of daily reflection for monks, quite apart from the specific Yogāvacara path, and one of the most evocative experiences when visiting a Buddhist temple is to hear the morning chanting just before dawn, when, following recollection of the Buddha, Dhamma, and Saṅgha, there follows this haunting and moving passage which for many meditators never fails to arouse pīti:[4]

> Rūpaṃ aniccaṃ.
> Vedanā aniccā.
> Saññā aniccā.
> Saṅkhārā aniccā.
> Viññāṇaṃ aniccaṃ.
> Rūpaṃ anattā.
> Vedanā anattā.

Saññā anattā.
Saṅkhārā anattā.
Viññāṇaṃ anattā.
Sabbe saṅkhārā aniccā.
Sabbe dhammā anattā ti.

Form is impermanent; feeling is impermanent; perception is impermanent; mental formations are impermanent; consciousness is impermanent.

Form is not-self; feeling is not-self; perception is not-self; mental formations are not-self; consciousness is not-self.

All formations are impermanent; all dhammas [phenomena] are not-self.

Followed by,

Te mayaṃ / otiṇṇāmha jātiyā jarā-maraṇena / sokehi paridevehi dukkhehi domanassehi upāyāsehi / dukkhotiṇṇā dukkha-paretā: / app' eva nām' imassa kevalassa dukkha-kkhandhassa antakiriyā paññāyethā ti. / Ciraparinibbutam pi taṃ Bhagavantaṃ saraṇaṃ gatā / dhammañ ca bhikkhu-saṅghañ ca. / Tassa Bhagavato sāsanaṃ / yathā-sati yathā-balaṃ manasikaroma / anupaṭipajjāma. / Sā sā no paṭipatti. / Imassa kevalassa dukkha-kkhandhassa antakiriyāya saṃvattatu.

All of us are subject to birth, aging and death, sorrow, lamentation, pain, grief, and despair. Bound by suffering, and obstructed by suffering. Let us aspire to complete freedom from suffering. The Exalted One who long ago attained parinibbāna is our refuge, so too the Dhamma and Saṅgha. Attentively we follow the Path of the Blessed One with all our mindfulness and strength.

May the cultivation of this practice lead us to the end
of all suffering.

The way chants such as this, dating back centuries, are able to
effectively disperse the hindrances in those listening and arouse
states normally only accessed in formal meditation is quite extraordinary and is a sign that profound states do not necessarily depend
on formal meditation techniques.

The yantra in Figure 10 is one of several depicting the embryo
with five branches, or the five khandhās. While the two in Figure 11
are yantras formed entirely by the Khom characters for the syllables
NA MO BU DDHA YA, these yantras are also often used as symbols
of mettā, or love.

To draw or execute a yantra, as continuously, smoothly, and with
as few strokes as possible, linked to the breath, is an act of samatha,
while simultaneously grasping its meaning is vipassanā.

BU DDHO ᨅᨘ ᨴᩪᩛ

As described in Chapter 2, mental repetition of BU DHO linked to
the breath is one of the oldest methods of developing jhāna. It was
practiced by Ajahn Mun, the figurehead of the Thai forest tradition, and is an ancient practice and part of the Yogāvacara as well
as boran kammaṭṭhāna (traditional meditation practices). For the
sake of completeness, the syllables in yantra form, shown before in
Figure 5 (Chapter 2), are repeated here in Figure 12.

Bu Ddho practice is still found in Southeast Asia, but silent
intonation of the syllables is also widely used as a mantra to recollect or invoke the qualities of the Buddha and the Path. BU, at the
center of this yantra, corresponds to the fire element as well as the
aggregate of perception in the Yogāvacara. In some Khmer texts,
it corresponds to one of the four purifications of sīla—namely
the "restraint of the six senses," described by the Buddha in the
Mahātaṇhāsaṅkhaya Sutta, or *Greater Discourse on the Destruction
of Craving*:

Fig. 10. Yan, khandhā.

Fig. 11. Two examples of yantras formed from the characters of
NA MO BU DDHA YA.

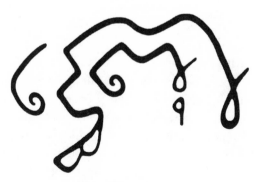

Fig. 12. Yan, BU DDHO.

Whenever the monk perceives a form with the eye, a
sound with the ear, an odour with the nose, a taste with
the tongue, an impression with the body, an object with
the mind, he neither adheres to the appearance as a whole,
nor to its parts. And he strives to ward off that through
which evil and unwholesome things, greed and sorrow,
would arise if he remained with unguarded senses: and
he watches over his senses, restrains his senses.[5]

Here the Buddha could also be describing the approach to jhāna
as outlined in earlier chapters, where the task for meditators is to
resist the habits of naming, recognition, liking and disliking, and
so on.

ME TTĀ

The syllables ME and TTĀ can be linked to the breath in a similar way as BU DDHO. With each in-breath, ME is intoned with
the intention to arouse and strengthen loving kindness (mettā),
while TTĀ is intoned on the out-breath while maintaining equanimity. After some practice, the feeling of mettā will strengthen
and develop to the point that not only does it suffuse the body but
during the intonation of TTĀ it progressively extends beyond the
body with the intention "may all beings be well and happy."

MA A U

These three syllables and characters—MA as in map, A as in hat,
and U as in up—occur together in many yantras. In the Yogāvacara,
MA represents the foundation, the body, the entire invocation, or
particularly the mother. A, the shortest vowel, "cuts" the stream of
consciousness, and in terms of jhāna meditation signals the transition from sensory consciousness to jhāna consciousness. The first
experience of jhāna is an event when something completely new,
unconditioned, and never-before-experienced arises, referred to in

the Yogāvacara as a "change of lineage," *gotrabhū*, when a person's life course is changed in a major and fundamental way. In Pāli, "a" preceding a word negates it, as in *attā* and *anattā*, self and no-self, while "u" or "upa" preceding a word indicates "higher," as in *upasampadā*, higher ordination. In the yantra tradition, U denotes the stage following A where the meditator adverts upward, as in attainment.

The sounds MA, A, and U are also used to represent different groups of threes in different yantras: such as dukkha, aniccā, and anattā; or in-breath (passāsa), out-breath (assāsa), and un-breath (nissāsa).

Together, MA A U represent the eternal essence of past, present, and future; or birth, life, and death inseparably intertwined; or as in the simple "Three Piṭakas" yantra shown in Figure 13, where they represent Sutta, Vinaya, and Abhidhamma. In another order they become the Tibetan and Indian OM (AUM), which is regarded as an invocation of spiritual power and the absolute.

Fig. 13. Yan, "Three Piṭakas."

A ᛘ

The character A has a magical cult all its own related to its ability, when placed before Pāli words, to remove whatever meaning follows, as in the already mentioned *attā* and *anattā* (self and no-self). Other examples include *vijjā/avijjā* (knowledge/absence of knowledge) and *rūpa/arūpa* (form/absence of form). This is subtly different from using the words *formless* and *ignorance*, which are discrete concepts or "things" rather than absences.

In the English language, also, *a-* is sometimes used in the same way (but pronounced as in *hay*). Take, for example, *apersonal*, a usage coming from a Greek root. It is also the first letter of the English alphabet, always a good starting point for the simple-minded meditator, and as the indefinite article it can stand for anything.

In Yogāvacara ritual or mantra, the character A signifies a break that allows adverting away from a name or concept to leave room for something entirely new to appear. Sounded in the throat, the vowel A can be extremely short, almost preceding audible sound. It cuts, and in cutting leaves a gap.

Groups of syllables are sometimes used together to utilize their different qualities. For example the syllables NA, MO, BU, DDHA, YA may be placed in order, starting with NA, at the tip of the nose, the epiglottis, the neck, the sternum, and the navel, in what is referred to in *The Path of Lanka* as the Yogāvacarin's "journey." At each stage the Yogāvacarin silently repeats the three fold mantra A RA HAM to evoke the "Dhamma treasure," the "Buddha treasure," and the "Sangha treasure" to strengthen and embed each of the NA, MO, BU, DDHA, YA syllables at the five locations, while peripherally holding nibbāna as the goal.

Some meditators practicing this visualization also find that pīti develops progressively through the five levels of intensity described earlier (Table 1, Chapter 3), as a sign of the body becoming integrated into a deepening and all-encompassing samādhi. When this five fold structure becomes stable within the body, the meditator may now visualize in sequence the constituent parts of the Khom

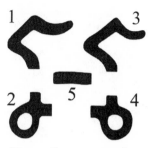

Fig. 14. Components of A.

character A in Figure 14, placing the syllables at the positions labeled one (NA) to five (YA). Position five, the center point, represents change of lineage (A) to either jhāna consciousness or the Path. The whole is ekaggatā citta, unification of mind.

This procedure is also a metaphor for establishing jhāna and is an interesting example of how much of the material in Yogāvacara texts likely reflects local traditions under a particular teacher, where techniques would have evolved to suit particular temperaments. For other temperaments, a far less directive instruction might be appropriate, as has been the case in much of the teachings behind the tradition that informs this book.

Rather than the five-branched usage shown in Figure 14, the symmetrical or mirror form of the Khmer character for A is sometimes used to illustrate its ability to make form disappear, as in Figure 15. With some creative imagination, the left and right parts, when flipped and superposed, cancel each other, reflecting the dual nature of mind, vijjā and avijjā, as the roots of suffering, while the character's unity is ekaggatā citta, unification of mind.

A RA HAṂ ដ ្ម ្ម ្ម

The syllables A RA HAṂ touched on above are a prominent feature in Yogāvacara texts, and like BU DDHO stand as epithets for the Buddha or the enlightened state. Used as silently intoned mantra, both are described in boran kammaṭṭhāna texts to invoke the

Fig. 15. Symmetry of A.

nimitta and experiences of pīti, which is in contrast to the Samatha Trust tradition, where the nimitta and pīti emerge naturally as ānāpānasati develops.

Also, similar to MA A U, the combination of three syllables in A RA HAṂ has a quite different "feel" to either binary combinations such as BU DDHO or ME TTĀ; isolated characters or syllables such as A or BU; or the five fold NA MO BU DDHA YA. The spatial nature of these different combinations is used in very creative ways in the Yogāvacara and is once again a reflection of the fine-material level of experience and loosening of the constraints of conventional language in the periphery of jhāna.

Thus, A is a precise mental act that "cuts" or negates, whereas BU DDHO and ME TTĀ are binary and are typically linked to in- and out-breaths to invoke the qualities the words represent. MA A U and A RA HAṂ, however, have the capacity to be three-dimensional, and apart from its links to groups of three in the Yogāvacara, MA A U for example is also commonly associated to the bodily forms of *Ong Phra* yantra to be described below.

In the Samatha Trust tradition, the syllables A RA HAṂ are sometimes used in a specific way to "spin" the nimitta using the "rrrr" quality of the central RA. Thus in exercises where the nimitta is associated with loving kindness, mettā, for example—where the mettā-nimitta is typically placed in the center of the body—silent intonation of A RA HAṂ may be used to stroke or spin the nimitta in much the same way as a spinning top, to spin away any imbalance, cloudiness, or illness located in the body, while allowing the nimitta and qualities of mettā to expand to suffuse the whole body, and then beyond to all beings.

NA Yantra (Thai, Na Yan)

The first character NA in the NA MO BU DDHA YA group also has a place in its own right: to represent the whole sentient being or its essence. The form of the character is sometimes depicted as being derived from the development of the embryo in the womb, as in the first part of Figure 16, the "spot," and it might be added that the whole of the Yogāvacara path is sometimes compared to a reworking of the journey of the developing embryo, but toward realization rather than repeated rebirths in the sensory world.

Based on NA, a little-known class of yantras developed known as NA yantras. Some examples (Figure 17) are humorous, some frankly rather odd, and it is again likely that they may have been drawn to illustrate a particular point of interest to a local regional group, with the original meaning long lost.

Some, however, suggest a relation to the subjective experience of pīti and energy flows in the body, as in the example at lower right in Figure 17. Here, with some variation, depending on the point being made, the central form is the "spot" (bindu) and vertical channel in the early stages of the fetus (Figure 16), with the energy flow from genital areas being redirected to activate first the diaphragm, then rising over the back of the spine to a region above the crown of the head. The development of pīti during jhāna practice is sometimes experienced subjectively in a similar way.

Fig. 16. Gestation of NA.

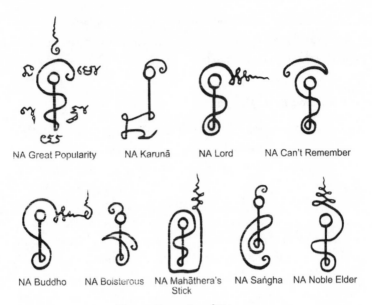

NA Great Popularity   NA Karunā   NA Lord   NA Can't Remember

NA Buddho   NA Boisterous   NA Mahāthera's Stick   NA Saṅgha   NA Noble Elder

Fig. 17. Examples of NA yan.

Ong Phra Yan

Ong is a linguistic classifier in Thai used to refer to a monk's or the Buddha's body, and this class of yantra is particularly relevant to a meditator. The left-hand example in Figure 18 has the characters NA MO BU DDHA YA placed inside the body, whereas they are below the body for the example at right. The characters MA A U are placed internally in the right-hand example and are around the head of the example at left.

The Khom character for U frequently appears inverted above the head in examples of Ong Phra yan, as it does in both these examples, in which case it is referred to as the *unalom* (*uṣṇīṣa* in Sanskrit) or flame of deliverance above the Buddha's head.

The simplest form of an Ong Phra yan would be that at right in Figure 18 but drawn without the characters and in one fluid movement as in Figure 19, left. The act of drawing is a mindfulness exercise integrating the three aspects sīla, samādhi, and paññā,

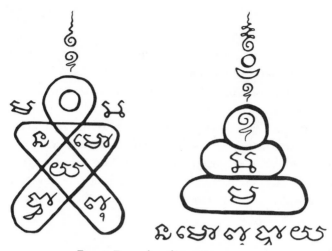

Fig. 18. Examples of Ong Phra yan.

Fig. 19. Drawing the Ong Phra yan as a meditation exercise.

or MA (foundation), A (change of lineage), and U (attainment). It doesn't matter about the order of these aspects (in fact the drawing usually begins at the top of the head and ends at the uppermost tip of the unalom).

Nor does the drawing have to be perfect. The attitude while drawing is simply the first two factors of attention, vitakka and vicāra for the first rūpa jhāna, or equally the first two bojjhaṅgas, sīla and dhamma-vicaya

The drawing may be repeated (as in Figure 19, right), paralleling repeated practice of meditation that gradually constructs an internal Dhammakāya, or body of dhamma, that can be recollected and returned to as necessary. Sometimes this recollection can usefully be employed when developing meditation, as though drawing the yantra within one's own body using the breath. Drawing a yantra is a useful lesson in not striving for perfection, including during meditation; it can lead to the realization that despite imperfections in individual practices, something quite beautiful can nevertheless eventually develop.

Yantras on Metal, Tattoos, and Amulets

In Thailand, Cambodia, Laos, and Burma, yantra are drawn on many materials for different purposes, sometimes as an aid to meditation as described above, sometimes on cloth to be hung in a shrine room, and sometimes on smaller pieces of paper or cloth to be carried or worn as a protection. Some of the most beautiful examples, however, are found inscribed on metal, often silver or mixed metals. And, strikingly, there are sacred tattoos drawn on the body.

Yantras Inscribed on Metal

Figure 20 shows two examples of multiple yantra inscribed on thin sheets of silver. The sheet at left was inscribed in honor of the Buddhist teacher Luang Por Suk of Wat Pa Klong Makham Thao (a temple around two hundred kilometers northwest of Bangkok), who was renowned for psychic power and making amulets. This sheet is dated around the time of his death in 1917 and shows many forms of yantras including examples of NA MO BU DDHA YA in yantra form, several Ong Phra yan, and other auspicious yantras.

The example at right was inscribed in 1932 to commemorate

Fig. 20. Yantras engraved on silver. *Left*: Luang Por Suk, 1917.
Right: Luang Por Derm, 1932. Both 35 × 24 cm.; author's collection.

Luang Por Derm of Wat Nong Po, around 250 kilometers northwest of Bangkok. This teacher was famous for psychic power and reputedly beloved by elephants. Again the sheet shows a mix of different forms, but note at center the NA MO BU DDHA YA Ong Phra yantra, with examples of small pīti yan (NA yan) on either side. Luang Por Derm died in 1951 at the age of ninety-two.

Figure 21 is an example using mixed metals overlaid on a silver sheet, to lend additional power to the yantras by virtue of the esoteric properties of different metals (this can be appreciated better in full color at www.shambhala.com/jhana-eeg).

This is a rare example again in honor of Luang Por Derm, and it is likely that both this and the smaller Luang Por Derm plaque in Figure 20 were produced in response to the 1932 revolution in Thailand (then Siam) that ended eight hundred years of absolute monarchy, as a meritorious act to encourage a positive outcome to the turmoil in Thai society at that time.

Fig. 21. Yantras engraved on silver with use of two other alloys.
Luang Por Derm, 1932, 62 × 35 cm.; author's collection.

Sacred Tattoos

Historically, an important medium for yantra has been the human body, with sacred tattoos popular in Thailand and Cambodia and other Asian countries for centuries. The tradition is known in Thai as *sak yan*, where *sak*, meaning "tap" in English, is equivalent to the Western "tattoo" (Figure 22). Historically such tattoos were closely linked to Buddhist practices as means of recollection and connection to the Dhamma, and many of the old tattoo masters were monks from inherited traditions. Associated uses outside the temple have been for protection, popular among the armed forces and Muay Thai boxers, as well as dubious practices related to black magic.

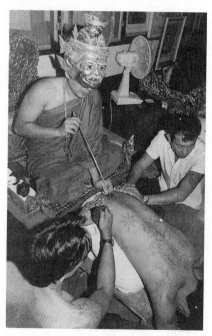

Fig. 22. Man receiving sak yan
from Buddhist tattoo master, Thailand,
date unknown.

Due to Western tourism, tattoos have become fashion statements in recent years, and little remains of the pre-reform traditions, except among some older monks. Also, since the 1960s as part of the reform movement in Thailand, tattooing has become frowned upon and forbidden for those working in government services or the armed forces, unless the designs are not visible.

The traditional method uses a long bamboo or metal instrument that the tattoo master uses to "tap" the design into the skin and draw in the ink, said to be much more painful than modern methods. The old Cambodian Khom script is used to depict Pāli words, and in northern Thailand, Lao or Shan characters are occasionally interspersed. The examples below are by kind permission of a number of Thai monks recorded in the late 1980s, who were happy to share their interest in yantras and sacred tattoos. Figure 23 is of a monk who was fortunate to meet one of the last tattoo mas-

Fig. 23. Sak yan example.

Fig. 24. Crown of Mongkut tattoo.

ters practicing in the northeast, who was himself experienced in meditation and would "transmit" the tattoo while at the threshold of jhāna, holding in mind the meaning of whichever form he was drawing. The somewhat erratic style reflects his almost trance-like state while performing the process.

The body of a monk, *ong*, is regarded as a vehicle or container of Buddha nature, with the head being the most sacred site. Only a few yantra are suitable to be tattooed on the head, such as the crown of Mongkut tattoo shown in Figure 24; visible for only a few days each month following the ritual shaving of the head before recitation of the Pāṭimokkha.

Figure 25 shows, left, an Ong Phra yan tattoo on the upper arm of a monk who had spent over thirty-five years in the robe, after abandoning a previous career as a well-known shaman; while at right are examples of "invulnerability" tattoos on a younger monk who had been a front-line soldier fighting the Khmer Rouge, who commented to me that such tattoos had failed many of his friends during the war.

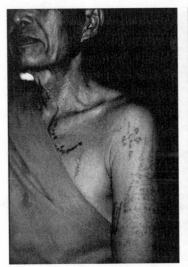

Fig. 25. More examples of sak yan.

Amulets

In Southeast Asian Buddhist countries amulets are traditional ways of commemorating monks renowned for skill in meditation and psychic power, and these are often issued to lay supporters in exchange for donations for repairs or extensions, or to have a new Buddha image cast, and so on. Often a mold is made by the monks themselves, and a limited number of amulets are made from it, then blessed in sometimes elaborate rituals. In some cases the amulets become highly prized in future years depending on their provenance. Some temples are also well known for amulet markets that spring up on their grounds in the evening or during festival days, where connoisseurs can search patiently for new treasures.

Most amulets are of fired clay, with additions of "potent" materials such as a dead monk's ashes, or the ashes from burned yantra drawn on paper, or with small amounts of gold dust, and so on. Sometimes a cavity is left inside in which a tiny relic is placed, which can be heard if the amulet is shaken. The examples in Figure

Fig. 26. Amulets from Thailand and Laos.

26 are from my own collection; all are over fifty years old and some much older. Amulets such as these all derive from samatha traditions and convey in different ways the fine-material experience in jhāna meditation.

8. The First Arūpa Jhāna: Infinity of Space

In Buddhist Suttas, the four rūpa jhānas are always followed by descriptions of four "immaterial liberations transcending form,"[1] typically referred to as the formless *āyatanas*, meaning "spheres" or "realms." However, because they are always associated with the rūpa jhānas in this way, they are often referred to as the arūpa or formless jhānas in later texts and commentaries. Also, because they are described following the fourth rūpa jhāna, with the same two jhāna factors—equanimity and unification of mind—they are often regarded as developments of the fourth rūpa jhāna. In what follows I use the terms *arūpas*, *āyatanas*, or *formless realms* interchangeably with *arūpa jhānas*.

Form, Fine-Material, and Formless Realms

In Buddhist models of consciousness such as the Abhidhamma, all forms of consciousness apart from the states of realization of nibbāna fall within either the sensory realm (kāma-loka), the fine-material realm (rūpa-loka) of the rūpa jhānas, or the formless realm (arūpa-loka) of the āyatanas, or arūpa jhānas.

It should be clear from the previous chapters that to practice jhāna meditation to disengage from sensory consciousness is a significant challenge. It also requires a parallel development of insight into the characteristics of sensory consciousness and a growing insight into the jhānas themselves. However, to move on to develop the arūpa jhānas is an entirely different but equally big challenge. Both the kāma-loka and rūpa-loka realms have something in common, which is form, no matter how fine or subtle this becomes in the fourth rūpa jhāna, but to develop beyond that into the formless states requires stepping outside the realm of form entirely.

As described in Chapter 6, the hindrances are signs that a practitioner is beginning to resist the habits of sensory consciousness in developing the rūpa jhānas. Those habits characterize living within a world of forms—rūpas—and they are the ongoing processes that fundamentally support a person's identity.

Subjectively, the habits of living within the everyday sensory world run deep and are difficult to resist—thinking, naming, comparing, liking and not-liking, wanting and not-wanting—until the benefits from disengaging—such as increased calm, happiness, and contentment—become preferable to the pull of the habits. From that point on, meditators develop more awareness and trust in the fine-material realm of the rūpa jhānas, including its characteristics described in Chapter 6, such as less dependence on formal language and more awareness of the feeling and symbolic realm.

In terms of the khandhās, the first rūpa jhāna involves working with attention, redirecting it away from sensory objects (that is, rūpas), and learning to sustain that stilled attention. Beyond the first rūpa jhāna, however, the focus turns to feeling, which is gradually refined to the point in the fourth rūpa jhāna where there is no longer any attachment to any "reward" of pleasant feeling, leaving just finely balanced and completely undisturbed equanimity. As we shall see in this and the following chapters, in the arūpa jhānas the focus shifts to working with and understanding perception, saññā.

To develop the rūpa jhānas requires a basic level of integrity of the "I" or persona to start with, to allow disengagement from the processes that support those structures, and it is one of the responsibilities of a teacher to make sure that basis is sufficient before teaching the rūpa jhānas. In a similar way, without in turn having developed a stable experience of the rūpa jhānas, to disengage further toward the formless realm can be unsettling and arouse fear—ultimately, the fear of loss of self.

Practices such as these could be dangerous or impossible for anyone with underlying character or personality issues. Even for individuals without such issues and who have a moderate experience of the rūpa jhānas, to develop the formless states requires letting go of the security of even that hard-won fine-material level of experience. Detaching from the world of rūpa entirely means letting go of all the anchors that we take for granted living in a sensory world—a reliable sense of time and space, a certain predictability of experience from one moment to the next—and all the factors that maintain our personal continuity, our sense of "I am" and "I do," a subtle trace of which remains even in the fourth rūpa jhāna due to the thread back through all the previous rūpa jhānas to the original sensory consciousness.

In pre-reform specialist meditation temples these cautions were well understood, but in addition there was no assumption that a monk would necessarily wish to develop the arūpas following the rūpa jhānas. Indeed, some monks might have been satisfied with some experience of the first and maybe the second rūpa jhāna and then gone no further, developing other interests apart from meditation; others might have aspired to practice all four rūpa jhānas, with not many reaching significant mastery; and of those who did manage to develop a good understanding of all four rūpa jhānas, only a portion might have gone further to develop the arūpa jhānas.

The same principles apply in the lay tradition that informs this book, perhaps even more so given the demands of attending to a normal lay life including families, children, work responsibilities, and so on. Also, teachers have a responsibility to know their meditators well enough to judge whether it is the right time, right person, and right circumstances to introduce the formless practices.

THE REALM OF THE INFINITY OF SPACE

In Pāli, the first arūpa jhāna is termed *Ākāsānañcāyatana*, where *ākāsā* is "space," *ānañcā* is "unlimited" or "infinite," and *āyatana* is "realm" or "sphere." Although the Pāli word *ākāsā* is normally translated as "space," this does not exactly mean empty space, or "nothing." Nor is it "something," since that would imply it had become a limited object or rūpa. Without the idea of space, however, we cannot imagine objects. Also, *ākāsā* derives from the Sanskrit root *kas*, "radiance," but in this case not light as an object, but rather as an alive potential. In some mystical traditions ākāsā is thought of as containing a record of everything that has ever happened, but also everything that will ever come to pass in the future.

The rūpa jhānas develop sequentially by transcending or mastering one or more of the jhāna factors, but the situation for the arūpas is quite different. The starting point is the fourth rūpa jhāna, but there is no longer any jhāna factor to transcend; the fourth rūpa jhāna is in itself complete as the highest development of the fine-material realm, rūpa-loka. The jhāna factors unification of mind and equanimity remain the same through all the arūpa jhānas—only the object changes. This leads to the question, how does a meditator conceptualize an object that is characterized by "infinity," unlimited or boundless?

The word *conceptualize* is generally used to refer to abstract ideas, and to express such an idea, either to oneself or to another, inevitably requires a comparison, which immediately makes clear the problem as far as the arūpas are concerned, since any comparison requires a boundary, or limit, to distinguish what something is being compared against. To some extent this touches on a question mentioned earlier in this book: How can something completely new, never experienced before, come into being? This question applies in different ways to the transition from sensory consciousness to the rūpa jhānas and now from the rūpa to the arūpa jhānas. Eventually it applies to the Path experience of realization itself.

The formless *āyatanas* are described by the Buddha on several occasions in the Nikāyas. The Pāli formulas, below for the first arūpa and in the following chapters for the further arūpas, are from the *Sallekha Sutta* in the Majjhima Nikāya.[2] As with the rūpa jhānas, the English translations are from *The Path of Purification: Visuddhimagga.*

In Pāli,

> idhekacco bhikkhu sabbaso rūpasaññānaṃ
> samatikkamā paṭighasaññānaṃ atthaṅgamā
> nānattasaññānaṃ amanasikārā 'ananto ākāso'ti
> ākāsānañcāyatanaṃ upasampajja vihāreyya.
>
> (Majjhima Nikāya 8)

> *With the complete surmounting of perceptions of matter,*
> *with the disappearance of perceptions of resistance,*
> *with non-attention to perceptions of variety, [aware of]*
> *"unbounded space," [the meditator] enters upon and*
> *dwells in the base consisting of boundless space.*
>
> (Vism. X, p. 323)

The starting point is the fourth rūpa jhāna, and the intent to completely surmount all perceptions of forms, or "matter" in the *Visuddhimagga* translation. This relates to a meditator, having gained experience practicing the fourth rūpa jhāna, realizing that despite its supremely subtle nature it is still a "held" state, and that the quality of "held" is a residual trace of the thread back through the preceding jhānas ultimately to the realm of form of the sensory world. In other words, the meditator becomes aware of a subtle limitation to the fourth rūpa jhāna in a residual dependence on the realm of form.

This recognition of the fourth rūpa jhāna as a held state is a difficult concept to grasp without direct experience, and ultimately any textual descriptions are secondary to the direct experience. However, once experienced it can be seen to correspond to the already mentioned description from the *Visuddhimagga* of being "finely balanced as on a razor's edge," alongside perfectly undisturbed equanimity. When a meditator grasps this, the alternative of a state that might be completely unbounded becomes possible to contemplate.

For a meditator of keen faculties, this realization alone may open the way to the first arūpa jhāna, since recognition of even this most subtle dependence on form automatically brings into conception an understanding that beyond this lies the counterpart—freedom from form. In other words, the meditator might understand directly at such a moment the beautiful symmetry of the rūpa and arūpa realms. Again depending on the meditator's keenness of faculties, this might then lead to the second and third factors in the Pāli formula above, *samatikkamā paṭighasaññānaṃ*, a letting-go of perceptions of sensory impingement, and *atthaṅgamā nānattasaññānaṃ*, non-attention to perceptions of diversity.

The actual impulse toward freedom from dependence on form depends on the meditator's maturity in understanding suffering as intimately related to impingements by or attachments to rūpas, either as objects or ideas, which, as I have commented several times, highlights the continuing interdependence between the jhānas and insight and eventually wisdom.

Although there have sometimes been debates about the possibility of attaining the formless experiences without prior development of the rūpa jhānas, it is difficult to imagine how this could be possible other than as a cognitive construction, without such a direct perception of the symmetry of the rūpa and arūpa realms.

Development in More Detail

Whether or not a person is of "keen faculties," it is important to understand in more detail what the processes above mean in practice, since understanding this first step into the formless realms is key to developing the higher arūpas, just as the first rūpa jhāna is key to developing the higher rūpa jhānas.

It is as though, for the person of keen faculties, that recognition of the most subtle degree of form in the fourth rūpa jhāna allows "formless" to be conceptualized, conceived, as its counterpart. This is different from the development of the rūpa jhānas, where for a person immersed in sensory consciousness there would be no way to conceptualize what the experience of jhāna might be—hence the requirement for a careful and staged disengagement from sensory consciousness in order to gradually understand the characteristics of jhāna and jhāna consciousness as distinct from sensory consciousness.

Because the fourth rūpa jhāna and the subsequent arūpas share the jhāna factors equanimity and unification of mind, a degree of conceptualization supported by equanimity can be helpful, and for most temperaments perhaps even essential. In fact, unlike the objects of meditation such as the kasinas or the breath used to develop the rūpa jhānas, the object for the first arūpa jhāna is a concept—the "infinity of space." Three approaches are described below.

By Letting Go of the Nimitta

In his explanatory guide to the *Abhidhammattha Saṅgaha*, Bhikkhu Bodhi describes the Abhidhamma model of developing the first arūpa jhāna following kasina meditation (such as a disk of earth), as follows:

> [A] meditator who has mastered the fifth fine-material jhāna [the fourth rūpa jhāna in the Suttas] based on a kasina object spreads out the counterpart sign of the kasina until it becomes immeasurable in extent. Then he removes the kasina by attending only to the space it pervaded, contemplating it as "infinite space." Through repeated attention given in this way, there eventually arises in absorption a citta having as object the concept of infinite space (ākāsapaññatti).[3]

This describes a form of conceptualization, but one far removed from the kind of thinking we are familiar with in sensory consciousness. It also takes place at the very threshold of the fourth rūpa jhāna, and incidentally illustrates the great subtlety and wieldiness of mind at this peak of development of the fine-material jhānas, and the ability of an experienced practitioner to rest in the deepest level of equanimity and undisturbed consciousness, but to nevertheless be able to move slightly from that position to conceptualize in this way. This form of conceptualization is more a matter of visualization and willpower, progressively letting go of perceptions of diversity, difference, or boundaries as the nimitta is extended until finally it has no limits.

It is difficult to know how common this approach was in pre-reform times, but it appears uncommon today. In my experience very few kasina practitioners develop mastery of the higher jhānas and the arūpa jhānas, and particularly for the arūpa jhānas experience difficulty in letting go of attachment to the nimitta of the kasina. Accordingly, many such practitioners transfer to ānāpāna-sati to develop the arūpa jhānas.

By Way of Invocation

I have already asserted that meditators cannot "think themselves" into the rūpa jhānas and for the arūpa jhānas this is even more so. A more direct approach is then to use invocation. After practicing the fourth rūpa jhāna and having become aware of it still as a "held" state, a meditator acknowledges a wish to experience the realm of infinite space, followed by silently intoning the syllables "ākāsa, ākāsa"—or, if preferred, "space, space."

Many practitioners also find it helpful to lengthen the breath to mark a transition away from the fourth rūpa jhāna, where the breath is usually so extremely fine and delicate as to be barely present, if at all, and to begin the first "ākāsa" during a first long in-breath. The long slow in-breath aids the sense of developing spaciousness. The word *ākāsā* is treated as containing the essence of infinite space, or

as a symbol of infinite space, such that if the invocation is successful and as the final sound of "a" comes to an end, then in the "gap"
created, infinite space appears. It is no accident that the related
invocation *Okāsa!* is used in Yogāvacara practices to express "let
it be made manifest." If the invocation is successful the length of
breath becomes immaterial, in both senses of the word.

In accordance with the Pāli formula described earlier, the meditator approaching the first arūpa jhāna resists any urge to look for
anything in the space created. If any discrimination of boundaries, limits, shapes, or other features creeps in, the silent invocation
"ākāsa" is repeated, and after progressing in this way several times
an increasing sense of limitless space may develop.

The meditator will be making use of the understanding gained
in the rūpa jhānas of resisting any move away from balance and
stillness, particularly its culmination in the perfect equanimity of
the fourth rūpa jhāna, with the added dimension of resisting any
urge to recognize a nimitta that, in the rūpa jhānas, is a necessary
core part of the jhāna experience to support unification of mind.
As already noted, letting go of dependence on the nimitta is usually
easier coming from a background of gradual progress in ānāpānasati, rather than from the kasinas.

By Dhamma-Vicaya and Visualization

A person who practices using invocation will usually benefit from
another approach on different occasions, using a method that taps
into the subtle use of dhamma-vicaya, investigation, that is possible
at the threshold of the fourth rūpa jhāna. This is not the same as
"thinking oneself" into jhāna, as by this time following the fourth
rūpa jhāna the meditator is far removed from crude discursive
thinking. It is the same quality of dhamma-vicaya that allows a
meditator, practicing recollection immediately after emerging
from one of the jhānas, to come to understand directly the jhāna
factors and "where he or she has been" without the usual comparative discursive thinking of sensory consciousness.

At this stage, though, the translation "investigation" does not exactly capture the quality that is possible at the threshold of the fourth rūpa jhāna, and something closer to insight and intuitive wisdom, or sati-sampajañña—mindfulness coupled with clear comprehension or knowing—might be more appropriate. This capacity is also an example of the close interrelatedness of the jhānas and wisdom in the parallel processes of samatha and vipassanā as the twin kammaṭṭhāna.

So, with variations, meditators practicing outside in the open air might emerge from the fourth rūpa jhāna and gaze at the sky, ideally a relatively cloudless sky, noticing with equanimity the empty spaces, the occasional cloud, and the boundaries or limits such as the horizon. Then, closing their eyes, they create a parallel experience of limitless sky with no features, and no boundaries, in a sense as an unbounded nimitta of the external experience.

After repeated practice in this way, each time letting go of any slightest feature, boundary, or even color (although interestingly a quality of light may remain for a while), a point will come where nothing remains to distinguish one part from another, no longer any "something," all the while maintaining equanimity. This eventually leads to an experience where meditators realize that for space to be truly limitless, with no boundaries and nothing to discriminate, they themselves have to *become* the experience of infinite space. At that moment all that discriminates form disappears, including any sense of body, or light, although with more familiarity subtle perception might be found to remain.

Challenging Subjectivity

When infinite space becomes the entire experience, with nothing to distinguish the meditator from it, subjectivity appears to completely disappear. If a sense of subjectivity were to reappear, the experience is lost and a subject-object pair is created with the implicit boundaries that that implies, and the meditator would be back in the form realm. As with early experiences of the rūpa jhānas, a meditator may not at first be able to sustain the experience for very long, but with repeated practice it becomes known through direct experience and can be sustained for longer.

In this first arūpa, the experience is of immense and unlimited spaciousness, with a corresponding freedom from any complexity, including the encumbrance of maintaining a sense of subjectivity. The experience is entirely of the object pole, in contrast to all previous experience of a linguistically based subject-object pair in sensory consciousness, and even the more subtle fine-material subject-object pair implicit in the "held" state of the fourth rūpa jhāna.

9. The Second Arūpa Jhāna: Infinity of Consciousness

The initial experience of the first arūpa can be as momentous a moment for a meditator as that of the first rūpa jhāna. To experience infinite space, with absolutely nothing to distinguish as an object and with a complete absence of subjectivity, is to discover a new freedom from even the most subtle dependence on form that remains in the fourth rūpa jhāna. This quality of freedom is a distinctive experience in the arūpa jhānas that distinguishes them from those of the fine-material realm.

At the same time, since the meditator is fully aware during the experience—that is, fully conscious—it is known intuitively that to simply interpret the experience as a disappearance of subjectivity is too crude or simplistic, rooted in the habits of labeling and perception within sensory consciousness. This realization is expressed beautifully by Lama Anagarika Govinda in his *Foundations of Tibetan Mysticism*:

> In the moment in which a being becomes conscious of his consciousness, he becomes conscious of space. In the moment in which he becomes conscious of the infinity of space, he realizes the infinity of consciousness.[1]

Given his broad experience of Theravāda Buddhist and Tibetan practices, Govinda's comment bridges Theravāda and Mahāyāna understandings of the formless jhānas, even though in this quotation the jhānas are not explicitly named. He describes a realization "in the moment"—that is, a direct, intuitive understanding outside conventional subject-object language.

THE REALM OF THE INFINITY OF CONSCIOUSNESS

Govinda's statement highlights a remarkable duality between infinite space and infinite consciousness, which is intuited directly by the meditator as a form of direct understanding. It is an understanding that can only be realized by developing and experiencing for oneself the first and second arūpa jhānas, which in a sense are two perspectives on a common reality.

In fact the second arūpa jhāna does not depend on establishing a conceptualization of infinite consciousness as object, as was required to establish infinite space for the first arūpa jhāna. In this second arūpa jhāna its object is not a concept at all, but rather the implicit understanding already there in the experience of the infinity of space, of the presence of infinite consciousness as the counterpart of limitless space, even though that consciousness is not attended to.

A meditator with sharp faculties may grasp this very quickly, even immediately, in which case it requires but a straightforward mental act of "adverting" to the consciousness of perceiving infinite space to immediately enter the subject position of infinite consciousness, which in Pāli is termed the *viññāṇancāyatana*. Here, *viññāṇa* is "consciousness," *ānañcā* is "unlimited" or "infinite," and *āyatana* is once again "realm" or "sphere." The formula in Pāli, below, illustrates this direct progression from the previous first arūpa jhāna:

In Pāli,

**idhekacco bhikkhu sabbaso ākāsānañcāyatanaṃ
samatikkamā 'anantaṃ viññāṇan'ti
viññāṇañcāyatanaṃ upasampajja vihareyya.**
(Majjhima Nikāya 8)

By completely surmounting the base consisting of
boundless space, [aware of] "unbounded consciousness,"
[the meditator] enters upon and dwells in the base
consisting of boundless consciousness. (Vism. X, p. 327)

For a meditator of less-than-sharp faculties, a similar procedure of invocation as described for the first arūpa jhāna can be
followed as a preliminary step to help the process along. The procedure might be something like the following, although meditators must each perform their own explorations to grasp the idea.
After bringing to mind a wish to experience the realm of infinite
consciousness following the first arūpa jhāna, the meditator having gained some experience of the realm of infinite space with-
draws just sufficiently to intone the words "viññāṇa, viññāṇa" or,
if preferred, "infinite consciousness, infinite consciousness." If the
invocation is successful and as the final sound fades, in that "gap"
infinite consciousness becomes the all-encompassing experience.
Here the meditator is once again applying the principle of *Okāsa!*
Let it be made manifest!

If the procedure of dhamma-vicaya is applied as a preliminary, it
needs to be very simple and minimal, more so than in developing
the first arūpa jhāna, since the second arūpa jhāna is even further
removed from linguistic conceptualization. A simple "question" on
emerging to the threshold of infinite space, as to where or what
is consciousness at that moment, similar to a Zen koan, may be
enough to trigger the realization.

SUBJECT-OBJECT BASIS OF CONSCIOUSNESS

Practicing the first two arūpa jhānas, it gradually becomes clear
that the arūpa states are an exceedingly creative way of disengaging
from attachment to the subject-object basis of consciousness, at
least for a while.

The first and second arūpa jhānas are inextricably interconnected, in a sense as two aspects of the same reality as Govinda rather beautifully expresses. To develop the first arūpa jhāna, to make the object—space—infinite, the meditator has to become one with it so that space is no longer a limited separate object, which in psychoanalytic parlance could be described as completely identifying with the object pole. But since consciousness requires both an object to be conscious of and a subject to experience that object, then in the first arūpa jhāna the subject pole must be present, but entirely unfocally conscious, or entirely unselfconscious, or both.

However, it would be a mistake to describe the subject pole as "unconscious," since consciousness requires both a subject and an object position, and one cannot be spoken of without the other. Similarly for the experience of the infinity of consciousness.

In sensory consciousness both poles arise automatically for any moment of consciousness, and to attempt to imagine an experience with just one pole would be merely an intellectual, cognitive construction. The procedure in the arūpa jhānas of making the meditation object infinite, and then adverting to the consciousness of that, is then a remarkable technique to *experientially* separate the subject and object poles to weaken attachment to subject-object duality.

To develop the arūpas therefore takes the meditator to the very roots of perception and the processes that underpin what we experience as consciousness, and it becomes increasingly clear that the arūpas following the rūpa jhānas are means of developing insight into what exactly constitutes our conscious experience and identity.

10. THE THIRD ARŪPA JHĀNA: NOTHINGNESS

The first two arūpa jhānas may be considered an interdependent pair, in that the meditator practicing these jhānas moves between the complementary poles of the process of perception. Even having moved to the pole of infinite consciousness, the other pole, infinite space, is both there and not there, since the second arūpa jhana arose from that base and has no ultimate reality except in counterpart. Awareness of this interdependence and the lack of ultimate reality in experiencing either position allows the meditator to conceive of moving to a central position identified with neither pole, although both are there in potential, which is the experience of the third arūpa jhāna known as the realm of nothingness, *Ākiñcaññāyatana*. Here, *ākiñca* is "nothing," and *āyatana* is again "realm" or "sphere."

In this sense the object of the third arūpa jhāna is a concept, as it was for the first arūpa jhāna, albeit now a very subtle concept. The concept is "neither subject nor object"—nothing, no-thing, nothingness, emptiness.

THE REALM OF NOTHINGNESS

Having developed and become familiar with the first two arūpas, the meditator can determine (as a mental act, adhiṭṭhāna) to take a middle position grasping neither—resisting any mental movement toward subjectivity, on the one hand, or toward discerning any object, on the other—and to then maintain that position with equanimity and unification of mind. These same two jhāna factors continue to support a parallel development of insight from the fourth rūpa jhāna onward, becoming ever more subtle as the arūpas develop.

For a meditator with keen faculties this equates to a direct realization of the equality of the two positions revealed by the previous first and second arūpa jhānas, followed by a mental movement to take up a middle position identifying with neither. This is expressed by the Pāli formula below, in which the phrase '*natthi kiñci'ti*—"there is nothing"—establishes the state of nothingness in much the same way as invocation.

In Pāli,

idhekacco bhikkhu sabbaso viññāṇañcāyatanaṃ samatikkamma 'natthi kiñcī'ti ākiñcaññāyatanaṃ upasampajja vihareyya. (Majjhima Nikāya 8)

By completely surmounting the base consisting of boundless consciousness, [aware that] "there is nothing," [the meditator] enters upon and dwells in the base consisting of nothingness. (Vism. X, p. 329)

If this does not develop in a straightforward manner, an overt act of invocation by intoning "ākiñca, ākiñca," or "nothing, nothing" as for the previous arūpas may help. The word *ākiñca* is particularly suited to invocation à la Yogāvacara since *kiñca* means "something" and *a-kiñca* means "not-something," and this is another example of the magical property of the letter *a* in the Pāli language to remove whatever follows, as described in Chapter 7.

If a meditator has progressed this far, a supplementary practice of conceptualization using a refined form of dhamma-vicaya should not be necessary; invocation is more direct, and preferred, if it is necessary at all.

THE NEUROSCIENCE OF THE ARŪPA JHĀNAS: PRELIMINARY FINDINGS

All the neuroscience examples described so far have been for the rūpa jhānas, and it was commented earlier that being recorded while meditating is a considerable challenge to a meditator's concentration and equanimity, particularly so when developing the higher jhānas and the arūpas.

The observer effect familiar in quantum physics recognizes that even the most subtle act of measurement profoundly affects what is being observed or measured. For example, a quantum of light in isolation has the potential to behave like a particle or as a wave, both states existing in potential as "superposed states" until, at the point of being observed, the system is triggered into one or other state— wave or particle. An act of measurement implies an observer, and for the meditator there is not only the external EEG technician-observer, but also the counterpart of an internalized "commentator" from which it is the task in meditation to disengage.

Attempts to record an EEG during arūpa jhāna have been almost entirely unsuccessful, and in an attempt to at least moderate the observer effect some experiments were tried where the meditator managed the recording. This at least removed a third party from the situation, but the pull toward becoming an internalized observer still remains, and only one recording so far might be considered a possible example of the effects on the brain of practicing the arūpa jhānas. In this recording the technician completed all the preparatory tests including fitting the head-cap, checking that the software and hardware were all functioning correctly, before leaving the meditator when ready to simply press a button to start the recording and to then enter meditation for a predetermined duration, in this case to attempt to develop the third arūpa jhāna.

The recording is described in more detail in Chapter 12, Part 2, but the immediate and most startling feature compared to any of the recordings of the rūpa jhānas was that strong slow-wave

158 — JHĀNA CONSCIOUSNESS

rhythms at frontal sites were almost mirror images of those at posterior sites. This suggested a near-perfect antiphase relationship between frontal and posterior sites, where energization of one balances and effectively cancels de-energization of the other.

Recollecting our earlier hypothesis that the subject-object nature of sensory consciousness involves a reciprocal relationship between posterior sites that carry the I/eye subject position, with frontal sites that relate to cognitive processing and features of the "object," this observation of an antiphase relationship might be seen as a reflection of this meditator's attempts in developing the third arūpa jhāna to resist identifying with either the subject or the object pole, but to hold a position of equanimity "in the middle."

By this stage in developing the arūpa jhānas, meditators might typically recognize a quite different process compared to the rūpa jhānas. Because the jhāna factors upekkhā (equanimity) and ekaggatā citta (unification of mind) remain the same, the quality of "jhāna" does not change; it remains essentially as it was in the fourth rūpa jhāna, although the quality of upekkhā becomes ever more subtle and refined, with an increasingly powerful quality of freedom. At the same time, the qualities of responsiveness and workability of mind develop with an accompanying realization that jhāna and insight are working together with no regression to thinking or coarse discrimination.

This is also related to realizing that what does change in the arūpa jhānas is the understanding and nature of perception, which carries with it a parallel realization of the illusory nature of subject-object, rūpa-arūpa, form and emptiness, and all dualities, which leads us to consider the fourth arūpa jhāna.

11. THE FOURTH ARŪPA JHĀNA: NEITHER PERCEPTION NOR NON-PERCEPTION

At this stage one might wonder, what could be more subtle, what else is there to let go of? This approaches the question "Who perceives?"—since the essence of perception is that there has to be a subject who perceives. Even in the fine balance of the third arūpa jhāna, any movement from that balance can result in a moment of consciousness, a moment of perception that creates a subject-object of the type we are familiar with. Yet the experience of progressing through ever more subtle stages of perception will have greatly weakened old habits and assumptions regarding self, other, perception, and consciousness.

This begins in the first arūpa jhāna, the infinity of space. To let go of the slightest perceptions of difference in how we conceive of space, to let go of all limits or restrictions, all qualities normally expressed in the language of "this" or "that," is a profound experience. Because it is unlimited and unbounded with nothing left of the old assumptions of difference, everything changes for the meditator who reaches this stage.

To then apply this same process to consciousness, deeply related to how we experience ourselves—to let go of all distinguishing characteristics of a personal identity, including our birth name—is an equally profound experience challenging the roots of subjectivity and sense of self.

One remarkable outcome of this is to realize the fundamental "sameness" of all qualities and experience, the fundamental sameness of all dualities—subject/object, form/emptiness, and even meditation/non-meditation—as well as the *a*- dualities—rūpa/ arūpa, niccā/aniccā, attā/anattā, kiñca/ākiñca, and so forth. One begins to understand, therefore, the illusory construction of difference as exemplified in everyday sensory consciousness by conventional language, in which any choice of *this* excludes uncountable *thats*, with a consequent restriction on what can be given attention or considered. And the meditator learns that even at the refined levels of perception reached in the arūpa jhānas, the realization of perception itself is ultimately binding and restrictive.

So where then to go from here? The dilemma is nicely summed up in this fragment from the *Salla Sutta* of the Khuddaka Nikāya:

"Yena yena hi maññanti tato taṁ hoti aññatha" (For, however they conceive it to be, it turns out to be otherwise).

THE REALM OF NEITHER PERCEPTION NOR NON-PERCEPTION

To maintain the "middle" position of the third arūpa jhāna, meditators have to restrain the impulse to perceive an object, no matter how subtle, or to perceive their own subjectivity, even at the most basic level of awareness of "something," which could be anything, given the growing understanding of sameness. In other words, the power of difference has faded to the extent that the activity of perception itself is revealed more clearly with a consequent weakening of attachment to that coarse form of perception.

To hold the middle position, perception necessarily becomes extremely refined, to become simply perception of the middle position itself rather than the previous coarser perceptions of either subject or object. At this stage this fine perception becomes intimately part of the quality of upekkhā, which itself has become correspondingly more subtle, to the point in fact that it becomes meaningless to speak of them separately at this stage.

Readers may notice a similarity here to the completion stage for the third rūpa jhāna, in which the distinction between the two qualities sukha and upekkhā also becomes increasingly meaningless and dissolves to reveal the perfection of upekkhā in the fourth rūpa jhāna.

In the case of the third arūpa jhāna, then, a direct realization or intuitive understanding may arise that even this most subtle level of perception is a restriction, allowing the meditator to intuit a direction to step back from even subtle perception, with its "near enemy" of coarse perception, to establish a liminal point of "neither perception nor non-perception," or *Nevasaññānasaññā*, in the fourth arūpa jhāna, which is described in the Suttas as follows:

In Pāli,

idhekacco bhikkhu sabbaso ākiñcaññāyatanaṃ samatikkamma nevasaññānasaññāyatanaṃ upasampajja vihāreyya. (Majjhima Nikāya 8)

By completely surmounting the base consisting of nothingness, [the meditator] enters upon and dwells in the base consisting of neither perception nor non-perception. (Vism. X, p. 330)

At this point I have no inclination to suggest a separate invocation along the lines of "Nevasaññānasaññā," "neva-n'a," or "neither-nor" to invoke the fourth arūpa. My sense is that distinctions of keen or less-than-keen faculties no longer apply at this stage, and that the fourth arūpa jhāna will emerge from the third rather like the fourth rūpa jhāna was described as emerging from the third rūpa jhāna, at the right time and given the right circumstances.

In this neither-nor description of perception, some vestige or liminal state of consciousness is necessarily retained, perhaps itself with a neither-nor nature. This may have some similarity to the liminal neither-nor feeling state of the fourth rūpa jhāna but is replaced now by the completely unbounded liminal neither-nor perception of the fourth arūpa jhāna.

With no impulse to perceive or to not-perceive, it is not possible to have even the most subtle reflection on the state while experiencing it, unlike the previous arūpas, and it is very difficult to conceive what kind of perception remains that can be neither-nor in this description. Again I am struck by the similarity to the idea in quantum physics of superposed states, a neither-nor realm that can exist only so long as it is not disturbed by an act of measurement or observation, or in this case by an impulse to perceive. In fact it could be said that letting go of even the most subtle impulse to perceive is what allows the neither-nor quality of the fourth arūpa to emerge. As a former physicist with an interest in quantum theory, I cannot help being aware that this same dilemma of maintaining a neither-nor state is a central problem in designing a quantum computer.

In the realm of the arūpas, this leads to the questions of where the impulse to perceive would come from and who perceives? The nature of the self that supports perception comes to the forefront in this question, and several meditators have recognized a similarity to the concept of anattā, not-self, which many have used as a meditation topic in the form of recollection of the three marks of existence—aniccā, impermanence; dukkha, suffering; and anattā, not-self—typically practiced after emerging from any of the jhānas. Again this highlights the increasingly close parallel development of the jhānas and wisdom.

INTEGRATION AND EMBEDDING OF THE JHĀNAS

Most meditators who practice beyond the rūpa jhānas into the arūpas find it helpful to alternate or move between the two realms once they have a reasonable understanding of at least the first two arūpa jhānas. This is similar to experiencing different routes through the stages of ānāpānasati and the rūpa jhānas, as described

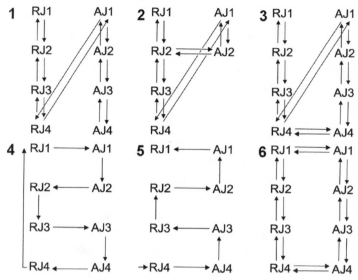

Fig. 27. Exploring routes through and between the
rūpa and arūpa jhānas.

in Chapter 6, with the added dimension of changing between the fine-material and formless realms as well as in the stages of the different jhānas.

Mostly this is a matter of personal exploration, and as with the stages of ānāpānasati and the rūpa jhānas there are several possible routes, some of which are shown in Figure 27, where the rūpa jhānas are designated RJ1, RJ2, RJ3, and RJ4, and the arūpas AJ1, AJ2, AJ3, and AJ4.

Route 1 is then the initial progressive route through the rūpa jhānas to RJ4, then to AJ1, AJ2, AJ3, and AJ4 before retracing in the reverse order AJ4, AJ3, AJ2, AJ1, RJ4, RJ3, RJ2, RJ1, and from there back to sensory consciousness by whatever route the meditator favors.

Route 2 starts from RJ1, and from there can progress either to RJ2, RJ3, RJ4, to AJ1 to AJ2, then back to RJ2, then RJ1; or from RJ1 to RJ2 to AJ2 to AJ1, back to AJ2 to RJ2 and RJ1. Route 3 is similar with direct transitions between RJ4 and AJ4, and although not drawn here another would be with transitions between RJ3 and AJ3.

Routes 4 and 5 focus even more on moving between rūpa and arūpa modes, while route 6 shows circular modes that can be practiced in forward or reverse order, and from different starting points.

Even if meditators do not feel inclined to explore as fully as this, most comment that moving from, say, the second arūpa jhāna to the second rūpa jhāna, and back, perhaps repeated several times, deepens the understanding of each realm in comparison to the other, helping meditators to understand their complementary nature and interdependence. This is also relevant to the comments above about the similarities in the transition from the third to the fourth rūpa jhāna, and from the third to the fourth arūpa jhāna.

Becoming familiar in this way with the felt experiences of the different jhānas within their own realm, as well as the different felt experiences in alternating realms, is a means of embedding these experiences in the body, which is an intriguing feature of Yogāvacara practices that recognize the crucial importance of the body in establishing unification of body-mind—that is, yoga.

Some boran kammaṭṭhāna texts describe other methods of embedding, such as visualizing different syllables, or elements, or the five pītis and placing them at specific points in the body.[1] In the Samatha Trust tradition, however, such directive instructions have been generally avoided to ensure preconceptions do not distort what develops in a direct and natural manner from practice. One method that has evolved and been found helpful, however, is described below.

THE WAX-TAPER PRACTICE

Both the *Yogāvacara's Manual* and *The Path of Lanka* include enigmatic references to a "wax-taper practice," but without detailed explanations. In the tradition that underpins this book, this practice developed in an intriguingly natural way out of direct experi-

Fig. 28. The wax-taper practice.

ence of some meditators in their explorations of the jhānas from
the early 1990s.

Figure 28 shows the basic arrangement of a slim beeswax candle
mounted on crossed bamboo pieces, bound together with *sai sin*
(Thai, "thread of sīla") and resting on a monk's bowl. Sai sin consists of nine strands of raw cotton and may be familiar to readers
who have taken part in pūja, or blessing ceremonies, where it is
often tied around the wrist as a protection and symbol of maintaining the precepts of sīla.

In Yogāvacara, the monk's bowl symbolizes the mother's womb;
the candle and crossed bamboo pieces, the body and limbs of the
practitioner, bound and protected by sīla; and the flame represents
consciousness.

Four weights rest on pins inserted into the candle at intervals in such a way that as the candle burns down and reaches a pin, the weight falls into the bowl making a characteristic sharp sound.

The wax-taper practice as it has emerged in this tradition can be used in several ways. A first and general use is as a test of a meditator's concentration. Normally if practicing alone a meditator has to make a resolution before starting as to how long to practice, or to rely on a reminder of some sort, or to simply wait until they emerge naturally. In guided practice the group leader ends the practice by typically sounding a bell. In the wax-taper practice no one is in control of the duration between the sounds of the weights falling, and there is no point in letting any anticipation develop, particularly given that handmade beeswax candles can be notorious in their unpredictable burning rates. So the test for the meditator is to let go completely of "expecting" or waiting for anything, which, once recognized, can allow very deep concentration to develop free from the sense of time that is more or less automatic in everyday sensory consciousness.

A second use of this practice is to "embed" the jhānas. The intention is established at the beginning, that after lighting the candle the meditator will develop the approach stages to jhāna, and when the first weight falls will immediately advert to enter the first rūpa jhāna; when the second weight falls will enter the second jhāna; and so on for the third and fourth rūpa jhānas. If the rūpa jhānas are established in a preparatory practice the same procedure can be used for the arūpa jhānas. There are more nuances to this practice, which is up to the "conductor" to articulate, or not.

Other uses of this ancient practice, or ritual, develop in response to stages of development of different groups, and beyond the jhānas become relevant to development of the Path and wisdom.

PART TWO

Modern Neuroscience, Consciousness, and an Ancient Path

12. Neuroscience of the Jhānas

In this chapter fuller descriptions are given of the EEG recordings referred to briefly in each of the chapters on the individual jhānas. Supplementary material is also available in color at www.shambhala.com/jhana-eeg, and readers wishing to pursue this material in even more depth can download my 2019 paper, "The Human Default Consciousness and Its Disruption: Insights from an EEG Study of Buddhist Jhāna Meditation," from the *Frontiers in Human Neuroscience* website.

The First Rūpa Jhāna

The challenges in being recorded during meditation center on an almost irresistible pull toward becoming overly self-conscious, which is in direct opposition to the need to let go of such concerns in order to disengage from sensory consciousness. The typical situation of wearing a head-cap with associated cables as shown in Figure 29 may give an idea of the actual recording situation.

Most of the subjects recorded handled these challenges very well, which is attested to by the consistent themes in EEG activity related to known characteristics of the jhānas that were observed during their meditation. The head-caps used in the study were connected to medical-grade amplifiers and analysis software, either hard-wired, as in Figure 29, or in some cases using a wireless amplifier. The electrode positions on the head are shown in Figure 30 and follow an internationally agreed protocol to allow experiments to be repeated with consistency. For more detailed information on equipment and methodology readers are referred to the *Frontiers* paper.

Fig. 29. EEG 31-electrode head-cap.

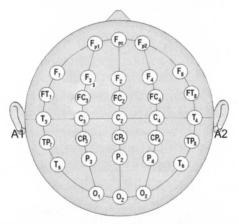

Fig. 30. Electrode positions. F frontal; T temporal; C central; P parietal; O occipital.

In previous chapters, I outlined how the defining characteristic of the first rūpa jhāna is the development of a deep understanding of attention. This development marks the beginning of the process of disengaging from the habits of sensory consciousness—in particular, discursive thinking, naming, mentally commentating, and liking/disliking. In Buddhist understandings of jhāna this involves two aspects of attention, described by the first two jhāna factors, vitakka and vicāra—placing attention on the meditation object and sustaining that attention. In this section we look at the two meditation practices Bu Ddho and ānāpānasati as examples of how brain activity is profoundly disrupted when redirecting attention inward, first to the breath and then to the increasingly mind-based object, the nimitta, mentioned earlier.

Bu Ddho

This first example from Bu Ddho practice was not reported in the peer-reviewed study, which focused entirely on ānāpānasati, the main modality taught by the Samatha Trust. However, some meditators have explored the Bu Ddho method, and it provides a fascinating comparison to ānāpānasati. Figure 31 shows a thirty-five-second segment from an EEG recording following the cue to begin Bu Ddho practice. The left-hand column lists electrode labels

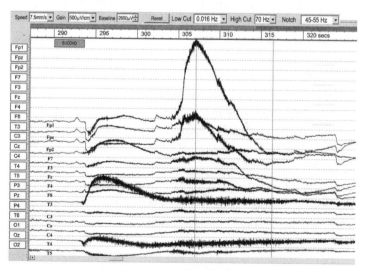

Fig. 31. EEG segment during Bu Ddho practice.

that correspond to positions shown in Figure 30, with frontal sites at the top, and posterior sites at the bottom.

The horizontal bar at the top shows time in seconds, and for this recording the intensity scale was set at 500 microvolts per centimeter (μV/cm) to show the full extent of the intense activity that follows. To put this into perspective, normal resting-state EEG activity is much weaker, typically 20–50 μV peak-to-peak. The whole record is also shifted down to show the full extent of the very high-intensity peak that develops at the frontal electrode Fp1.

Within two to three seconds following the cue to begin, frontal electrical activity is suppressed by around 300–400 μV, while activity at temporal sites T3 and T4 is strongly increased—at T4, for example, by around 1,000 μV, a very high intensity by normal EEG standards. It can hardly be a coincidence that this occurs at the time the meditator silently intones the syllable BU, and that the temporal lobe sites T3 and T4 are precisely the location of the auditory cortex of the brain, demonstrating a direct link to those brain networks being activated during intonation of BU.

About ten seconds later, during which time the meditator is now sounding the syllable DDHO, a massive excitation develops at frontal sites, reaching over 2,000 μV at Fp1, again almost unheard of in EEG research, let alone as the result of a person's willed intention. In Buddhist jhāna theory, however, this fits well with the purpose of Bu Ddho being to arouse high levels of pīti, energization, which is then tranquilized into, eventually, jhāna.

The whole procedure of Bu Ddho is a good example of the interactive relationship between the first three jhāna factors— vitakka, vicāra and pīti—as well as the first five bojjhaṅgas. BU establishes mindfulness, or sati (the first bojjhaṅga), and vitakka (placing attention, the first jhāna factor) as a moment in time. The slow intonation of DDHO adds vicāra (sustained attention, the second jhāna factor) in the same manner as the fading reverberation of the bell in the bell simile. In terms of the bojjhaṅgas, sustained attention is related to salience, which requires a degree of dhamma-vicaya, or investigation, the second bojjhaṅga; and the whole endeavor of the Bu Ddho practice requires willpower, or vigor, the third bojjhaṅga. The high energization of pīti (the third jhāna factor and the fourth bojjhaṅga) is calmed during the DDHO phase into a deepening stillness and peace in the approach to the absorption of jhāna, reflecting the activity of the fifth bojjhaṅga, passaddhi, tranquilization.

From the EEG study of Ānāpānasati

Across the total group of twenty-nine meditators, of varying levels of experience, three themes were identified as meditators developed the first and then higher jhānas. As noted earlier, the most common theme was the occurrence of spindles, a surprising finding given their more usual occurrence in light sleep, anesthesia, or situations of conflicted attention. The frequency of their occurrence suggested a relationship to the early stages of developing jhāna and disengagement from sensory consciousness.

Spindles are disruptions of the brain's alpha rhythm (around 8–12 Hz), which is normally mostly random and located near the back of the head as a sign of a relaxed resting state, particularly when the eyes are closed. When a person opens their eyes to re-engage with the visual world, the alpha rhythm is suppressed, and faster rhythms develop related to thinking and cognitive processes. Figures 32 and 33 show two examples of spindles during meditation, where both figures follow the same format regarding electrode positions and so on, as in Figure 30.

"Spindles" may be an unfamiliar term to many readers, but they are simply very brief symmetrical or near-symmetrical bursts of activity in the EEG. Figure 32 shows an example where spindles are very prolific, with a broad distribution across large areas of this subject's head, whereas Figure 33 shows them occurring mainly toward the back of a subject's head. The enlarged extract at the bottom of Figure 33 shows their characteristic symmetrical "wave-packet" form when they are well-developed, compared to the normally more irregular non-meditating alpha rhythm, also

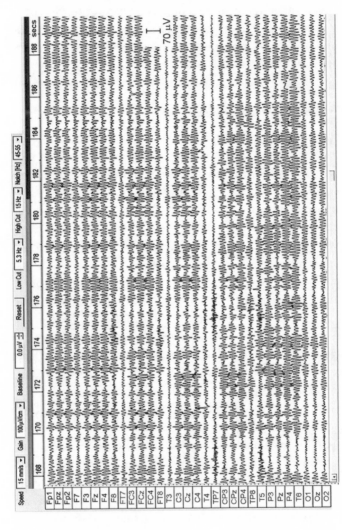

Fig. 32. An example of meditation spindles occurring as a broad distribution across the head; subject 1, 2015.

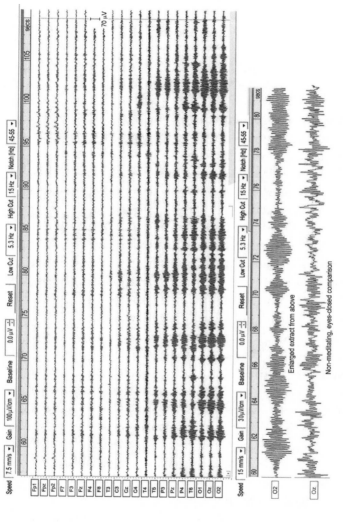

Fig. 33: *Top:* Localized spindles at the back of the head in meditation; subject 13, 2016. *Bottom:* enlarged section with comparison to non-meditating condition.

shown. Across the whole group of meditators who showed spindles, significant spindle activity was always seen to some degree at the back of the head.

Meditation spindles differ significantly from those in early-stage sleep; the wave-packet shape is similar, but in meditation they are of longer duration (approximately seven times longer) and are far more prolific (about ten times more prolific) than those in sleep. They also differ from those in early-stage anesthesia, which are mostly restricted to the front of the head. However, the most striking difference appears when the underlying cortical sources driving the spindle activity are examined.

This procedure, known as a Loreta or e-Loreta analysis,[1] is described more fully in the *Frontiers* paper and finds an intriguing distribution of underlying sources falling into regions of interest (ROIs) shown in Table 3. The labels B6, B10, and so on refer to the conventional Brodmann area locations of neuroscience, which are a system of categorization and location to allow findings to be compared across studies internationally. They are included here simply for the sake of completeness in case any reader wishes to pursue the broader significance of these different regions.

For reasons that will become apparent in a moment, activity at the very front of the head in the forehead area (column 1, Brodmann sites B10, B11, and B47) is separated from activity in higher frontal sites (column 2, B6, B4, B3, and B5) toward the top of the head, while column 3 shows activity around or just posterior to the top of the head (B7, B40, and B19). Column 4 shows activity in more central, limbic or core regions of the brain, while column 5 covers temporal lobe sites at the side of the head. Activity in occipital sites at the back of the head is shown in column 6. (More detail can be found in the *Frontiers* paper.)

Since spindles appeared to some degree in posterior (occipital) areas for all subjects, it is no surprise that Table 3 shows occipital activity amounting to 23.2% of total activity compared to only 8.8% at the opposite side of the head in the most frontal sites. The remainder activity, however, falls into two very interesting

Table 3: Meditation Spindles, Cortical Sources

Cortical Source Analysis for Meditation Spindles Regions of Interest (ROIs) Normalized to 100% Total Cortical Activity					
Fronto-frontal 8.8%	Upper-frontal 8.3%	Parietal 23.5%	Limbic 10.6%	Temporal 25.6%	Occipital 23.2%
(inc. B10/B11/B47)	(inc. B6/B4/B3/B5)	(inc. B7/B40/B19)	(inc. B30/B31 and limbic sites)	(inc. B20/B21/B22/B37/B40/B42)	(inc. B17/B18/B19)
	DORSAL PATHWAY 31.8%		VENTRAL PATHWAY 36.2%		

ROIs known in neuroscience as the dorsal and ventral attention/ perception streams,[2] in this case each carrying over 30% of total brain electrical activity. Taken together, these networks amount to 68% of brain activity located in areas well known to have high involvement in attention.

This demonstrates that as attention in meditation moves away from engagement with the outer sensory world, both of these attention streams of neuroscience are disrupted, indicated by the occurrence of spindles. Also, since these two attention networks are the backbone of everyday sensory consciousness, there is an interesting correspondence to Buddhist theories of jhāna as requiring disengagement from sensory consciousness. Even more intriguing is to find correspondences between the two attention streams of modern neuroscience and the two aspects of attention, vitakka and vicāra, that have been known within Buddhist meditational practices for over 2,500 years. This becomes clearer when referring to Figure 34, which shows the two attention streams of neuroscience and their main characteristics.

The dorsal network links posterior occipital sites to frontal sites via upper (dorsal, like a shark's fin) parietal regions of the brain, and is known to be fast and short-term, rather like the RAM in a computer. This network represents basic moment-to-moment attention, which corresponds well to the function of the jhāna factor vitakka, placing attention and establishing both a moment of mindfulness (sati, the first bojjhaṅga) as well as a position in the time sequence of cortical attention processes.

The ventral stream also links occipital to frontal sites, but via core (limbic) and side (temporal) areas of the brain related to long-term memory, feelings, and emotions, that add meaning and salience to attention, linking information in both time and space. The timescale is longer than for the dorsal stream and corresponds well to the functions of the second jhāna factor, vicāra, sustained attention, as well as to the second bojjhaṅga, dhamma-vicaya, investigation.

In both cases information flows between the back and the front of the head, either via upper parietal sites for the dorsal stream or

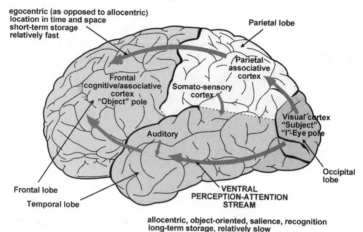

Fig. 34. The dorsal and ventral attention-perception streams
of neuroscience.

via central (limbic) and side (temporal) sites for the ventral stream.
This is the reason frontal sites were separated in the manner of
Table 3.

The prevalence of spindle activity suggests that disruption to
the brain's attention networks is the main effect during the early
stages of disengaging from sensory consciousness. This in turn suggests that attention likely forms an early stage, and possibly the
most basic underpinning characteristic, in the development of consciousness, which will be considered in more depth in Chapter 13.

Looking back at Figures 32 and 33, it is also intriguing to wonder why for some meditators a very broad distribution of spindles
suggests disruption of very extensive areas of brain activity, whereas
others show spindles predominantly at the rear of the head, which,
as we will see later, is likely to be the locus of the subject "I/eye"
pole of the subject-object processes of sensory consciousness. A
possible explanation might be that some meditators are unconsciously drawn to focus their disengagement from sensory con-

sciousness on the subject "I/eye" networks of the occipital visual cortex, whereas others might instinctively attempt to suppress all sensory consciousness activity across widely distributed networks. This might correspond to the sense I had in directing this study that individuals use their brains in subtly different ways to aim toward the same outcome.

THE SECOND RŪPA JHĀNA

As a meditator becomes more skillful in the first rūpa jhāna, attention becomes sufficiently stabilized on the meditation object that vitakka and vicāra effectively function automatically, or become part of the foundations to open the way to the second rūpa jhāna. At this stage feelings and affect come into prominence as a meditator continues to give attention to the breath and nimitta, as do the third and fourth jhāna factors, pīti and sukha. This is particularly the case for pīti, which becomes the primary jhāna factor for the second rūpa jhāna.

In earlier chapters, pīti was considered to be closely related to energization in the body and the second-most prevalent theme in meditators' EEG—namely, strong and very slow rhythmic activity, which was interpreted as likely evidence of such energization.

Figures 35 and 36 show two examples of these slow waves, which at first sight have superficial similarity to slow waves in the deepest stages of sleep, anesthesia, or coma. However, the slow waves in meditation were much slower, hence termed infraslow waves (ISWs), as well as in some cases reaching high levels of intensity unprecedented in existing neuroscience research. Both these features are also quite different from much more benign EEG activity typically seen in the many reported studies of other forms of meditation, often little different from everyday sensory consciousness activity apart from a moderately enhanced level of alpha activity as a sign of deeper relaxation.

The recording in Figure 35 shows intense ISWs at frontal, occipital, and central-temporal sites, with a steady rhythmic alternation

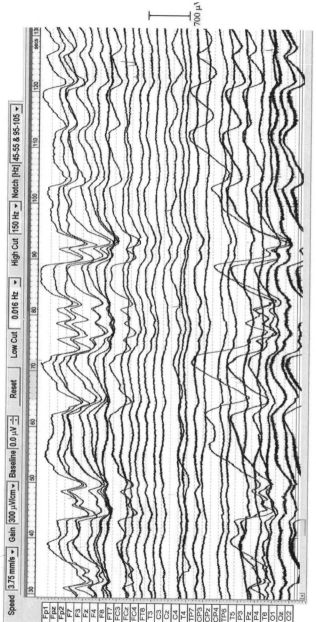

Fig. 35. An example of infraslow waves in meditation; subject 5, 2014.

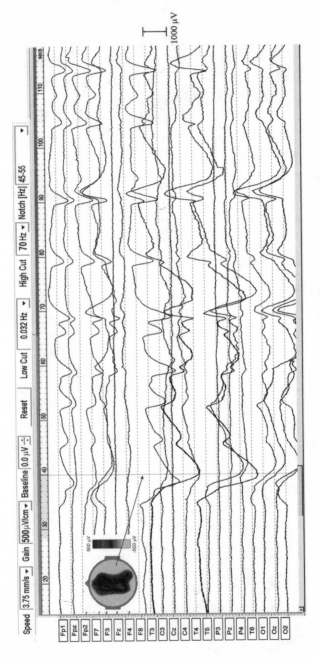

Fig. 36. An example of rapid onset of infraslow waves in meditation; subject 17, 2016.

between excitation and inhibition, such that overall energy is conserved. The intensity scale in Figure 35 is 300 μV/cm, and it can be seen that the ISWs reach intensity levels of around 1,000 μV p-p (peak-to-peak) at times. Figure 36 is another example of very intense ISWs, but also illustrates how for some meditators the onset of the ISWs can be quite rapid following the cue, and then the intention, to develop the jhānas (in this case to develop the second and higher rūpa jhānas). At approximately thirty-five seconds following the cue to begin, a massive inhibition of activity develops around central areas, which is illustrated by the inset intensity map at upper-left that shows an annulus of suppression around central sites at the forty-second point (this can be seen more clearly in color plots in the *Frontiers* paper and also at www.shambhala.com/jhana-eeg). The sequence of ISWs that then follows at times reach remarkable intensities exceeding 2,000 μV p-p.[3]

Overall, three features from these and other examples stand out:

· First, the ISWs show slow and alternating patterns of strong inhibition and suppression of large areas of the cortex, where faster activity more typical of sensory consciousness is either suppressed or effectively disappears.
· Second, across subjects more experienced in this mode, a localized hot-spot of excitation near the vertex develops. Such increased energization near the crown of the head is a theme that develops for experienced meditators working to develop the second and higher rūpa jhānas and will become a major theme in describing the higher jhānas.
· Third, Figure 36 is an example of remarkable responsiveness of brain activity to a meditator focusing attention on the nimitta, similar to the equally fast response seen in Bu Ddho meditation when a meditator focuses attention on intoning the syllable BU. Increased responsiveness is an intriguing observation for a significant number of meditators, and may reflect the description in ancient texts on the jhānas that they develop not only stability and deep calm,

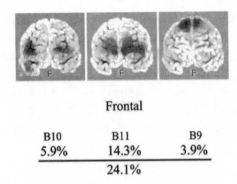

Frontal

B10	B11	B9
5.9%	14.3%	3.9%
	24.1%	

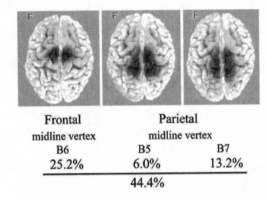

Frontal midline vertex	Parietal midline vertex	
B6	B5	B7
25.2%	6.0%	13.2%
	44.4%	

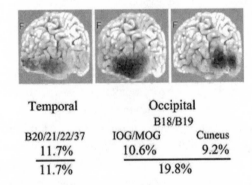

Temporal	Occipital B18/B19	
B20/21/22/37	IOG/MOG	Cuneus
11.7%	10.6%	9.2%
11.7%	19.8%	

Fig. 37. Cortical sources responsible for ISWs. Mean 3D plots from seven independent recordings (>2,500 secs. data).

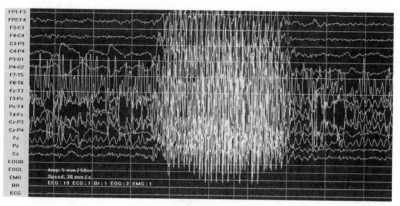

Fig. 38. EEG activity during intentional arousal of strong pīti. 2010, 19 electrodes, 0.5–30 Hz.

but also workability and malleability of mind—which, based on these results, extends also to the brain.

As with spindles, the analysis then turned to examine the underlying cortical regions responsible for these infraslow waves, and Figure 37 shows the results from an e-Loreta analysis of seven independent recordings totaling more than 2,500 seconds of data and showing the strongest and most clearly defined ISWs. The regions of interest (ROIs) are shown as mean 3D plots, and Brodmann site labels are included for reference purposes as in Table 3.

The results for this sub-group of experienced meditators show three regions of interest (ROIs). The left-hand plots show frontal activity extending upward toward the vertex amounting to 24.1% of the total brain activity. The three central plots show strong intensity around the vertex, or crown of the head, an area that includes the frontal-parietal divide, together contributing 44.4% to the total activity. The third ROI at right shows temporal and occipital activity amounting to 11.7% and 19.8% respectively.

Activity around the vertex/crown of head for this subgroup of experienced meditators accounts for almost half of the total EEG activity in the brain. In the *Frontiers* paper, this focused intensity near the vertex was interpreted as a developing vertical axis of jhāna consciousness, beginning with the second rūpa jhāna and eventually dominating the overall brain activity in the higher jhānas to the exclusion of the previous networks of sensory consciousness. We will investigate this further in the next two sections dealing with the higher jhānas.

In the *Frontiers* paper, the posterior and frontal regions of interest in Figure 37 were hypothesized to represent the subject and object poles of normal sensory consciousness respectively—the posterior visual cortex functioning as the "I/eye" subject position, while the frontal cortex specialized for executive/cognitive functions represents the object position.[4]

The Deliberate Arousal of Pīti and Its Tranquilization, Passaddhi

While strong pīti develops quite naturally for some practitioners, some meditators find it helpful to explore this area of energization more actively, and the Yogāvacara oral traditions teach methods to do this. As already noted, the Bu Ddho technique is effective in arousing strong energy, and it can be practiced without using the syllables if carried out with the intention to arouse and "collect" energy during successive in-breaths in order to strengthen and brighten the nimitta. More focused versions concentrate the energy in the stomach/diaphragm area before leading it upward toward the crown of the head. Since these are strongly physical and body-based practices, guidance from a teacher is essential to avoid misunderstandings, and demonstrations in a group context can be helpful to ease any initial anxiety.

In what follows we explore EEG recordings of meditators practicing these specialized energization techniques. Figure 38 is an early example, recorded as part of a pilot study in 2010–11. The equipment at that time was prone to movement artifacts, making it difficult to separate cortical activity from the effects of movement of electrode wires during strong pīti, but the recording was

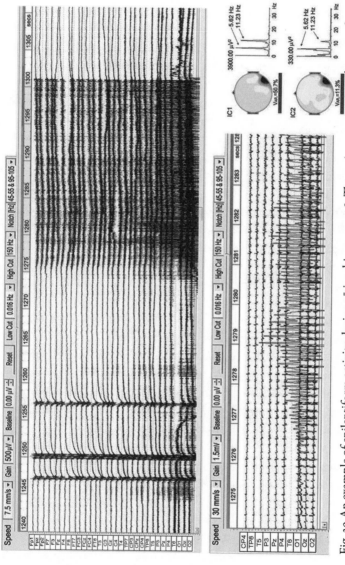

Fig. 39. An example of epileptiform activity during piti; subject 15, 2018. The main ~25-sec. episode occurs from 1,275–1,300 secs., with occipital activity expanded below, with plots of the main underlying cortical sources.

nevertheless so intriguing and unexpected as to lead me to develop the study further over the following years with more sophisticated equipment. Even at that time and given the limitations of the equipment, the strong bursts of energization shown in Figure 38 were reminiscent of seizures in epilepsy, even though the meditators performing this practice were composed and fully conscious.

Figure 39 (page 187) is a more recent example using highly stable medical-grade head-caps and recording amplifiers, equipment far less prone to movement artifacts. The subject in this example is experienced in the practice and was able to balance the intensity in such a way that the cortical effects in the brain can be discerned easily without undue confusion with movement artifacts. Strictly speaking, the description that follows is outside the main remit of this book exploring the jhānas, but on the other hand practices such as these have a long history in esoteric traditions, including the Yogāvacara, as means to master pīti and develop the higher jhānas. Such practices as described here illustrate the rather remarkable latent power that can be released by acts of will by someone skilled in jhāna meditation.

In this example the first sign of increasing energization is the development of occipital spike-waves,[5] bottom left, as an initial sign of instability, followed immediately by a roughly half-second global ictal burst. *Ictal* is a term used in epilepsy research to denote a brief burst of EEG activity associated with physical movement, such as a jerk or spasm. Ictal bursts usually precede the main *clonic* seizure of mostly unconscious shaking or spasms.

The initial ictal burst in Figure 39 is followed by another burst three seconds later, then another around seven seconds later, and finally by the main body of what resembles an epileptiform "seizure" fifteen seconds later.

The term "epileptiform" is a deliberate choice to make the point that examples such as this are *not* examples of epileptic seizures triggered by meditation; there are some features such as spike-waves that are also seen in epilepsy, but in examples such as this during meditation the subject is composed, fully aware, and experiencing no discomfort. Someone experienced in the technique is able to develop the state at will and emerge with no discomfort.

During the main phase in this example, the meditator shows mild clonic jerks or bodily vibration, mainly along a vertical bodily axis (rather than side to side). If deliberately developed further, these can lead to the body jumping in the air (usually only a small distance) from a cross-legged position, similar to descriptions of powerful pīti in some Yogāvacara texts. The expanded section lower down in Figure 39 shows occipital spike-waves at the rearmost posterior sites, O1, O2, and Oz, apparently synchronized with a near-sinusoidal rhythm at the right temporal site T6. This latter rhythm reaches extremely high levels of intensity, close to 3,000 μV peak to peak. The head-plots and frequency spectra at right were calculated for the two strongest independent components from an e-Loreta source analysis for the main event lasting 1,275–1,300 seconds and show the underlying source to be located in the middle temporal gyrus, Brodmann site B37. The spike-waves have a frequency 5.62 Hz, and the more rhythmic and near-sinusoidal temporal-lobe activity has a frequency at the harmonic, 11.23 Hz.

Recordings such as this were explored to better understand the mechanisms of arousing high levels of energization—pīti in Buddhist jhāna terminology—but this particular example and the intriguing temporal lobe harmonic activity has clear relevance for epilepsy studies, within which the temporal lobe is often the site of epileptic instability. However, I stress the point that this is not an example of a seizure proper triggered by meditation, but the fact that such activity can be deliberately aroused by acts of will, and then calmed back to tranquility at will, raises the interesting question as to whether anything can be learned from such practices that might benefit epilepsy sufferers.

The most likely explanation for this developed ability to arouse and manage pīti in this way might lie in the highly precise development and control of attention in the early stages of developing jhāna, as well as the central features of samatha meditation in general: calmness, peace, and the ability to hold a position of balance and equanimity, eventually upekkhā.

It might also be said that mastering the processes of pīti parallels the stages of mastery of jhāna described in earlier chapters. The first stage for pīti would be mastery of its arousal, then managing its duration, followed by the ability to tranquilize the energization and return to normal functioning with no problems or aftereffects. Gradually the nature of pīti becomes clear, and rather than any false pride in being able to arouse strong pīti at will, meditators realize that the far more valuable skill is to manage the subtle processes of its tranquilization, passaddhi, into a deeper mind-body (or brain-body) samādhi.

THE THIRD RŪPA JHĀNA

The EEG evidence for the third and fourth jhānas shows considerable similarity, possibly reflecting how they are both described in the Suttas as including a quality of being "completely conscious" or "completely aware," with the only difference being in the roles of sukha, bliss, and upekkhā, equanimity. However, as far as the EEG evidence is concerned there may be a distinction in the intensity and timescale of the very slow wave activity, described in this and the next section. The examples in Figures 40 and 41 are from a meditator recorded in 2016 and then re-recorded in 2017 after an interval of one year to illustrate how the second and higher jhānas develop as subjects gain more experience. The 2016 segment (Figure 40) shows strong infraslow waves (ISWs) mainly at occipital sites, and the inset maps show the intensity distributions across the head for the single large ISW at the far right, highlighted gray in the top time-bar at 212–16 seconds.

The inset maps show an annulus of ISW inhibition-excitation enclosing central areas. The high intensity of around 500 μV peak-to-peak and very slow rhythmicity of this annulus—around ten seconds—completely overshadows any remaining faster rhythms of normal everyday sensory processing. Brief periods of enhanced

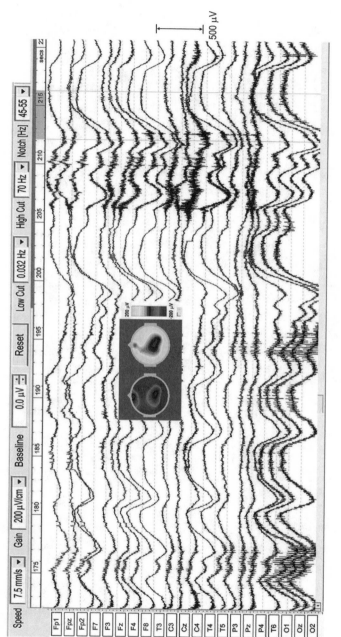

Fig. 40. EEG recording of subject 24, 2016.

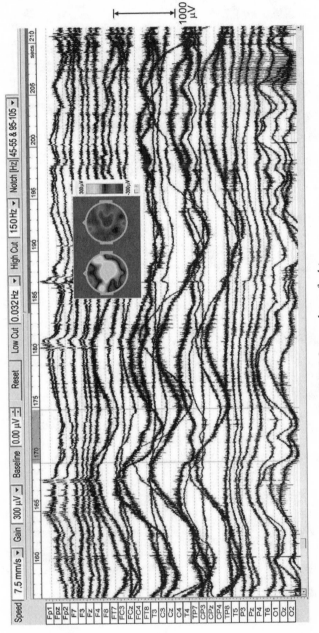

Fig. 41. EEG recording of subject 24, 2017.

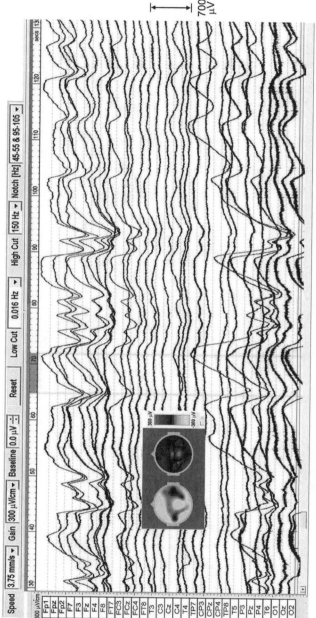

Fig. 42. EEG recording of subject 5, 2014. The inset scalp maps correspond to the start and end-points of the gray-highlighted ISW at 65–72 secs.

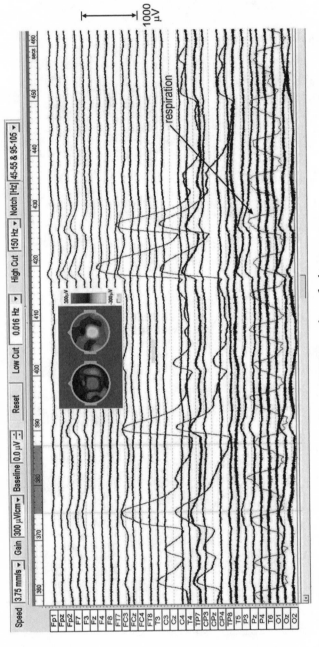

Fig. 43. EEG recording of subject 5, 2017.

high-frequency gamma activity can also be seen (for example, at 206–12 secs.), as well as spike-wave bursts lasting two to six seconds at posterior occipital sites. Such very fast gamma activity is not well understood in neuroscience, but it has been suggested by some to represent high-order unconscious processes that might have a subtle synchronizing role across the brain. Spike-waves have been mentioned elsewhere, and most likely represent momentary brief periods of instability of untranquilized pīti.

Figure 41 (page 192) shows a 55-second extract for the same subject recorded one year later in 2017, and the inset scalp maps now show much stronger and highly focused ISW activity at sites around the vertex compared to 2016. Activity across the rest of the head is much reduced in comparison to the crown-of-head activity. Occipital ISWs are still present, as well as significant fast gamma activity, and spike-wave bursts at occipital sites as in 2016.

This subject was one of the group of meditators showing strong and rhythmic ISWs, whose EEGs formed the collective data for the 3D intensity plots shown in Figure 37. The average across the group showed 44.4% ISW dominance around the vertex, with the remaining activity made up of 24.1% in frontal sites and 31.5% in occipital and temporal lobe sites. In the *Frontiers* paper, this was interpreted as a developing vertical axis of jhāna consciousness, with the frontal and occipital activity related to residual sensory consciousness activity, and as a group these subjects were at various stages in developing the second rūpa jhāna characterized by high intensity (pīti) ISW activity, with moments touching on the higher jhānas.

If we assume that complete vertex dominance might correspond to the description of the third rūpa jhāna as "completely conscious," then the recording of subject 24 in 2017 (Figure 41) would suggest that this meditator is on the threshold of, or at moments touching on, the third rūpa jhāna; and in line with the discussion on instability in the previous chapter, the sporadic spike-wave activity at lower-right likely reflects the last stages before pīti becomes tranquilized into consistent deep absorption.

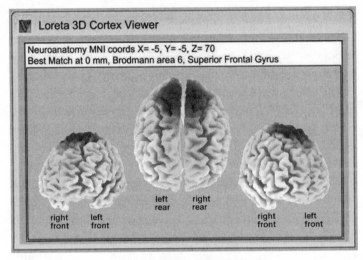

Fig. 44. 3D cortex plots of the vertex ROI, subject 5, 2017
(600-sec. sample; 0.016–150 Hz).

Figures 42 and 43 (pages 193 and 194) are from recordings of
subject 5 in 2014 and then three years later in 2017. Figure 42 was
previously shown as Figure 35 but is reproduced here with some
additions to compare to the recording three years later in 2017. In
this version, the inset scalp maps in Figure 42 correspond to the
ISW at 65–72 seconds and show that the vertex region of interest
is already apparent in 2014, with signs of an incomplete annulus
around it, but the focus is not nearly as dominant compared to that
for subject 24 in 2017 (Figure 41).

However, three years later (Figure 43) and with greater experience of developing the jhānas, the vertex source for subject 5 is
now almost completely dominant. Figure 43 also shows the very
regular respiration rhythm of this meditator during meditation,
and in the published paper it was commented that there is significant correlation between the rhythms of respiration and the ISWs,
unlike the slow waves in deep sleep, which are related more to the
cardiac rhythm.

Table 4: Contributions of All Possible Independent Cortical Sources to the Total Signals' Variance

2014 % Contribution to total EEG signals' variance	Source Locations	2017 % Contribution to total EEG signals' variance
5.7%	Frontal B11, B47 SFG, MFG, IFG	0.2%
92.8%	Vertex Fronto-parietal B4, B5, B6, B7 MFG, SFG, PCL, PCG	99.7%
1.5%	Occipital B18, B19 Cun, MOG	0.1%

*Subject 5, 2014 and 2017; 600-sec. recording, bandwidth 0.016–150 Hz.

The underlying cortical activity driving the vertex focus of ISWs was investigated, again using an e-Loreta analysis, and is shown in the 3D cortex plots of Figure 44. More distributed activity typical of everyday sensory consciousness seems to have disappeared in these plots, which represent the first published visual evidence of the neural correlates of a vertical axis of jhāna consciousness.

To look more closely at just how dominant the crown-of-head focus has become in this example, the e-Loreta analysis was extended for both the 2014 and 2017 recordings of subject 5 to identify all possible underlying cortical sources from the strongest to the weakest. This analysis was carried out across the full bandwidth of frequencies 0.016–150 Hz so as not to exclude any of the total brain activity, resulting in the summary shown in Table 4. The abbreviations SFG, MFG, IFG, PCL, PCG, Cun, and MOG correspond to the superior, medial, and inferior frontal gyri; the paracentral lobule and postcentral gyrus; and the cuneus and middle occipital gyrus of the brain, respectively. The individual details of these locations need not concern us here—it is the overall pattern that is significant. This total activity averages to the percentages shown in Table 4 for frontal, occipital/posterior, and near-vertex regions of the brain.

The figures in Table 4 show that the vertex dominance in "source-space" (as distinct from the surface scalp EEG, known as "electrode space") is even stronger than the surface activity alone would suggest. Already highly dominant in 2014 when it accounted for 92.8% of the total activity, this percentage had increased to an extraordinary 99.7% in 2017, with only very weak 0.2% and 0.1% contributions remaining at frontal and occipital sites respectively.

Also, as noted in Chapter 4, the frequency structure of the vertex source was found to be overwhelmingly made up of very slow (ISW) activity, with some evidence of not only a very slow rhythm with a mean periodicity of around eight seconds, but an even slower component with a rhythm around twenty to fifty seconds, which is extremely slow by neuroscience standards, as well as being only very rarely observed. Across the whole group of meditators these two rhythms correspond to a frequency range 0.02–0.13 Hz. Such very slow rhythms suggest an involvement of metabolic bodily processes—which follow much slower timescales than faster neuronal processes (typically 1–50 Hz and higher during sensory consciousness)—during the deeper stages of samādhi in the higher jhānas.

The only other activity that could be detected apart from the ISWs was a far weaker background of much faster activity in the gamma band of neuroscience, extending beyond 100 Hz, but very weak, less than one part in 15,000 compared to the dominant vertex ISW activity. Gamma activity is not well understood in neuroscience, and is not pursued here, since it is in any case so weak. The crucial point, though, is that activity typical of our default sensory consciousness that falls in the intermediate delta, theta, alpha, and beta bands of neuroscience that range from about 1–30 Hz, had effectively disappeared.[6]

Table 5: Development of the Vertex ISW Source

Source locations	Mean across 7 subjects 2014–17 (>2,500 secs.) % of total EEG	Subject 24 2017 % of total EEG (~80 secs.)	Subject 5 2014 % of total EEG (~500 secs.)	Subject 5 2017 % of total EEG (~500 secs.)
Frontal B1, B47, B9 SFG, MFG, IFG	24.1%	1.1%	5.7%	0.2%
Vertex Fronto-parietal B4, B5, B6, B7 MFG, PCL, PCG	44.4%	78.4%	92.8%	99.7%
Occipital B18, B19, Cun	19.8%	15.3%	1.5%	0.1%
Temporal B20/21/22/37	11.7%	2.7%	-	-

*Column 2 data are from Figure 37; column 3 data for subject 24 are based on similar data to that in Figure 41; columns 4 and 5 for subject 5 are from Table 4.

This raises questions about the nature of jhāna consciousness, as well as implications for understanding the frequency patterns of both sensory consciousness and jhāna consciousness, which will be pursued in the following chapter.

THE FOURTH RŪPA JHĀNA

Table 5 (page 199) summarizes the available information from the EEG study as to how the vertex source develops from the second rūpa jhāna onward. The figures in column 2 are taken from Figure 37 and are average percentages from more than 2,500 seconds of recordings from seven meditators showing particularly strong ISWs. For this group as a whole the mean vertex activity accounts for 44.4% of the total EEG signals' intensity.

Columns 4 and 5 show the figures for subject 5, recorded in 2014 and 2017, reproduced from Table 4, where vertex activity increased from 92.8% to an extraordinary 99.7%. Column 3 is based on a similar analysis for subject 24 in 2017, based on a slightly longer extract than that shown in Figure 40. The vertex activity here amounts to 78.4%, intermediate between the 44.4% for the group of seven as a whole, and the much higher percentages for subject 5 in columns 4 and 5.

These figures are consistent with the fact that subjects making up the data in column 2 represent a range of experience of jhāna, and overall were developing their understanding of pīti evidenced by high-energy ISW activity. The mean vertex activity (44.4%) suggests that on average those meditators were developing the second rūpa jhāna, and perhaps touching on the third jhāna at times, confirmed by subjects 5 and 24 (columns 3–5) being members of this group.

Subject 5 in 2014 (column 4) shows very powerful vertex activity of 92.8%, which so dominates the EEG that distributed higher frequency activity typical of normal sensory consciousness has all but completely disappeared. Subjective feedback after the recording suggests this subject had been developing the third rūpa jhāna, and

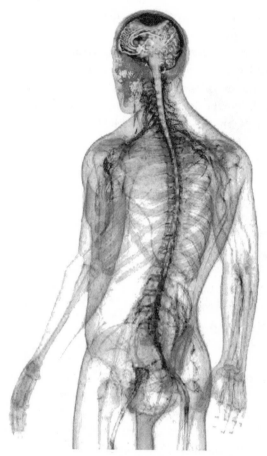

Fig. 45. Brain-body axis, conceptual illustration.

perhaps at times the fourth given that the activity was maintained for more than twenty minutes with segments of near perfect rhythmicity. The recording of this same subject three years later in 2017 (column 5) was even more consistent, again for more than twenty minutes, with an extraordinary 99.7% vertex activity, which might well correspond to the phrase "completely conscious" in either the third or fourth rūpa jhānas.

This same subject was one of the few mentioned earlier who showed evidence of an even slower twenty- to fifty-second rhythm (in 2017) compared to the mean ISW rhythm of approximately eight seconds, which raises the intriguing question of whether the transition from the third to the fourth rūpa jhāna might be associated with a shift to the significantly slower activity. If so, this would be consistent with one of the features of hierarchical structures described in Chapter 13, where each higher level in a hierarchy (in this case the fourth jhāna) is predicted to have a larger spatial scale and a slower timescale than the lower level (in this case the third jhāna). This might be something to explore in future recordings.

For meditators who developed strong ISW activity, the most agreed upon description for their subjective experience was "embodied presence," rather than any consciousness of "this" or "that" typical of everyday sensory consciousness. And for those who developed strong and highly focused vertex activity, the phrase "nothing is left out" as an alternative to "completely conscious" was also suggested by some meditators.

Subject 24, column 3, was able to maintain a vertex focus of up to 78.4%, for medium length durations of 60–100 seconds, suggesting partial but not complete development of the third rūpa jhāna. Between periods of well-developed vertex activity, short bursts of spike-wave activity (lower right, Figure 41) suggest difficulty in maintaining the focus with moments of regression to the second rūpa jhāna and instability of pīti.

A Brain-Body Axis of Jhāna Consciousness

The crown-of-head/vertex focus covers neurological sites that include the supplementary motor area (SMA), strongly connected down to core regions of the brain, including the thalamus, and projecting further to the upper brain stem and spinal cord. It is also highly connected to the medial parietal associative cortex, which has dense links to the cingulate, thalamus, and brain stem. Recent neuroscience research has also identified the closely related

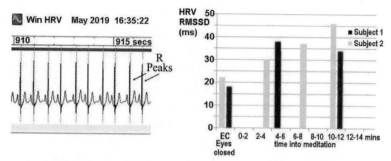

Fig. 46. *Left*: ECG segment showing R peaks of the heartbeat; *right*: changes in HRV from before to during meditation.

anterior cingulate cortex as an area that relates presence to agency, which resonates with meditators' descriptions of "embodied presence" during the deeper stages of jhāna.[7]

This vertical axis also suggests involvement of the ascending reticular activating system (ARAS) of neuroscience, previously mentioned in Chapter 5, with its known involvement in processes of arousal and consciousness. It is also known that disruptions to the ARAS and to cingulate connectivity can cause unconsciousness, yet meditators developing this vertical axis connectivity during jhāna remain fully conscious throughout their practices.[8]

Development of a vertical brain-body axis, rather than the frontal-occipital axis of our everyday sensory consciousness as hypothesized in the published study, together with the observation of even slower underlying infraslow waves with frequencies around 0.02–0.05 Hz, suggests that as jhāna consciousness develops, fast neuronal systems in the brain interact via intermediate brain-stem areas with the much slower visceral nervous systems in the body, including the complex and tree-like vagus nerve networks. Figure 45 (page 201) is a conceptual illustration of the situation based on medical imaging of internal bodily structures. This might also be the reason that many meditators in this tradition have described an increasing awareness of the importance of the body and its role in meditation (in contrast to descriptions in some post-reform traditions of the body effectively disappearing in jhāna).

The vagus networks in the body regulate the autonomic nervous system balance between sympathetic and parasympathetic activity. The former is the basis for adrenaline-fueled fight-flight reactions, while the latter becomes dominant in deeply relaxed states. It is possible to test this balance to see if it is affected during meditation by measuring the heart-rate variability (HRV), which is sensitive to the sympathetic-parasympathetic balance.[9] Put simply, when the adrenaline system readies the body for action, the resulting tension causes the heart rate to become more fixed, with a reduction in inter-beat variability.

Figure 46 (page 203) shows preliminary results from such a test on two subjects from the original study who were recorded again in 2019 together with their electrocardiograms (ECGs).

At left is a short section of a subject's ECG, showing what are called the R peaks in the heart rhythm, where variation of the interval (R-R) between peaks is the measure of heart-rate variability. The bar charts at right show changes in heart-rate variability (HRV) for these two meditators, immediately before meditation compared to within meditation. The actual measure adopted for HRV is the root-mean-square of the time differences between successive R peaks (RMSSD), which can be seen to increase by 75–100% as meditation develops, which strongly suggests that the reported experience of "embodied presence" in jhāna is indeed an experience of deep peace in the body as much as in the mind.

THE ARŪPA JHĀNAS

The challenge of being recorded and the "observer effect" noted in Chapters 5 and 10 is believed to have limited the ability of some meditators when being recorded to access the higher jhānas quite as fully as they might in their individual practices when not being recorded. This was particularly so for the arūpa jhānas, which is why all the neuroscience examples described in previous chapters and in the published study have been for the rūpa jhānas.

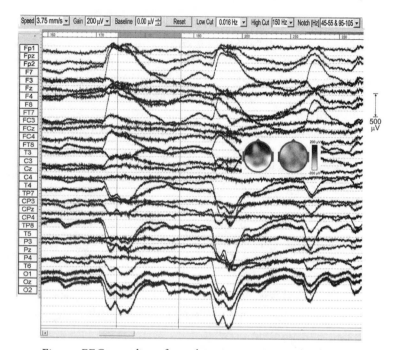

Fig. 47. EEG recording of a meditator attempting to develop
the arūpa jhānas.

One recording of arūpa jhāna meditation does exist, however,
using a protocol where everything was set up by the researcher in
such a way that the meditator, with no "observer" present, was able
to simply press a button to start the recording. From that point
the meditator determined to enter meditation for a predetermined
duration and to attempt to develop, in this case, the third arūpa
jhāna, putting aside as far as possible any concerns about being
recorded. This recording is described here for the first time.

Figure 47 shows a one-minute segment from the recording, dominated by strong infraslow waves reaching peak-to-peak intensities
of more than 500 μV, comparable to intensities shown during the
rūpa jhānas described above. The inset scalp-intensity maps correspond to the start and end points for the gray-highlighted segment

at around 174–187 seconds, in the upper time bar. Looking at these EEG traces in comparison to previous examples recorded during the rūpa jhānas (Figures 36, 37, 41, 42, 43, and 44), a very striking difference is that the strong slow-wave rhythms at the top frontal sites in Figure 47 are almost mirror images of those at posterior sites—that is, they appear to be in antiphase.

The left-hand scalp map that corresponds to the point of peak intensity for the first strong slow wave illustrates this clearly. Frontal sites are highly energized (black) while posterior sites are equally strongly de-energized (white), in almost exact antiphase, effectively, one might suppose, cancelling each other out. This energization–de-energization phase then fades toward the stage of the right-hand scalp map, which shows a near-neutral distribution across the whole head. This pattern repeats approximately every twenty seconds for some fifteen minutes.

Although this is just a single recording from a single meditator, with as yet no others to compare, it is so startling and was at the time so unexpected that it is included here to consider what it might mean.

For the rūpa jhānas, earlier chapters described how strong infraslow waves develop at the crown of the head beyond the first rūpa jhāna, defining a vertical axis of jhāna consciousness, while at the same time the more widely distributed networks typical of sensory consciousness simplify to residual regions of activity at mostly posterior and frontal sites, with a weaker temporal lobe component (Figure 37). And it was hypothesized that the posterior sites, which include the brain's primary visual cortex, represent the subject I/eye pole of consciousness, while frontal sites carry the discriminatory characteristics of the object pole.

Relating this to Figure 47, the pattern appears to be an almost perfectly antiphase relationship between frontal and posterior sites, where energization of one balances and effectively cancels de-energization of the other, which, given the meditator's subjective description of attempting to develop the third arūpa jhāna,

is highly suggestive of being related to the intention not to identify with either subject or object position. The then-much-reduced
activity across the head following each episode of the antiphase
frontal-posterior relationship, shown by the right-hand scalp map
in Figure 47, would nicely correspond to the meditator holding
a middle position identified with neither, for a while, before the
sequence needs to be re-established as a sign of incomplete mastery
of the process.

Looking more closely at the raw EEG traces in Figure 47, it is
also interesting that posterior sites alternate between being highly
de-energized to relatively neutral, whereas frontal sites alternate
between being strongly energized to relatively neutral. In other
words, we do not see an antiphase balance where frontal sites are
de-energized and posterior sites are highly energized. This suggests
that the meditator's primary focus is to not react to any impulse to
identify with either position, corresponding to a de-energization
of any (posterior) subject-mode activity, and that the corresponding energization of frontal sites is required to conserve the overall
energy balance in the brain's networks.

By this stage in developing the arūpa jhānas, the meditator
will be recognizing a quite different process compared to the rūpa
jhānas. Because the jhāna factors of equanimity and unification
of mind remain the same, the quality of jhāna does not change; it
remains essentially as it was in the fourth rūpa jhāna although the
quality of upekkhā becomes ever more subtle and refined, with an
increasingly powerful quality of freedom. This quality of freedom
is characteristic of the arūpas in comparison to the rūpa jhānas.
At the same time, the qualities of responsiveness and workability
of mind develop with an accompanying realization that jhāna and
insight are working together, with no regression to thinking or
coarse discrimination.

This latter realization of the parallel activities of samatha and
vipassanā is also associated with a deeper understanding and realization of the nature of perception: that the arūpa jhānas take a

meditator to the very threshold of perception, which carries with it a parallel realization of the illusory nature of subject and object, rūpa and arūpa, form and emptiness, and indeed all dualities.

A final comment is needed regarding the absence in Figure 47 of an intense vertex/crown-of-head focus in this example of a meditator developing the third arūpa jhāna. On the contrary, it appears that the activity is concentrated in those areas of the brain related to the subject-object positions of sensory consciousness that normally support our sense of "I am." It is as though following the perfectly balanced equanimity of the fourth rūpa jhāna, the intensity of the rūpa jhāna is allowed to ease, to be replaced by processes of developing insight into the nature of identity and perception. This may relate to an enigmatic comment made by Nai Boonman when introducing the arūpas: that meditators would find themselves at times needing to use their brains as much as their minds in this phase of their practice.

13. Consciousness

Referring to the samatha division of Buddhism, the writer and meditation practitioner Alan Wallace commented in 1999 that the "mind and consciousness itself are the primary subjects of introspective investigation within the [samatha] Buddhist tradition."[1] Based on the descriptions in this book, jhāna meditation specifically might be seen as a science of mind, centered on sophisticated meditation practices to explore the mechanisms of cognition and consciousness.[2] Although ultimately motivated by a wish to understand and find an end to suffering, once a person commits to a core meditation practice it is a natural development to become increasingly aware of the subtlety of processes of perception, feeling, and consciousness. The arūpa jhānas in particular reach to the very foundations of consciousness and the nature of subject-object interactions and perception.

The EEG study of meditators practicing jhāna confirmed that to develop the jhānas requires disengagement from sensory consciousness, and brain activity in the approach to jhāna indicates steady development of a new mode of cortical network interactions along a vertical axis that characterizes jhāna consciousness. Such a concept was completely new to neuroscience, and in this chapter I contrast and compare these two modes—sensory consciousness and jhāna consciousness—and discuss some of the insights that emerge from a cross-discipline study of consciousness bridging ancient Buddhist understandings with modern neuroscience.

In the next sections sensory consciousness is described first from a Buddhist perspective and then from recent developments in modern neuroscience. This is then extended to summarize additional insights from observing its disruption during jhāna meditation, including how the banded frequency structure of sensory consciousness reflects how thought and consciousness develop. I will also consider how these two modes of consciousness—sensory consciousness and jhāna consciousness—are part of much more extensive hierarchies linking all scales of life.

The final section describes the subjective experience of jhāna consciousness, with some comments on the illusory nature of our sense of "I."

SENSORY CONSCIOUSNESS: A BUDDHIST MODEL

Although not usually described as such, the Buddhist model of dependent origination describes the conditional links that make up a person's engagement with the sensory world, which is essentially a description of sensory consciousness. Probably the earliest and most succinct description of dependent causation is the statement by the Elder Assaji soon after the Buddha's enlightenment, when asked by Upatissa (the future chief disciple of the Buddha, Sariputta), "What does your teacher teach?"

Ye dhammā hetuppa bhavā, tesam hetum tathāgato āha. Tesañ ca yo nirodho, evam vādi mahā samaṇo.

The Tathāgata has declared the cause and also the cessation of all phenomena which arise from a cause. This is the doctrine held by the Great Samaṇa.[3]

Which is paralleled in the *Bahudhātuka Sutta* by this statement:

When this exists, that comes to be; with this arising of this, that arises. When this does not exist, that does not come to be; with the cessation of this, that ceases.[4]

This is a statement of causation: that dependent on causes and conditions, either this or that comes to be, which we shall see later is effectively equivalent to modern neuroscience models of active inference and the free-energy principle. While these early statements are rather abstract, not long after they were made the Buddha gave a fuller description of the familiar twelve-stage model of dependent origination, which more clearly describes the conditions of human life in a sensory world.[5] These are listed below and in Figure 48.

1. ignorance (*avijjā*)
2. mental formations or fabrication (*sankhārā*)
3. consciousness (*viññāṇa*)
4. mentality and materiality (*nāmarūpa*)
5. sixfold sense-bases (*saḷāyatana*)
6. contact (*phassa*)
7. feeling (*vedanā*)
8. craving (*taṇhā*)
9. clinging (*upādāna*)
10. becoming (*bhava*)
11. birth (*jāti*)
12. aging and death (*jarāmaraṇa*)

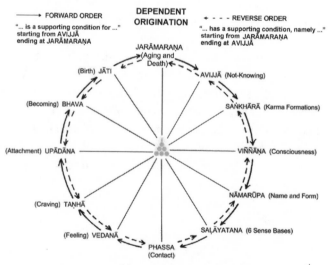

Fig. 48. Buddhist dependent origination. &#x1F;

The starting point can be anywhere, either in the forward order, in which each link is a supporting condition for the one that follows, or in the reverse order, in which each link has a supporting condition in the previous link that gives rise to its existence. Usually, the starting point is taken as *avijjā*, ignorance or not knowing, and the end point as *jarāmaraṇa*, aging and death. The two stages of birth, *jāti*, and aging and death, *jarāmaraṇa*, are the start and end points of a single human life, which due to the factor *avijjā*, ignorance, repeats endlessly. Ignorance, here, does not refer to any kind of cognitive inadequacy or lack of learning; instead it refers to a primary restlessness or the need and urge to know "something" in order to "Be." This primary urge activates awareness of past experiences—kamma (Sanskrit, *karma*) formations—in relation to present conditions and possibilities or implications for the future, in an urge to orient oneself in the flow of consciousness within the world. In neuroscience terms, it is connected to the notion of *temporal depth* as a deep underpinning of everyday consciousness that gives continuity to our sense of "I" in the world. This will be developed further in the next section.

The primary urge of avijjā leads to consciousness (viññāṇa), with its implicit subject-object (nāma-rūpa) duality, and interaction, or contact (phassa), with the outer sensory world or inner world of ideas via the six sense-bases (saḷāyatana): vision, hearing, touch, taste, smell, and mind. Which in turn leads to feeling (vedanā), craving (taṇhā), and attachment (upādāna)—followed by actions or "becoming" (bhava), whether mental, physical, or both.

"Becoming" is similar in some ways to the saṅkhārā, or *formations*, one of the five khandhās or aggregates of a sentient being described earlier. Both are involved in continuing the repetitive cycle of birth, aging, and death.

SENSORY CONSCIOUSNESS FROM A NEUROSCIENCE PERSPECTIVE

During the first few years of the EEG study of jhāna meditation, beginning in 2010–11, I learned that far-reaching and related developments were taking place elsewhere within neuroscience. These initiatives centered around Karl Friston's "free-energy" theory, but they rapidly evolved into detailed models of "active inference" with implications for understanding how all biological systems, in particular self-organizing systems such as human beings, adapt to living in a sensory world.[6] Put simply, the idea is that every organism or biological system only exists in relation to its environment. There has to be an *inner* and an *outer* and some form of self-organization—otherwise a system cannot continue to exist independently, whether at the microscale of a single cell, or at the larger scale of a human being.

For a human being, Figure 49 illustrates the principles of active inference in neuroscience. "Inputs" (left) are received from the outer world via our senses, in particular sight, hearing, and touch, together with information about the immediate state of our body by sensation, including interoceptive information via the brain stem about the nervous system balance in the body and condition of its internal organs.

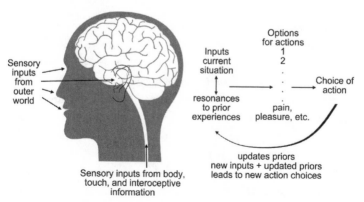

Fig. 49. Active inference in neuroscience.

This constantly changing flux of information is processed (right) largely unconsciously and very quickly in relation to prior experiences, mostly held in memory, leading to possible action choices. For a self-organizing system to be viable, to survive and resist entropy processes that would otherwise lead to dissolution or chaos, means that any action choice needs to assess all possible outcomes to make the most efficient use of available energy. Neuroscience theory describes this as a requirement to minimize free energy, while at the same time minimizing prediction error ("surprise," or unexpected shocks to the organism)—and ultimately to keep entropy within bounds.

Readers will notice this is beginning to sound much like dependent origination. Whatever action is chosen immediately becomes part of the "priors," so that sensory inputs are constantly updated in a self-directed and continuous feedback process. In his 2018 paper "Am I Self-Conscious?" the leading neuroscientist Karl Friston points out that for active inference to succeed in minimizing prediction errors, the inference process must have *temporal depth* in order to link memories of past experiences to current sensory information from the world, in order to predict future outcomes, which "necessarily lends (active) inference a purposeful and self-centered aspect that has the hallmarks of consciousness (and necessarily implies self-consciousness because I am the author of my actions)."[7]

In other words, theories such as active inference are much more than mathematical models—they are beginning to consider the emergence of consciousness itself.[8] Action-choice in active inference requires an *agent* or *subject* to manage choices, and subjectivity has been linked to arousal processes well known in neuroscience that define wakefulness. This theory also suggests that it is our capacity to *feel* and experience affect that defines consciousness—that feelings and affect are *precisely* the qualia of consciousness. It is therefore suggested that the most basic form of consciousness is *affect consciousness*, which may or may not develop further into self-reflective consciousness. If it does develop further, the process is envisaged as follows: following the initial affect response, attention to an idea or sensory input leads to further cognitive processing and comparison to memories of previous experiences, which in turn leads to discrimination and recognition of characteristics as well as formation of a basic subject-object construct, and affect consciousness evolves to become *perceptual consciousness*, since it is the nature of perception that a subject is required to perceive. Further reflective re-presentations facilitated by language might then lead to *cognitive consciousness*, which we might equally term self-reflective consciousness if the subject becomes aware of being the subject of his or her own thoughts.

Here again there are fascinating parallels to the Buddhist model of dependent origination, which presents a similar chain of links that construct our conscious experience of life: inputs from a sensory world create feelings based on past experience, in turn causing attraction or aversion to different action choices, and ultimately resulting in a repetitive, cyclical process. Both models also describe interactions that are conditional, and in that sense both the agent in the neuroscience model and what we assume to be individual person, or locus of subjectivity, in dependent origination may be seen as largely illusory, reactive to circumstances, inseparable from the environment, and impermanent—more *processes* than *things*.

This can then be compared with Buddhist understandings of jhāna, where the necessary disengagement from sensory consciousness begins with resisting these same cognitive processes of thinking, including their feeling impact, while redirecting attention inward first to the breath, and then increasingly to the *felt* qualia of consciousness itself, or to the nimitta in jhāna terminology.

DISRUPTION OF SENSORY CONSCIOUSNESS BY JHĀNA MEDITATION

Until quite recently, neuroscience research focused heavily on trying to identify areas of activity in the brain that might somehow have the capacity to generate consciousness, the so-called "neural correlates of consciousness" (NCC). The EEG study of jhāna meditation, on the other hand, provided a completely different window into these networks through observing their disruption as jhāna meditation develops. In fact it was the profound nature of those disruptions that led me to coin the phrase "human default sensory consciousness" to highlight that neuroscience research into the NCC was likely dealing with but one possible mode of brain-network organization.

Historically, sensory consciousness networks are described by EEG frequency bands, which until relatively recently have not been well understood. Roughly speaking, these are the delta band (1–4 Hz) seen in sleep, the theta band (4.5–7.5 Hz) intermediate between sleep and waking, the alpha band (8–12 Hz) as a default "idling" rhythm and sign of relaxation, and the beta band (15–30 Hz) related to thinking and cognitive processing. These are the networks that are disrupted as meditators practice to develop the jhānas.

Table 6 summarizes the main themes of disruption (column 1) described in previous chapters, with their significance in terms of the jhāna factors in column 2, and implications from a neuroscience perspective in column 3.

As described in Chapters 2 and 12, meditation spindles were identified as signs of disruption to sensory attention networks. Spindles also highlight the importance of the alpha rhythm as in many ways being the *signature* of our default sensory consciousness. The mid-frequency of the alpha rhythm, 10 Hz, corresponds to a time period of 100 milliseconds, which is the typical fastest human reaction time—that is, the shortest time between first contact with a sensory input and its *affectual*, or felt, registration in the body. I suggest that this 100-millisecond "alpha moment" could be the "most basic conscious thought" in the sense of affect consciousness mentioned in the previous section—or, alternatively, to correspond to the first two stages of form (rūpa) and feeling (vedanā) in the Buddhist khandhās, where attention is drawn to contact a rūpa, as object, followed by a consequent vedanā, feeling, reaction—or

Table 6: Disruption of Sensory Consciousness during Development of Jhāna

Features of EEG Disruption	Significance from a Meditation Perspective	Implications from a Neuroscience Perspective
Spindles	Signs of disruption to the default attention networks of sensory consciousness; related to activity of vitakka and vicāra	Highlights the role of the alpha α rhythm as the "signature" of sensory consciousness
Infraslow Waves	Signs of increased energization, pīti	Highlights an increase in available energy as sensory networks simplify toward jhāna consciousness
Spike-Waves	Signs of untranquilized pīti	A harmonic structure to meditation spike-waves suggests a repertoire of frequency structures beyond the default bands of sensory consciousness

equally to the contact and feeling stages in Buddhist dependent origination.

Just as the 100-millisecond alpha moment may be related to the most basic form of thought, I further hypothesized that the other frequency bands of sensory consciousness relate to different stages of the development of thought and consciousness. These frequency bands are an example of what is called scaled activity in complex systems, where potentially chaotic systems in the presence of an "attractor" are drawn to operate in bands which may be harmonic or characterized by similar scaled patterns. The "attractor" in this case was suggested to be the time-scale factor of the alpha rhythm. When it was then observed that meditation spike-waves (unlike spike-waves in epilepsy) showed harmonic frequency structure, different for different meditators, it was realized that the structure of the delta, theta, alpha, and beta bands of sensory consciousness might be just one possibility among many.[9]

Hierarchical Structures beyond Sensory and Jhāna Consciousness

The years 2014–19 during the EEG study coincided with the far-reaching developments in neuroscience of active inference, with their almost uncanny similarities to Buddhist dependent origination that I have described. By 2016–17, active inference led on to another fascinating and related area of research into hierarchical structures, described by the intriguing concept of Markov blankets. The background to this is again the principle that in order to exist at all, all biological or living systems need to be distinguished from their environment by a boundary, without which a prototype entity could not survive and would ultimately dissipate or die according to the laws of entropy and thermodynamics. Such a boundary is termed a Markov blanket, an evocative term attributed to Judea Pearl, a computer scientist and philosopher, in 1988. Recent years have seen a flurry of papers dealing with, among other aspects, the "Markov blankets of life."[10]

Theory predicts that all systems interact with each other across hierarchies, from the micro-scale of the simplest organisms such as a single cell or virus up through, for example, the development of a fertilized egg in the womb, the interaction of a baby with mother, an individual in society, societies to their encompassing countries, and at the highest level between societies worldwide and planet Earth. Some of these systems are listed in Table 7, from the micro-scale at the bottom moving up to ever-larger scales in the hierarchy, and it can immediately be seen that jhāna is a special case compared to all the others in that there is no "outside" state beyond the body.

However, from our explorations of the rūpa jhānas we can recognize in them also a hierarchical structure, in the progressive ways in which the jhāna factors are transcended as they are developed from

Table 7: Some Markov Blanket Hierarchies

Markov Blanket System	Inner State	Outer States	Form of Consciousness
Societies–Planet Earth	Societies	Planet Earth	"Gaia" consciousness
Jhāna	Mind/brain	Body	Jhāna consciousness
Individual–Society	Individual	Society	Early to fully developed sensory consciousness
Baby–Mother/Father	Baby	Mother/Father	
Fetus–Mother	Fetus	Mother's womb	
Sperm–Ovum	Sperm	Ovum	Reactive, adaptive
Virus–Host	Virus	Host cell	Reactive, adaptive

the first rūpa jhāna to the fourth. This cannot be said, however, for the arūpa jhānas since they share just the two jhāna factors of equanimity, upekkhā, and unification of mind, ekaggatā citta, as developments from the fourth rūpa jhāna.

The theory of Markov blankets is well-established and predicts specific and characteristic features of levels and their interrelationships that are highly relevant to our understanding of the rūpa jhānas. First is the feature that all levels are interconnected, and that it is meaningless to consider any level in isolation. This supports our discussion earlier in this book that the jhānas to some degree develop interactively, and that as soon as a meditator begins to make progress in developing any one of the rūpa jhānas they are also to some degree developing the others.

Second, and related to this interconnectedness, is the feature that each successively higher level in a hierarchy develops larger scale and slower dynamics. This may relate to the evidence for two rhythms in the infraslow wave activity (ISW) in the EEG at the stages of working with the third and fourth rūpa jhānas: first a rhythm shown by most of the meditators developing the higher jhānas with a time period of about eight seconds, and second a much slower rhythm of around twenty to fifty seconds shown by only very few meditators. Two of the latter group were those who developed exceptionally high dominance of the crown-of-head focus, and it is tempting to consider that the second very slow rhythm might indicate they were experiencing the higher fourth jhāna level in the rūpa jhānas hierarchy. This can only be a provisional suggestion, given the very great difficulty in recording and analyzing such extremely slow rhythms, which require long and consistent recordings.

The third feature of hierarchies predicted in Markov blanket theory is that different and adjacent levels in a hierarchy tend toward "self-similarity." A good example from Table 7 is the mother-baby Markov blanket system, where, in a healthy interactive relationship between them (i.e., between the "outer" and "inner" levels of their Markov blanket system), the baby may learn and repeat many characteristics of the mother. Also from Table 7, we might consider how in the individuals-society Markov blanket system, the higher level in the hierarchy, such as a country or region, might develop a language or dialect that individuals at the "lower" subordinate level mimic and repeat. In both these examples it is important to note that the theory only predicts *similarity*—does not predict that levels tend to become *identical* since that would prevent individuality or anything new developing. In the case of the jhānas hierarchy, the tending toward self-similarity might correspond to the progressive deepening of mindfulness and concentration from the first rūpa jhāna to the fully developed upekkhā of the fourth rūpa jhāna.

At an even higher scale than the hierarchies in Table 7, we might also wonder how the realms of Buddhist cosmology fit into all this, governed as they are in Abhidhamma descriptions by durations of rebirth in units of *mahākappas* (aeons) that follow an ascending harmonic scale according to the three levels of mastery of the different jhānas: ⅓, ½, and 1 mahākappas for the first rūpa jhāna; 2, 4, and 8 mahākappas for the second; 16, 32, and 64 for the third; and 1,000, 2,000, 4,000, 8,000, and 16,000 for persons attained by faith, energy, mindfulness, concentration, and wisdom respectively for the fourth rūpa jhāna.[11]

It is as though in the ancient traditions of Buddhism there has been for millennia an intuitive recognition of the interconnectedness of all these phenomena and hierarchies of existence.

JHĀNA CONSCIOUSNESS

As jhāna develops beyond the initial stages of the first rūpa jhāna, infraslow waves (ISWs) develop to eventually replace the rhythms of sensory consciousness, as a sign of disengaging from sensory consciousness. It then follows, from the earlier discussion of dependent origination and active inference as models of sensory consciousness, that while absorbed in jhāna consciousness a meditator is at least temporarily free from the twelve-stage cycle of mundane (i.e., sensory) dependent origination (see Chapter 14 for a discussion of transcendent dependent origination). We can speculate that such temporary freedom from the mainly unconscious processes of dependent origination might well be the major benefit of regular practice of jhāna meditation, leading to a progressive weakening of craving and attachment and taking practitioners steadily forward toward the stages of realization of the Buddhist Path.

The Subjective Experience of Jhāna Consciousness

It is consistent with the much greater spatial scale and much slower timescale factor corresponding to the ISWs that meditators experience jhāna consciousness as an almost timeless "presence," quite different from everyday consciousness of "this" or "that" dominated by cognitive processing, liking, and disliking. The experience of jhāna is free of the constraints of language and is also more all-encompassing of the whole person—brain, body, and mind—hence "embodied presence," and also the term *yoga* as in *Yogāvacara*.[12]

The subjective sense of embodiment also corresponds to the fact that, unlike in neuroscience models of active inference, there are no "inputs" from an "outer" world beyond the body. This is a crucial difference. It is sensory information from the outer world that supports the inner mental and brain processes of sensory consciousness, whereas the processes of jhāna are apparently contained entirely within the body and brain. The vertical axis of jhāna consciousness described in earlier chapters suggests that it is the body itself that supports the "inner" mental processes of jhāna consciousness.

For the situation of jhāna, then, the equivalent to sensory information from the outer world is most likely to be *interoceptive* information about the condition of a person's nervous and visceral systems of the body. This also explains the different timescale factor of jhāna, due to the meditator's biological and visceral bodily processes being 100–300 times slower than the rapid neural processes involved in sensory processing.

Furthermore, so long as the brain-body system of jhāna consciousness can be maintained, with its almost timeless, subjective equanimity, then not only will a practitioner be temporarily free from the constraints of Buddhist dependent origination, but in the neuroscience language of free energy and active inference there will be no prediction error; all that is redundant, distracting, or unnecessarily complex will have been dissolved, with expected free energy absolutely minimized until the experience of jhāna comes to a natural close—in some cases after a few minutes, or in the case of experienced meditators, potentially after several hours.

The experience of deep and almost timeless, undisturbed tranquility raises an intriguing question as to the subject-object nature of jhāna consciousness. By definition, consciousness requires an object to be conscious of, so what kind of consciousness is this? Two views have been expressed in the oral jhāna tradition, the first being that each moment of consciousness becomes the object of the next, creating the illusion of perfectly continuous, undisturbed consciousness. This is envisaged as a high-level and very fast process, so fast indeed that we might wonder at the role of the much higher frequency rhythms of the weak background EEG gamma activity mentioned several times in this book, including brief gamma bursts that were observed at those transition points where meditators were given a cue to move to the next stage in their meditation. This may imply a very fast flickering between moments of jhāna absorption, each followed by an immediate (non-discursive) reflection on the immediately preceding state (corresponding to the "reviewing" stage described under the heading of "Preparation and Mastery" in Chapter 3), then re-establishing absorption.

A second view, which I favor, is that the experience of "embodied presence" might correspond to the body itself being the supporting object of jhāna consciousness as part of a deep metabolic integration, which might relate to the intriguing term "body-witness" encountered in the *Vimuttimagga* and *Visuddhimagga*. The term refers to a meditator who has made much of developing concentration and has experience of all four rūpa jhānas and the four arūpas. To this we can add the following quotation from the *Rohitassa*

Sutta, with its own intriguing reference to an outermost hierarchy of the cosmos:

> it is just within this fathom-long body, with its percep-
> tion and intellect, that I declare that there is the cosmos,
> the origination of the cosmos, the cessation of the cos-
> mos, and the path of practice leading to the cessation of
> the cosmos.[13]

THE ILLUSION OF "I"

As a meditator's experience of the jhānas develops, "presence" deepens and progressively replaces self-referential assumptions of "I am." The less that consciousness depends on the limiting assump-tions of "I," the more vivid and all-encompassing does the experi-ence of "presence" become. This is consistent with Buddhist views of our sense of "I" as an illusion, and that it is freedom from the deeply embedded habits of such assumptions during jhāna med-itation that leads to deepening insight into attachment and the human condition.

Neuroscience may be converging with this view of the illusory nature of "I," in how its three-stage taxonomy of affect conscious-ness, perceptual consciousness, and reflective consciousness is interpreted. In the third stage where reflective re-presentations lead to self-consciousness, we might consider the likely possibility of such re-presentations attaching to the imaginal structure of a person's own body as "I" or "mine," similar to what the psychologist Brian L. Lancaster termed the "I-tag."[14] A rather similar allusion is made in the puppet simile described in the *Vimuttimagga*:

> These puppets are called bodies; the master of pup-
> pets is the past defilement by which this body is made
> complete; the strings are the tendons; the clay is flesh;
> the paint is the skin; the interstices are space. [By] jew-
> els, raiment and ornaments [they] are called men and

women. Thoughts [of men and women] are to be known as the tugging by the element of air. Thus they walk, dwell, go out, or come in, stretch out, draw in, converse or speak.[15]

It might then be argued that both Buddhist and active inference models support the view that the cognitive conclusion that "I am" and "I do" is both impermanent and has no ultimate reality. Nevertheless, in everyday life the continuity of this illusion serves a valuable purpose, particularly in allowing a person to predict outcomes from past experience, so that we should not be surprised that the process of disengaging to develop the jhānas is a challenging undertaking.

14. An Ancient Path

Coming to the end of a journey, and this final chapter, helps to make clear the beginning, confirming to me that there was already some subliminal awareness of the end from the start, even if not yet fully conscious—which reminds me of the comment of the monk at Heathrow airport in 1974, about the Dhamma being beautiful in the beginning, in the middle, and at the end.

The primary example of knowing something about the end, even in the beginning, is knowing from an early age that at some point we will die, while not yet knowing exactly what that means. For meditators the starting point for developing the jhānas is the moment of vitakka, transferring attention away from the outer sensory world inward. The experience is then refined by vicāra, sustained attention, directed first toward the breath and its associated nimitta, or sign, and eventually toward perception and consciousness itself. Vitakka and vicāra together lead to the further jhāna factors of energization (pīti), happiness or bliss (sukha), and ekaggatā citta (unification of mind), and in the third and fourth rūpa jhānas to absorption, concentration (samādhi), and equanimity (upekkhā).

The very basic moment of vitakka at the beginning establishes mindfulness (sati), which by the end of the process, in the fourth rūpa jhāna, has matured into perfect mindfulness, the seventh factor of the Noble Eightfold Path. Similarly, the concentration developed in the first rūpa jhāna leading to the first experience of unification of mind (ekaggatā citta), becomes, in the fourth rūpa jhāna, the eighth factor on the Eightfold Path: right concentration.

In the description of the factors of enlightenment (bojjhaṅgas), the starting point is also a moment of mindfulness (sati), which is then consolidated by investigation (dhamma-vicaya), leading to vigor (viriya), energization (pīti), and tranquilization (passaddhi), and finally as in the jhānas to concentration (samādhi) and equanimity (upekkhā). As with the jhānas, the final developments of concentration and equanimity are already presaged in the early establishments of mindfulness and investigation.

Even in the most sublime experience of perfect equanimity in the fourth rūpa jhāna, there is a thread reaching back to the very beginning, the beginning of a process to disengage from sensory consciousness; it is this thread, no matter its subtlety, which is behind the sense of the fourth jhāna as still a "held" state, still with a subtle connection to the world of form. And by reciprocal logic, at the beginning of the journey there must also be a thread, even if only in potential, but which nevertheless has its own reality and form, connecting forward to the end of the journey. Which again, from the perspective of ordinary logic, tells us that the beginning and end are inextricably linked, just as form is to formless, or something to nothing, or forward to backward, as in the forward and reverse orders in which the jhānas may be practiced or the stages of dependent origination contemplated.

Occasionally we glimpse this same reality in situations of everyday life. Sometimes setting out on a long-haul journey at the moment of boarding a plane, travelers might experience a strange dissociation of simultaneously experiencing themselves disembarking at the end of the journey, or embarking for the return journey.

And speaking of journeys, I am reminded of a question Nai Boonman asked beginners over fifty-five years ago, as to whether a person would start meditation at all if they knew what it would entail and where it might lead—particularly if they knew that at some point there would be no going back. I suspect that those who do start and commit themselves to practice do in fact know at some deep level what they are taking on, and perhaps Boonman's question might have had the effect of activating that awareness at some level.

The journey I have taken in this book has deliberately broadened the discussion of the jhānas to also include the bojjhaṅgas, brief mentions of the Eightfold Path, and Nai Boonman's early descriptions of meditation as essentially a balance between concentration and mindfulness. These aspects are summarized together in Table 8.

Table 8: The Bojjhaṅgas, the Jhānas, and the Eightfold Path

Samatha-Vipassanā	Bojjhaṅgas	RJ1	RJ2	RJ3	RJ4	Eightfold Path Factors
Concentration	Upekkhā Equanimity				Upekkhā	**Sammā Samādhi** Right Concentration
	Samādhi Concentration/Absorption	Ekagattā	Ekagattā citta	Samādhi		**Sammā Sati** Right Mindfulness; **Sammā Vāyāma** Right Effort
	Passaddhi Tranquilization	Sukha	Sukha	Sukha		**Sammā Ājiva** Right Livelihood
	Piti Energization, Joy	Piti	Piti	(Piti)	(Piti)	**Sammā Kammanta** Right Action
Mindfulness	Viriya Vigour					**Sammā Vācā** Right Speech
	Dhamma-vicaya Investigation	Vicāra Sustained attention	(Vicāra)	(Vicāra)	(Vicāra)	**Sammā Saṅkappa** Right Intention
	Sati Mindfulness	Vitakka Placed attention	(Vitakka)	(Vitakka)	(Vitakka)	**Sammā Diṭṭhi** Right View

The Rūpa Jhānas (RJ) and Their Factors

Columns 2 through 6 show the correspondences between the jhāna factors and the bojjhaṅgas aligned in the respective rows as described in earlier chapters. The dominant jhāna factors for each jhāna are shown bold, and those placed in parentheses indicate they have been mastered in one of the preceding jhānas. Together this scheme illustrates the progressive development from an initial moment of sati in the bojjhaṅgas scheme or vitakka as the first jhāna factor, to the culmination in upekkhā in the fourth rūpa jhāna.

Column 1, left, is the overall encompassing simplified structure taught by Nai Boonman in the early years of this tradition, of a balance between concentration and mindfulness, which I interpret as an alternative description of the twin kammaṭṭhāna of the Yogāvacara, samatha and vipassanā developed equally alongside each other. For completion, the Eightfold Path factors are shown in column 7 as an alternative view of all the qualities being developed alongside the bojjhaṅgas and the jhānas. The Eightfold Path factors develop interactively with each other and, together with mindfulness and concentration in column 1, are encompassing structures not meant to align with the individual bojjhaṅgas or jhāna factors in columns 2 through 6.

In following one's individual path through these structures, there is often a sense in the Yogāvacara of an alternative reality—something "nearby," just off-center, not quite in view. Perhaps this is one of the attractions or fascinations of the Yogāvacara, a reflection of the fine-material sphere of the jhānas, an increasing awareness of an alternate mode of consciousness as a meditator lets go of the familiar anchors of sensory consciousness. It is remarkably powerful to experience such alternate modes of consciousness, and it is a sobering thought that the centuries-old practice traditions that provide access to such states were nearly wiped out in the twentieth century.

THE SAṄGHA AND A PATH ALMOST LOST

In an article dealing with the concepts of jhāna in the Suttas and Abhidhamma, Bhikkhu Brahmāli quotes the following extract from the *Saddhammappatirūpaka Sutta* of the Saṃyutta Nikāya:

> The true Dhamma does not disappear all at once in the way a ship sinks. There are, Kassapa, five detrimental things that lead to the decay and disappearance of the true Dhamma. What are the five? Here the bhikkhus, the bhikkunīs, the male lay followers, the female lay followers dwell without reverence and deference towards the Teacher . . . towards the Dhamma . . . towards the Saṅgha . . . towards the training . . . towards concentration (samādhi). These are the five detrimental things that lead to the decay and disappearance of the Dhamma.[1]

This warns of a breakdown in the functioning of the Saṅgha together with devaluing samādhi, which seems to be precisely what developed in Thailand from the early 1830s and particularly from the 1950s onward. Bhikkhu Brahmāli also recognizes the significance of samādhi being included in the list rather than, for example, wisdom. This may be because samādhi is the seventh factor of the Eightfold Path required to be fulfilled before the eighth factor, wisdom, can come to fulfillment.

It is said that without the Buddha there would be no Dhamma, but without the Saṅgha there would also be no Dhamma. It has always been the role of the Saṅgha to preserve the teachings and protect the lineage from the time of the Buddha to the present day. That the Saṅgha has been largely successful for more than two millennia is a remarkable achievement. Someone practicing samatha and vipassanā today will recognize even in enigmatic and ancient textual descriptions the same experiences they find in their own present-day meditation practice. And yet, these descriptions alone do not preserve the tradition. Given that the core of Buddhist spiritual experiences—whether of jhānas or the Path—are unconditioned and largely formless compared to default sensory processing, no amount of words or texts alone are sufficient to preserve the heart of a tradition. So it is all the more remarkable then that the people composing the Saṅgha throughout the centuries have mostly succeeded in this work of preservation.

In practice, the monastic Saṅgha, certainly in contemporary Southeast Asia, is an eclectic mix of characters comprised of scholar-monks, monks involved in pastoral and educative roles in society, monks immersed in Vinaya and inter- and intra-Saṅgha relations, and monks drawn to meditation. There is also a sprinkling of men seeking temporary refuge from social or marital problems, including in recent times refugees from wars, some even of dubious character, as well as always a number seeking temporary ordination as a rite of passage or to satisfy societal expectations.

Yet each month at the full moon, after shaving the head and after a ritual confession of infractions of Vinaya to fellow monks and being forgiven those transgressions, those monks cease to be flawed individuals and come together as a ritually purified Saṅgha to take part in the age-old recitation of the Pāṭimokkha, thereby re-establishing their connection to the Buddha's lineage.

Looking back almost two centuries, the formation of a second sect and ordination line in Thailand in 1833 under the label "reform" was a severe blow to the coherence and identity of the Saṅgha. Some have even wondered at how that action sits in relation to one of the most serious, *pārājika* or defeat, offenses in the Vinaya—that of causing a schism in the Saṅgha. After much reflection over thirty to forty years I believe those events set in motion a near destruction of some of the most valuable and subtle understandings of Buddhist meditation, in particular jhāna meditation.

I am not alone in that opinion. Writing about the changing politics of Thailand's Buddhist elite during the 1950s–1970s in a 2012 article entitled "The Changing Politics of Thailand's Bud-

dhist Order," the scholar Duncan McCargo describes the disarray of the Saṅgha hierarchy in Thailand as being a consequence
of Mongkut's reforms dating back to the 1830s, resulting in long-
standing tensions between the rival Thammayut and Mahānikāy
sects and "a dearth of moral and administrative leadership that
paralyzed the Thai monkhood and rendered it seemingly incapable
of reforming itself."[2]

It was not until writing this book and filling in historical gaps that
I realized reforms similar to those in Thailand had also taken place
in Burma from the mid-1880s, partly as a response to British colonial
rule but also affected by Western scientific and Christian mission-
ary influences.[3] The leading figure behind the reforms in Burma
was Ledi Sayadaw (1846–1923), one of a line of eminent scholar-
monks who, while acknowledging to some extent the value of jhāna,
claimed that only a minimal level of moment-to-moment concentration, what he termed *khaṇika samādhi*, was sufficient for full development of insight (and by implication the Path). Somewhat later,
Mingun Sayadaw (1868–1955) further sidelined jhāna practices by
promoting vipassanā without jhāna, and not surprisingly his pupil
Mahāsi Sayadaw (1904–1982) continued this model of what came
to be known as "dry" insight, or "new vipassanā." Those eminent
scholar-monks also wrote at great length about the Abhidhamma,
sometimes using it to justify their claims regarding vipassanā as a
complete practice in its own right, and it is not clear whether there
existed at that time a strong tradition and in-depth knowledge of
jhāna meditation to balance their academic views.

Mahāsi Sayadaw and "Dry" Vipassanā

After establishing a large following in Burma, Mahāsi Sayadaw
toured Thailand in 1951, and his influence grew considerably after
Burma hosted the Sixth Buddhist Council in 1954–55. Like his pre-
decessors the Ledi and Mingun Sayadaws, he taught that samatha
meditation, in particular the practice of jhāna, was not necessary,

and even an impediment to developing insight and wisdom. His new version of vipassanā came to be referred to as "dry" insight, as it was not "moistened" by the pīti and sukha of jhāna.

Mahāsi Sayadaw had a number of highly connected and influential students within the Thai Saṅgha, and his new vipassanā movement quickly spread into Thailand and eventually worldwide. This happened so quickly that the disarray within the Saṅgha, mentioned earlier as a consequence of Mongkut's reforms, manifested in ineffective and confused responses, with leaders of both Mahānikāy and Thammayut sects vying with each other for influence in the newly developing vipassanā movement. There appears to have been no clear meditational authority—including within the "forest tradition" that might have been expected to defend the importance of jhāna—capable of unifying the Saṅgha to resist the heavy political promotion of this new movement that presented a major challenge to meditation practices and understandings that had existed across Southeast Asia for centuries.

In effect, the new movement represented a massive devaluation of jhāna, and hence samādhi, exactly as warned by the quotation at the beginning of this section as the precursors for decay and disappearance of the true Dhamma. That this could happen seems extraordinary given that samādhi is defined as precisely the four rūpa jhānas in the Suttas, and much of the confusion at the time seems to have been around how the new vipassanā movement understood samādhi and concentration.

In his 1945 book, *Manual of Insight*, Mahāsi Sayadaw writes:

> There are three types of concentration that entail purification of mind: access or neighbourhood concentration (upacārasamādhi), absorption concentration (appanāsamādhi), and momentary concentration (khaṇikasamādhi).[4]

And later in the same work:

One who develops insight based on a foundation
of access or absorption concentration is called "one
who takes the vehicle of tranquillity to nibbāna"
(samathāyānika) . . . A person who takes the vehicle of
insight uses only momentary concentration to bring
about the necessary purification, and his or her insight
practice is then based on that mental purification.[5]

The terms *upacārasamādhi* and *khaṇikasamādhi* do not appear
in the original Buddhist Suttas, where samādhi, with no qualifiers,
is simply and unequivocally the rūpa jhānas. The terms Mahāsi
Sayadaw uses are later concepts developed in the Abhidhamma
and commentaries such as the *Visuddhimagga*, both of which figure prominently in his writings. It is also not clear what exactly
is meant by "purification of mind" for these different degrees of
concentration noted in the first extract.

The second extract above is clear in stating that the new Burmese vipassanā practice is based on momentary concentration,
aligning with his predecessor Ledi Sayadaw's statement. Yet in his
later *Practical Insight Meditation* (1971), while the level of concentration is not clearly specified in the main text, the endnotes that
quote extensively from the Buddhist commentaries indicate the
required level to be "access concentration," closer to jhāna. Also,
several excerpts in the main text sound very much like the development of pīti and the nimitta in the approach to jhāna—for example,

Again, as a result of insight, a brilliant light will appear
to the meditator. There arises also in him rapture, causing "goose-flesh," falling of tears, tremor in the limbs
[and] there arises tranquility of mind and along with it
appears mental agility, etc.[6]

Although this appears under the heading "Corruptions of
insight," and apart from the fact that "a brilliant light" would be

understood to be the result of concentration and not insight in pre-reform Yogāvacara or boran kammaṭṭhāna practices, the statement at least indicates an awareness of subjective experiences very similar to the threshold stages of developing the first rūpa jhāna. This might indicate a shift in Mahāsi Sayadaw's understanding in his later years, less dependent on the influences of his teachers, with a clearer recognition of the role of at least access concentration and some development of the approach stages to jhāna.

However, both terms "momentary" and "access" were often used interchangeably during various retreats led by Mahāsi Sayadaw, including one of his late retreats in the West that I attended in Oxford in 1979. The Oxford retreat attracted many monk participants as well as a number of lay meditators. My motivation for attending was a wish to understand exactly what this "dry vipassanā" practice consisted of, which required me to resist any urge to develop the jhānas and to follow the new vipassanā technique exactly as taught. The experience led me to believe that some practitioners of this method do in fact have a momentary—but not sustained—experience of at least access, and maybe a momentary experience of the first rūpa jhāna. However, the senior teachers of the Mahāsi method appeared to have very little understanding of the jhāna factors or how jhāna develops, judging from the Dhamma talks and informal discussions at that time.

Having witnessed some of the damage done to the old practices in Thailand from the late 1960s onward, as well as taking part in one of the last intensive retreats led by Mahāsi Sayadaw, I was often struck by the rigidity and dogmatic attachment to views in even the most supposedly advanced practitioners of the Burmese method. This also extended to what appeared to be, in my opinion, gross overestimations of progress on the Path, with many of the Burmese monk practitioners convinced they had attained the third Path of anāgāmin, or non-returner—a practitioner destined for only one more life in the heaven of the Pure Abodes before attaining full enlightenment. Mahāsi Sayadaw himself of course was regarded as an arahat, or fully enlightened being.

In fact in the late-1960s to early-1970s period when the Burmese vipassanā movement was at its height, courses were offered in Burma that were claimed would lead to the first Path, sotāpanna, stream-enterer, within a month—without the need for jhāna. Some centers even gave certificates to verify the attainment, a practice that not surprisingly aroused criticism and didn't last long, and which is now mostly forgotten or denied.

In later years, as I became interested and eventually trained in psychoanalysis, the underlying psychological mechanisms in play behind the reform conflicts began to interest me. The parallels between the Buddhist reforms and what happens when a family structure becomes dysfunctional are striking, given the description of the Saṅgha ceasing to function as a coherent, responsible whole. The symptoms of growing dysfunction in organizations or families typically vary from confusion, doubt, and anxiety to dissociation, delusion, denial, and even psychotic splits and severe disconnection from reality.[7] In the case of the reform disruptions of the Saṅgha, consequences of denial and forgetting seem particularly relevant, raising the question as to the extent to which age-old practices were not only grossly devalued, but partially or in some respects actually forgotten.

Intentional Forgetting

> "The most dangerous of all falsehoods is a slightly distorted truth."
>
> —Georg Christoph Lichtenberg (1742–99), *Aphorisms*

The mechanism of intentional forgetting or denial is well known in psychoanalysis, stemming largely from Freud's early work, particularly in his 1895 *Project for a Scientific Psychology*, in which he outlines his then emerging understanding of conscious and unconscious processes, and particularly the defensive process of intentional forgetting or denial as a defense against inner conflict or psychic pain.[8]

If there is a traumatic aspect to what is being denied, intentional forgetting is mostly an unconscious mechanism that underlies many mental health conditions. Sometimes, however, intentional forgetting is not simply a crude defense (or attack) but can be a largely conscious strategy to reduce a clutter or confusion of ideas.[9] The promotion of Burmese dry vipassanā in the 1950s may have been rationalized in this way, with the traditional practices being seen as flawed, superstitious, or obsolete, while the far-reaching consequences of the reforms were denied or not fully realized. It is also relevant that intentional forgetting is frequently associated with delusional and often rigid attachment to a particular view, which rationalizes and justifies the process of forgetting.

The organizational context highlights the importance of the larger organization carrying an "organizational memory" of what has been forgotten in order to manage cues that might cause it to be remembered, or not. In the case of the Saṅgha, "organizational memory" would correspond to its historic role of protecting and preserving the teachings of the Buddha, symbolically renewed each full moon in the Pāṭimokkha recitation. This organizational memory, particularly of the oral traditions of jhāna and the Yogāvacara, appears to have failed progressively from the 1830s, reaching a climax of failure in the reforms of the 1950s.

An intriguing question: At what point does an individual or organization forget that at some point in the past they chose to forget something important? Has it then disappeared forever? There is an old saying that we may not realize the value of something until we lose it, but that depends on someone, or an organization, remembering what has been discarded or lost in the first place.

Self-Delusion and Self-Fulfilled Expectations

Related to but slightly different from intentional forgetting is self-delusion, which, it turns out, is greatly facilitated by the neuroscience processes of active inference described in the previous chapter.

The dynamic balance between inputs from the sensory world and chosen actions in the active inference model is strongly influenced by the personal element of likes and dislikes and by previous experience. It then becomes immediately clear that if a person strongly wishes for a particular outcome, then it may become a self-fulfilling process by virtue of feedback reinforcement.

This can lead to negative outcomes as in psychological illness, often accompanied by rumination, which is precisely a form of negative feedback reinforcement, although it can also lead to positive outcomes as practiced for example in "positive psychology" to encourage more constructive thought patterns.

Thinking back, then, to how the Burmese vipassanā movement was promoted from the mid-1950s onward: it is a fact that the methods of practice and the aspired-to stages of insight were described in great detail and with great conviction by highly respected and authoritative scholar-monks, who sometimes appeared to borrow the authority of the Abhidhamma to justify their claims, with little acknowledgment of other views regarding the jhānas and paññā (wisdom) in the Suttas. It is then not a great leap to understand how some new practitioners—monks, nuns, and laypeople alike—might well have come to experience what they wished for or expected as a largely cognitive "construction," rather than as fully embodied experience, and to then also greatly overestimate their attainments. This is the same mechanism of cognitive reinforcement described in Chapter 6 that can lead to "facsimile jhāna," a superficially convincing but ultimately fragile construction. Of course it also has to be acknowledged that even given those risks, for some the experiences can undoubtedly be genuine.

THE BUDDHA, THE JHĀNAS, AND WISDOM

Given how central jhāna meditation is to the Path in the Suttas, it is extraordinary that the "reforms" of the early 1800s and then the 1950s almost succeeded in destroying these ancient practices and, by implication, knowledge of the Path. And what is this Path, exactly? It is not simply an invention of the Buddha. As the Buddha states in the *Nagara Sutta*:

> It is as if while travelling through a great forest, one should come upon an ancient path, an ancient road traversed by people of former days . . . Even so have I, monks, seen an ancient path, an ancient road traversed by the rightly enlightened ones of former times.[10]

The Buddha spoke these words soon after his enlightenment, or realization, over 2,500 years ago, describing an ancient Path discovered, lost, and rediscovered throughout history by others before him. He spent the rest of his life teaching how to develop and practice this Path, which spread over vast areas of Asia, eventually and more recently to the West. In each new location where the Path has emerged, it is a process of transmission—the planting of a seed by someone with direct experience of the Path. In each case as new shoots develop, they are required to adapt to new contexts, with fascinating creative possibilities.

Once asked to describe the essence of the Buddha's teaching in a round-table multi-faith radio broadcast in the 1970s, Nai Boonman, after a long pause following the lengthy talks by other members of the panel, finally commented that "the heart of the Buddha's teaching is suffering," which was received by a rather stunned silence given that the previous contributions had been focused on ideas more readily recognizable as religious in nature.

Of course Boonman was prevailed upon to say a little more about the core Buddhist teaching, and he responded with some words about the Four Noble Truths—the reality of suffering, how it arises from attachment and craving, the reality of its cessation, and the way, or Path, that leads to this cessation. But nevertheless it is a great leveler that the origin of the teaching is simply the very human experience of suffering. The Buddha's teaching is universal rather than political or dogmatic.

Nai Boonman was simply restating the Buddha's own words from the *Alagaddupama Sutta*: "I teach only suffering and the cessation of suffering." The Four Noble Truths of Suffering constitute the core of Dhamma, and their deep realization becomes actualized at the moment of attaining the Path. In a monk's life they are recollected at the start of each day in the morning chanting, where, after recollection of the Buddha, Dhamma, and Saṅgha, there come the beautifully evocative stanzas mentioned earlier in Chapter 7, but repeated here:

Rūpaṃ aniccaṃ.
Vedanā aniccā.
Saññā aniccā.
Saṅkhārā aniccā.
Viññāṇaṃ aniccaṃ.
Rūpaṃ anattā.
Vedanā anattā.
Saññā anattā.
Saṅkhārā anattā.
Viññāṇaṃ anattā.
Sabbe saṅkhārā aniccā.
Sabbe dhammā anattā ti.

Form is impermanent; feeling is impermanent; perception is impermanent; mental formations are impermanent; consciousness is impermanent.

Form is not-self; feeling is not-self; perception is not-self; mental formations are not-self; consciousness is not-self.

All formations are impermanent; all dhammas [phenomena] are not-self.

This is a reminder that, ultimately, the quest to experience the jhānas and the Path are responses to human suffering. The process cannot be rushed. As Nai Boonman once said, it requires the right person, right place, and right time.

Realization, or enlightenment (Pāli, nibbāna; Sanskrit, nirvāna), is often translated as "blowing out" (as in a candle) or "quenching" (as in thirst). But what exactly is blown out, and what, if anything, remains? The usual answer to this is that the three root tendencies of greed, hate, and delusion (lobha, dosa, moha) are extinguished, without remainder. But clearly, as in the examples of the Buddha and his noble disciples (those who attained one of the four stages of the Path), the person certainly does not disappear, and in fact appears to become more vividly "present." Nevertheless, the person has to have become radically transformed if consciousness is to be no longer motivated or dominated by greed, hatred, and delusion.

Nibbāna, and the Path to it, is therefore a psychological and ethical reality, where the transformed state is characterized by deep peace, compassion, and a refined and subtle awareness within which negative mental states and emotions such as doubt, worry, anxiety, and fear are absent.

But how is this transformed state achieved, beyond the jhānas, particularly given that nibbāna is described in Buddhist texts as unconditioned, meaning it cannot be cognitively constructed? As with the jhānas, a person cannot think themselves into nibbāna. This once again raises the fascinating question as to how anything completely new and different, never experienced before, can ever be experienced at all? From the sciences to the arts, even the most profound discoveries and breakthroughs, if examined closely, are generally conditioned by previous thought or experience and are rarely, if ever, completely new.

The Sākyan Prince Gotama, as a young man before he became the Buddha, also struggled with this dilemma and for many years followed austere yoga teachers in attempts to create conditions from which the release from suffering might arise. Finally, before his enlightenment, Gotama rejected such practices because he realized they were rooted in aversion to the body. Having abandoned asceticism, he turned instead to his early memory of experiencing the first rūpa jhāna as a young boy, and this turning away from asceticism and toward the practice of jhāna eventually led him to his enlightenment experience. When he began teaching others how to experience enlightenment for themselves, his teachings centered on developing the jhānas as a basis for wisdom.

The Jhānas and Wisdom

After rejecting the path of austerities, the Buddha's teachings centered on detailed practice and experience of the jhānas and the twin kammaṭṭhāna, which came to be known as samatha and vipassanā. The centrality of jhāna in the Buddha's teachings cannot be overemphasized—as for example this extract from the *Gaṅgā-Peyyālo Sutta*:

> Just as, monks, the river Ganges flows to the east, slides to the east, tends to the east, even so a monk by cultivating the four trances [jhānas], making much of the four trances [jhānas], flows, slides and tends to nibbāna.[11]

A further example is *Dhammapada* verse 372:

> Natthi jhānaṃ apaññassa, paññā natthi ajhāyato.
> Yamhi jhānañca paññā ca, sa ve nibbānasantike.

There is no jhāna for one without wisdom. Nor wisdom for one without jhāna. But for one with both jhāna and wisdom Nibbāna truly is near.

Here wisdom, or paññā, is a common epithet for the Path, but the true significance of this brief statement is the equal importance given to jhāna and wisdom. This relates to the subjective experience from the very first stages of approaching the first rūpa jhāna, of how vipassanā develops alongside jhāna from the beginning. To disengage from sensory consciousness encounters resistance, experienced as the hindrances, and it is only when a meditator has sufficient insight into how to let go of wanting or not-wanting, how to weaken the habits of attachment and craving, that the way opens to experience the unification of mind that characterizes jhāna.

The Jhānas and the Four Paths

My understanding, based on extensive experience with the old practices and practitioners, is that the jhānas (although not explicitly described as such in any texts, as far as I am aware) can be understood as temporary experiences of the stages of realization of the Buddhist Path. The four stages of realization are attained by four categories of persons: the sotāpanna, stream-enterer; the sakadāgāmin, once-returner; the anāgāmin, non-returner; and the arahat, fully realized. These are listed in Table 9.

At each stage the "fetters" binding a person to repeated cycles of rebirth are progressively transcended, and these are listed along with the future rebirths in the table. Those who fully (i.e., permanently) attain one of these Paths become members of the Ariyā Saṅgha, technically senior to members of the Bhikkhu Saṅgha if the latter have not yet attained to one of the Paths.

The Sotāpanna and "the Threes"

In Chapter 3, three levels of mastery were described for at least the first three of the four rūpa jhānas, and those same three levels are traditionally believed to lead to increasingly long durations of rebirth in the realms corresponding to each jhāna (see Chapter 13's discussion of hierarchies). The situation for the fourth rūpa jhāna is believed by some to be different, in that because that jhāna has reached perfection of equanimity, with nothing further to be done, there cannot therefore be gradations in its experience.

In terms of the Paths as listed in Table 9, the first rūpa jhāna as the first experience of the Path is of particular interest. Corresponding to the three stages of mastery of the first jhāna, the

Table 9: Stages of the Path

Stage of the Path	Fetters Abandoned		Rebirths
Sotāpanna Stream-enterer	1. False view of self 2. Doubt 3. Attachment to rituals or asceticism	Lower fetters	· 6 rebirths in higher realms before final human rebirth (weak faculty) · 2 or 3 more human rebirths (middle faculty) · 1 more human rebirth (keen faculty)
Sakadāgāmin Once-returner	As above, + weakened: 4. Sense desire 5. Ill will	Lower fetters	Once more as a human
Anāgāmin Non-returner	Totally abandoned: 4. Sense desire 5. Ill will	Lower fetters	Once more in a heavenly realm (pure abode)
Arahat Fully realized	Totally abandoned: 6. Attachment to the rūpa jhānas 7. Attachment to the arūpa jhānas 8. Conceit 9. Restlessness 10. Ignorance	Higher fetters	No more rebirths

sotāpanna is described in *Vimuttimagga* XII as being of three types: one of weak faculty who will be born in higher realms for six births before a final human birth to complete the Path; one of middling faculty who will be born two or three times as human before completing the Path; and one of keen faculty who will be born once more as human to complete the Path in that life.[12]

This latter course is not elaborated in written texts but suggests that the life experiences during that single life for such a person carry the same weight and impact as what might otherwise require seven lives. The significance of seven lives rather than two or twenty is related to working through and developing the seven factors of enlightenment, the bojjhaṅgas.

In the case of a sotāpanna who is reborn, that person will need to re-experience the Path for it to become embodied once more in the new birth (i.e., body), but that experience will be subtly different from its first occurrence in a previous life. Although there will be no contextual memory of the prior experience of attainment (unless the person has mastered recollection of previous lives, perhaps unlikely for a first-stage sotāpanna), the re-experience may happen surprisingly easily, and may take some time to be fully understood as to its meaning and significance. However, even if not fully understood, until perhaps confirmed by someone able to do so, it is said to be characterized by an acute and sometimes sobering and even painful awareness of what has not yet been achieved, what remains to be done, rather than pride in having attained something special.

Ledi Sayadaw in his early writings mentions a term, *bon-sin-san*, as the lowest level of sotāpanna, which, given the background of the vipassanā practices he advocated that did not require development of jhāna, might refer to a person who through well-developed sīla (sin) and faith has ensured a favorable next birth, but perhaps has many, many more lives before finally attaining arahatship, unlike the more familiar sotāpanna described in Table 9, who has at most seven future lives. Although the term is not found in the suttas, common Burmese understanding of *bon-sin-san* is that the person has progressed sufficiently to guarantee reaching arahatship at some point in the future, hence Ledi Sayadaw's use of the term as a type of sotāpanna.

The Jhānas, the Arūpas, and the Paths

Practicing the jhānas and the formless arūpas allows a meditator to directly experience a degree of freedom from sensory consciousness, with growing insight into attachment and the roots of suffering. Table 10 summarizes the factors that characterize the parallels between each of these stages and the four Paths of realization.

An initial experience of the first rūpa jhāna can be a major experience in a person's life, the realization of another realm of experience quite different to sensory consciousness, which breaks the illusion of a permanent "I." Wrong view of self dissolves, and doubt and attachment to rites and rituals disappears to be replaced by a deeper confidence that a Path does indeed exist. This equates to a temporary experience of the sotāpanna stage and is held in balance by the power of stabilized vitakka and vicāra.

To develop the second rūpa jhāna requires a much greater degree of mastery of attachment than is required for the first rūpa jhāna. This is particularly so in regard to bodily disturbance, or untranquilized pīti. Eventually the meditator becomes aware of even the slightest disturbance as an obstacle to increasing peacefulness and stillness, which is then quickly tranquilized by passaddhi into deepening samādhi. This might then be regarded as a temporary experience of the sakadāgāmin Path characterized by weakened aversion, dosa, and attachment, or wanting, lobha. In daily life, if it becomes permanent, it would equate to being able to quickly tranquilize any arousing of greed or hatred should they arise.

The third rūpa jhāna goes further—the meditator attains the point of all-encompassing sukha, or mental bliss, experienced without attachment within deep equanimity, upekkhā. So all-encompassing is this experience of bliss within equanimity, described in texts such as the *Visuddhimagga* as "perfectly conscious," that there is now no room for even the slightest disturbance to either the body or the mind. This might then be regarded as a temporary experience of the anāgāmin Path, characterized by total absence of dosa and lobha, which if it became fully realized and permanent would equate in everyday life to complete tranquility or evenness in the face of any provocation toward dosa or lobha.

In the fourth rūpa jhāna, samādhi and upekkhā become complete; all attachment has been let go, even attachment to happiness. This fully perfected equanimity, upekkhā, and freedom from any attachment, which completes the rūpa jhānas with no further development possible within the realm of form, might then be regarded as a temporary experience of the arahat Path.

It is said that full experience of the Path can arise at any time if conditions and the meditator are "ripe," and this is particularly so at moments of establishing one of the jhānas, which is described as a change of lineage, gotrabhu, just as attainment of one of the stages of the Path is also described as a change of lineage. In the gradual Path of ānāpānasati and the Yogāvacara, there should be no urgency to this process, as any such contrived direction or intent negates the possibility of attainment—the Path can only arise if unconditioned. Practicing the jhānas, whether the Path arises or not, is like drawing an Ong Phra yantra repeatedly until it eventually takes the form of a Dhammakāya body. It is a gradual, cumulative process.

If the Path does not arise in conjunction with one of the rūpa jhānas, then the arūpa formless practices can take a meditator even closer, as described in Table 9, due to the truly unbounded nature of the arūpas. Thus in developing the first arūpa, the infinity of space, a meditator can only do so by completely letting go of the security of a subject position, which requires a high development of non-attachment and a corresponding understanding of impermanence and the nature of suffering. At that point of establishing the arūpa experience, if it is truly unbounded, nothing remains to interfere with a complete attainment of the first sotāpanna Path, with the same principle applying for the other arūpas and the fur-

Table 10: The Jhānas and the Arūpas in Relation to the Stages of the Path

The Jhānas and Arūpas	In Relation to the Stages of the Path
1st Rūpa Jhāna	The change of lineage in disengaging from sensory consciousness = *temporary* experience of first **sotāpanna**, stream-enterer stage. Dosa/lobha/moha (ill will/greed/delusion) suspended and held in check by activity of vitakka and vicāra, although still nearby as near-enemies.
2nd Rūpa Jhāna	Pīti and all bodily disturbance progressively tranquilized; any tendency to disturbance through dosa or lobha quickly mastered by passaddhi = temporary **sakadāgāmin**, once-returner.
3rd Rūpa Jhāna	"Fully conscious" = no falling back. No trace of dosa or lobha remains within the jhāna = temporary **anāgāmin**, non-returner.
4th Rūpa Jhāna	Equanimity, upekkhā, fully developed, no longer any attachment based on naming, liking, disliking, wanting or not wanting = temporary **arahat**.
Infinity of Space	Experience of object pole as infinite removes enchantment with the world, establishing right view. If perfected (i.e., unlimited) = permanent **sotāpanna**.
Infinity of Consciousness	Experience of subject pole as infinite removes the "I" construct, and dosa and lobha related to that = permanent **sakadāgāmin** if perfected.
Nothingness	Detachment from both subject and object positions establishes freedom from attachment to the sensory world = permanent **anāgāmin** if perfected.
Neither Perception Nor Non-perception	No longer being drawn to perceive, or to not perceive, removes all attachment to any assumptions of a "self" = freedom = permanent **arahat** if perfected.

ther Paths. The question of "truly unbounded" is then very interesting; how can it be known to be so? Might it be the case that attainment of the Path at such a moment is the only sure way for that to be confirmed?

TRANSCENDENT DEPENDENT ORIGINATION

In the previous chapter, the Buddhist model of dependent origination and the neuroscience model of active inference were described as two formulations of the repetitive and cyclic nature of living within sensory consciousness. Disengaging from sensory consciousness therefore means that in the experience of the jhānas, a meditator breaks the cycle of dependent origination, at least for the duration of the jhāna. This also means that in that mode, new kamma is not made, since it is the repetitive cycle of response to the sensory world that leads to action choices based on prior experience—and kamma is essentially action. This is a related factor to the thesis of the jhānas as temporary experiences of the Path.

Dependent origination is usually qualified as mundane dependent origination, meaning it is a description of life within sensory consciousness. But there is another formulation known as transcendent dependent origination that describes in detail the processes that finally break the mundane cycle to reveal the Path. This is illustrated in Figure 50, and is my formulation based on Bhikkhu Bodhi's 1995 translation of the *Upanisa Sutta* of the Saṃyutta Nikāya. This detailed understanding of dependent origination is often referred to as the heart of the Buddha's teaching, as in the *Mahā-hatthipadopama Sutta*, in which the Buddha proclaims, "He who sees dependent arising sees the Dhamma; he who sees the Dhamma sees dependent arising."[13]

The lower circular series in Figure 50 is the same as that shown in the previous chapter (Figure 48) for the mundane process, except that in the *Upanisa Sutta* the stage "aging and death" is replaced by "dukkha (suffering)." In fact, in the Suttas, the formula for mundane dependent origination often ends with the refrain "with birth as condition, aging-and-death, sorrow, lamentation, pain, grief, and despair arise. Such is the origination of this entire mass of suffering."

Suffering by itself may lead to a deep unease and disillusionment with the repetitive patterns of striving based on wanting or not-wanting, but to trigger a radical new direction requires something more. The first link in the transcendent mode, "suffering is the supporting condition for faith,"[14] identifies the importance of encountering a teaching that can inspire faith sufficiently to stimulate effort in a new direction. Many meditators would recognize such a moment, either in encountering the Dhamma in written works or from hearing a talk, or more often by meeting a teacher with some connection to an authentic path.

Following this first step on the transcendent path—the arousing of saddhā, faith—there are then two ways, perhaps more, of interpreting the entire series of stages in Figure 50 that follow.

In the first, which I believe is the one described by Bhikkhu Bodhi, the stages pāmojja (gladdening), pīti, passaddhi, and sukha lead to the next stage, samādhi, the absorption of jhāna (it is unspecified whether this is the first rūpa jhāna or the whole series of the rūpa jhānas and arūpas). The subsequent stages are then progressive stages of insight, which at virāga, dispassion, become supramundane, meaning they have passed beyond the sensory, fine-material, or formless realms to become unconditioned. From here the four Paths unfold, culminating in vimutti, freedom, followed by the final stage of āsavakkayeñāṇa, knowledge of destruction of the āsavas, which can also be interpreted as looking back at all that has gone before.

The interrelatedness of stages described for the different models—the bojjhangas, the jhānas, the Eightfold Path, and now the links of transcendent dependent origination—allow for several more detailed interpretations, with the following most in correspondence with the discussion so far as described in Tables 8, 9, and 10.

Again starting from saddhā, faith, contact with an authentic path offers a degree of hope, gives relief from hopelessness, and establishes a new direction forward that gladdens the mind, pāmojja. The new direction forward is equivalent to establishing vitakka and vicāra, and together with gladdening (and when followed through) leads to the first rūpa jhāna. The next two links, pīti and passaddhi, describe development of the second rūpa jhāna, as detailed in Chapter 3, followed by sukha, bliss, for the third rūpa jhāna, as described in Chapter 4, and then samādhi for the fourth rūpa jhāna. In Chapter 5 we followed the tradition of the jhāna factors to name upekkhā as the characterizing factor of the fourth rūpa jhāna, but samādhi as fully developed concentration in the sense of the seventh factor of the Eightfold Path is equally valid.

So the right-facing arc in Figure 50 in this interpretation describes progression through the four rūpa jhānas, and the left-facing arc that then follows is concerned with the formless arūpa stages and their interrelatedness with the Paths as in Table 10.

The next stage then is ñāṇadassana, knowledge and vision "of things as they are," which corresponds to the dismantling of the habitual subject-object processes of "I" to realize a new level of reality in the first arūpa, the infinity of space, as a temporary experience of the first sotāpanna (stream-entry) Path, which, if the experience is truly boundless, will be a permanent realization. The next stage, nibbidā, disenchantment, then corresponds to the second arūpa, the infinity of consciousness, which effectively breaks the "spell" of "I" consciousness sufficiently to develop a temporary experience of the second Path of the sakadāgāmin, or once-returner—again, a permanent attainment if truly boundless.

Virāga, dispassion, then corresponds to the third arūpa, nothingness, where a meditator separates completely from both subject and object poles, with no clinging to either, as a temporary experience of the third Path of the anāgāmin, or non-returner—once again, permanent if truly unbounded.

Virāga is followed by vimutti, freedom, corresponding to the freedom from all attachment in the fourth arūpa of neither perception nor non-perception and the stage of the fully realized arahat.

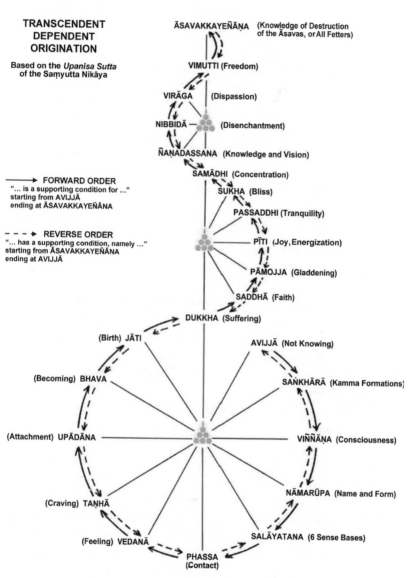

Fig. 50. Transcendent dependent origination.

The final stage, āsavakkayeñāṇa, knowledge of the destruction of the āsavas, or all fetters, is the stage of looking back at everything that has led up to the final stage of completion. In the case of the Buddha's own experience, this would correspond to the second week after his enlightenment when he stood to face the Bodhi tree from a distance to reflect for seven days on everything that had gone before, "unmoving and with steady gaze."[15]

For the Buddha, the "looking back" would have included not only what had gone before in his current life, but all preceding lives also. Although in that sense and in the scheme of transcendent dependent origination it represents the peak of realization, the practice of recollection following formal meditation, described earlier in this book, is not unrelated as a starting point.

An Accelerated Path

The Yogāvacara with its focus on mastering jhāna has similarities to the Tibetan view of an accelerated Path that, in some circumstances, might be completed in one lifetime. This idea of an accelerated path is very different from the view that prevailed during the Buddhist reforms of the 1830s in Thailand that the Path was already lost.

The possibility of an accelerated path lies in the capacity or quality of jhāna to "disperse" (Pāli, apacaya-gāmiṃ) kamma. This process is almost alchemical in nature and is related to many repeated sequences of disengagement from sensory consciousness into the stillness of jhāna consciousness, where the normal processes of action—and therefore creation of more kamma—are temporarily suspended. The repeated "frictions" created in this process appear to loosen subtle memories of past actions and experiences mostly held in the body, not unlike, but seemingly more powerful than, the effect of psychoanalysis on suppressed memories.

This is quite a challenge to a lay meditator. One may find oneself working through issues of kamma brought into consciousness sooner than might otherwise happen. However, in both traditions, Tibetan and Yogāvacara, there appears to be an embodied understanding of how to manage such experiences within the Saṅgha, whether a monastic Saṅgha or a lay Saṅgha. Also, given the detailed understanding of the jhāna factor pīti common to both traditions, it may also be a factor that the near-automatic ability to tranquilize and incorporate pīti into deeper stillness may also allow the emergence of such deeper karmic effects to be managed in a similar manner.

In this way, if episodes of powerful emotions from the past do resurface, they can dissolve on their own if viewed with a degree of equanimity.

Reflecting on how pre-reform practices have re-emerged in this tradition over the last almost sixty years, I am struck by three themes in particular that I believe highlight what was almost lost in the "reforms," but which have been firmly re-established. The most significant has to be the importance given to balancing mindfulness and concentration, which is my earliest recollection of how Nai Boonman introduced these practices in the 1960s. Based on the discussions in this book, I believe this apparently simple instruction carries the essence of the "twin kammaṭṭhāna" of the Yogāvacara. When embarking on practice, "concentration" stands for establishing an initial reference point, vitakka, while "mindfulness" establishes the necessary context and salience, dhammavicaya or vicāra, without which a still point of concentration is in fact meaningless.

And when practice comes to fulfilment in the experience of jhāna, concentration and mindfulness have become perfectly balanced and unified samatha and vipassanā, reminiscent of superposed states in quantum theory, which resolve at the moment of emergence into direct seeing, even paññā. Even the minimal goal of experiencing just the first rūpa jhāna makes the significance of this balance between concentration and mindfulness, between samatha and vipassanā, vividly clear, and highlights how neglecting this balance, as in the reforms that dispensed with jhāna meditation, can have far-reaching consequences.

The second theme related to this is the role of pīti in energizing and effectively waking the body to become fully incorporated into a mind-body samādhi, where "nothing is left out," while the third theme is the ancient skill of using different lengths of breath to facilitate disengagement from sensory consciousness.

The "reforms" of the 1830s and 1950s onward came very close to destroying centuries-old practices, particularly jhāna meditation, at the heart of the Buddhist Path for over 2,500 years. It is somewhat ironic that the damage caused by those reforms, rationalized as more modern and "scientific," might only now be in the process of being repaired, aided by detailed understandings of brain processes from the most recent (scientific) developments in neuroscience in this twenty-first century.

Notes

Preface

1. Various scholars have explored the effects of the "reforms"; see for example McCargo (2012), who writes of the changing politics of Saṅgha affairs during this period.

Introduction

1. The Abhidhamma is the third of the three divisions of Buddhist texts: the Suttas, or discourses of the Buddha; the Vinaya rules and ethical code of conduct; and the Abhidhamma, or higher doctrine. It was composed by a Sri Lankan monk, Ācariya Anuruddha, sometime between the eighth and twelfth centuries.
2. The original work was published in Pāli and Sinhala (Rhys Davids 1896) and later translated into English as *Manual of a Mystic* (Woodward 1916), both by the Pāli Text Society. Many believe the original work to date back to the eighteenth century following the Thai mission to Sri Lanka in 1753 to re-establish the lost ordination line, with the new ordination line being referred to as the Siam Nikāya.
3. *The Path of Lanka* (Bizot 1992) is one of several publications of l'École française d'Extrême-Orient based on analysis of palm-leaf manuscripts found mostly in Cambodia. More recent boran kammaṭṭhāna research conducted by academics and ethnologists can be found in Crosby (2000; 2013; 2021).
4. At the time of writing this book (mid-2021), the paper (Dennison 2019) had attracted over 15,000 reads, placing it in the top 5% of all research outputs worldwide scored by Altimetric; it can be downloaded for free at www.frontiersin.org/articles/10.3389/fnhum.2019.00178/full.

CHAPTER 1. INVOCATION

1. The Vinaya is believed to have been recited by Upāli, one of the chief disciples, at the First Council not long after the Buddha's death. For a description of the 227 rules for monks, see Pruitt (2001).
2. These and other material on chanting can be found in the Samatha Trust's Chanting Book, available at www.samatha.org.
3. See for example Phra Chuntawongso, "Samanera Ordination Chanting in Pali-Thai," *Dhamma Wheel Buddhist Forum*, www.dhammawheel. com/viewtopic.php?p=95604&sid=dcddc93443f43dc4c09f8e6291d-e1267#p95604, May 2, 2010.
4. For an introduction to Buddhism and the Noble Eightfold Path see Harvey (2013), and for a discussion of the interrelated nature of the jhānas and the bojjhaṅgas see Dennison (2020).
5. *Ānāpānasati Sutta,* Majjhima Nikāya 118, translated from the Pāli by Ñāṇamoli Thera (1952, p. 3).

CHAPTER 2. THE FIRST RŪPA JHĀNA: ATTENTION, VITAKKA, AND VICĀRA

1. *The Path of Lanka* and the *Yogāvacara's Manual* appear to be more aligned to a later fivefold model of the jhānas described in the eighth–twelfth-century Abhidhamma, which will be described later in Chapter 5.
2. The jhāna formulas or "pericopes" appear frequently in the Buddhist Nikāyas, and the Pāli extracts for the four rūpa jhānas in Chapters 2 through 5 are from the *Samaññaphala Sutta*, Digha Nikāya 2 (PTS D i 47). English translations vary slightly, and those in this book are from the *The Path of Purification: Visuddhimagga* (Buddhaghosa 1999).
3. This was pointed out by Cousins (1973).
4. My interest in the Bu Ddho technique paralleled my interest in techniques for arousing strong pīti from the late 1960s. My understanding was later greatly helped by exchanging experiences with older monks I met in the late 1970s while practicing in Ajahn Thate's monastery, Wat Hing Mak Peng, in the far north of Thailand, and later in 1992 as a monk in rural Suphanburi, Thailand.
5. Trungpa (1995, p. 69.)
6. This process of using the nimitta as a guide predates modern understandings of neurofeedback by over two and a half millennia, on which see Dennison (2012b).

7. The thirteen dhutaṅgas are (1) wearing patched robes; (2) wearing only three robes; (3) going for alms; (4) not omitting any house on the alms round; (5) eating at one sitting; (6) eating only from the alms bowl; (7) refusing any further food; (8) living in the forest; (9) living under a tree; (10) living in the open air; (11) living in a cemetery; (12) being satisfied with any dwelling; and (13) sleeping in a sitting position. See also Khantipalo Bhikkhu (1965).

8. *Visuddhimagga* VIII (Buddhaghosa [1999, p. 184]).]

9. Driver distraction is an example of conflicted attention and does not necessarily imply that a driver is drowsy, and so is a different mode to the early stages of sleep (Sonnleitner et al., 2012).

CHAPTER 3. THE SECOND RŪPA JHĀNA: PĪTI, ENERGIZATION

1. This extract is from an exposition of, and commentary on, the *Upanisa Sutta* (Saṃyutta Nikāya 12.23) by Bhikkhu Bodhi (1980, p. 11).

2. The phrase "door of the eye" is easily understood when the object of meditation is one of the kasinas, an external object, where it is literally via the eyes and normal vision that the parikamma nimitta begins to develop.

3. *Tummo* as a method to arouse heat has also attracted interest in neuroscience quarters, as in Kozhevnikov et al. (2013).

CHAPTER 4. THE THIRD RŪPA JHĀNA: SUKHA, "FULLY CONSCIOUS"

1. A fuller description of the khandhās can be found in either Gethin (1986) or Harvey (2021).

2. There are many possible references to writings on the Buddhist Abhidhamma, but Bhikkhu Bodhi's (2000) authoritative work is particularly comprehensive.

3. Interoception is the perception of sensations from inside the body and includes the perception of physical sensations related to internal organ function such as heartbeat, respiration, and satiety, as well as the autonomic nervous system activity related to emotions (Price and Hooven 2018).

4. I am grateful for conversations with Peter Harvey as helpful in clarifying my understanding of kāya. See also Harvey (1995, 116–17).

5. *Visuddhimagga* IV (Buddhaghosa [1999, p. 155]).

6. There are many practices that aim to link the qualities of the Buddha to a meditator's own body, of which the embedding or placing of syllables described in boran kammaṭṭhāna texts is just one example. It is likely these have varied across time and location according to specific interests of indi-

vidual teachers. Two important examples are visualization and internalization of the qualities of a Buddha image, familiar to many practitioners in the Samatha Trust tradition, and sometimes augmented by relating different aspects to the "32 Marks of the Great Man" (e.g., in the *Brahmāyu Sutta*, Majjhima Nikāya 91).

7. *Vimuttimagga* VIII (Upatissa [1961, p. 108]).

CHAPTER 5. THE FOURTH RŪPA JHĀNA: UPEKKHĀ

1. *Visuddhimagga* IV (Buddhaghosa [1999, pp. 154–55]).
2. *Vimuttimagga* VIII (Upatissa [1961, p. 111]).
3. *Visuddhimagga* IV (Buddhaghosa [1999, p. 154]).
4. *Vimuttimagga* VIII (Upatissa [1961, p. 112]).

CHAPTER 6. SUMMARY OF THE FOUR RŪPA JHĀNAS

1. The terms *Deva* and *Brahmā* relate to Buddhist cosmology models of different planes of existence; see for example Kloetzli (1983).
2. The wake-sleep transition in neuroscience is still the subject of much research and is not yet fully understood; see Blumberg et al. (2014).

CHAPTER 7. TWILIGHT LANGUAGE, SYLLABLES, AND YANTRAS

1. Leibnitz (1896, p. 368).
2. This quotation comes very early in Freud's work, in his *Psychical (or Mental) Treatment* (1890, p. 283).
3. Suppes and colleagues (1997) pioneered the study of brain activity correlates of individual words.
4. The extracts from the Theravada Buddhist chants here are readily available from multiple sources online—see for example the Samatha Trust's Chanting Book, available at www.samatha.org, or the website of Amaravati Buddhist monastery, www.amaravati.org.
5. The translation of this extract from the *Mahātaṇhāsaṅkhaya Sutta*, Majjhima Nikāya 38, is taken from Nyanatiloka Thera (1998, s.v. Sikkhāpada, moral rules).

CHAPTER 8. THE FIRST ARŪPA JHĀNA: INFINITY OF SPACE

1. The immaterial states are mentioned in several suttas, for example the *Anupada Sutta* in Majjhima Nikāya 111 (PTS: M iii 25) translated by Thanissaro Bhikkhu, 2007, and available at www.accesstoinsight.org/tipitaka/mn/mn.111.than.html

2. *The Sallekha Sutta*, Majjhima Nikāya 8 (PTS M i 40).
3. From Bhikkhu Bodhi's (2000) guide to stanzas 22–24, section I of the Abhidhammattha Sangaha.

CHAPTER 9. THE SECOND ARŪPA JHĀNA: INFINITY OF CONSCIOUSNESS

1. Govinda (1969, p. 116).

CHAPTER 11. THE FOURTH ARŪPA JHĀNA: NEITHER PERCEPTION NOR NON-PERCEPTION

1. See for example Crosby (2021), or the various works by Bizot under the umbrella of l'École française d'Extrême-Orient, including *The Path of Lanka* (1992).

CHAPTER 12. NEUROSCIENCE OF THE JHĀNAS

1. Loreta analysis—or its latest version, e-Loreta (Pascual-Marqui 2002; 2007)—is a rather beautiful mathematical algorithm that translates EEG surface activity from n electrodes into the same number n of underlying cortical sources, in decreasing order of significance, responsible for the surface scalp electrical activity. For the analysis of spindles or infraslow waves described in the published paper (Dennison 2019), this equates to thirty-one possible cortical sources, of varying significance.
2. The attention/perception streams of neuroscience have been well researched in the field, originally to understand the visual processing pathways but in recent years to understand attention and perception processes more generally. See, for example, Petersen and Posner (2012) and Milner (2017).
3. Such intensities are unprecedented in neuroscience and EEG studies, to the extent that a preliminary report on this study in 2017 was rejected out of hand by a well-known academic journal whose peer reviewers simply did not believe these levels of intensity. It is to the credit of the *Frontiers* group of journals that their more experienced reviewers endorsed the much longer 2019 paper after careful peer review of the detailed analysis.
4. It is no accident that in everyday sensory consciousness it is the visual cortex that carries perhaps the bulk of the role of the subject position, in comparison to the other sensory modes, either in actually seeing and monitoring "the world" or in visualizing possibilities or ideas.
5. Spike-waves are well-known in epilepsy studies, but those that occur in meditation are significantly different, as described in the published

study (Dennison 2019). See also the further discussion in Chapter 13, "Consciousness."

6. Early in the history of EEG it was realized that electrical activity fell into frequency "bands" rather than being spread across all frequencies, which gave rise to the following conventions: delta δ band ~1–4 Hz; theta θ band ~4.5–7.5 Hz; alpha α band ~8–12 Hz; beta β band ~15–30 Hz; and gamma λ band ~35–150 Hz or higher.

7. During preparation of the published EEG study, it was interesting to find that parallel developments in neuroscience models of active-inference (Seth and Friston 2016) were also becoming interested in the idea of "presence."

8. For more information on the ascending reticular activating system (ARAS) see Maldonato (2014), and for the posterior cingulate see Herbet et al. (2014).

9. See Laborde et al. (2017) for more information on the measurement of heart-rate variability.

CHAPTER 13. CONSCIOUSNESS

1. Wallace (1999, p. 176).

2. Many scholars have debated whether Buddhism should be regarded as a religion, a philosophy, or a science, and it may be one or another or all of these to different people at different times.

3. *Dhammapada*, verse 392 (trans. Daw Mya Tin, 1986).

4. This extract is from Majjhima Nikāya 115, trans. Bodhi and Ñāṇamoli (1995, p. 927). In Pāli, it reads: *imasmiṃ sati idaṃ hoti, imassuppādā idaṃ uppajjati, imasmiṃ asati idaṃ ha hoti, imassa nirodhā idaṃ nirujjhati.*

5. Saṃyutta Nikāya 12.2.

6. In 2010, Karl Friston published his free-energy theory to explain how self-organizing systems use the available energy as effectively as possible to prevent decay into chaos, and to resist the processes of entropy (Guevara et al. 2016).

7. Friston (2018, 8).

8. Following Friston's 2010 theory, creative developments rapidly followed, in particular regarding predictive and active inference models (e.g., Seth and Friston 2016) and the implications for consciousness (e.g., Solms and Friston 2018; Solms 2019).

9. Dennison (2021b) and the preprint https://doi.org/10.31219/osf.io/djsk6 enlarges on some of these ideas.

10. For more on Markov blankets see Kirchhoff et al. (2018) and Friston et al. (2020).

11. There appears to be some kind of intuitive understanding of harmonics and hierarchies in Buddhist cosmology, even though it is far from understood; see Suvanno (2001) for example.

12. The word "mind" is used here, even though not clearly defined, as a less limited term than the impermanent and largely illusory experience of "I" (see below) in default sensory consciousness, closer to an idea of a core sense of self.

13. This translation of the *Rohitassa Sutta* from the Anguttara Nikāya 4.45 (PTS: A ii 47) by Thanissaro Bhikkhu (1997) is available at https://www.accesstoinsight.org/tipitaka/an/ano4/ano4.045.than.html.

14. Lancaster (1997, p. 129).

15. *Vimuttimagga* (Upatissa [1961, p. 204]).

Chapter 14. An Ancient Path

1. Brahmāli (2007, p. 86).

2. McCargo (2012, p. 627).

3. Erik Braun (2014), for example, describes how British colonial rule triggered a new populist vipassanā movement in an attempt to make meditation more widely accessible to the masses in Burma and to restore a semblance of Buddhist identity, in reaction to Western pressures similar to those in Mongkut's Thailand in the 1830s.

4. Mahāsi Sayadaw ([1945] 2016, p. 45).

5. Mahāsi Sayadaw ([1945] 2016, p. 46).

6. Mahāsi Sayadaw ([1971] 1998, p. 24).

7. For a description of how these processes play out across the hierarchies in teams, particularly in community mental health teams, see Dennison and Carson (2008) and Dennison (2012a).

8. The ways in which language can be manipulated, mostly unconsciously, often underpin the mechanisms of intentional forgetting and self-delusion; see for example Dennison (1997).

9. This was described by Kluge and Gronau (2018) as a strategy in some organizations to minimize connections to obsolete ideas to allow new directions to emerge.

10. This translation of an excerpt from the *Nagara Sutta*, Saṃyutta Nikāya 12.65 (PTS: S ii 104), is taken from Kornfield (2008), available at jackkornfield.com/finding-the-middle-way.

11. This is F. L. Woodward's translation of the *Gaṅgā Peyyala Sutta*, Saṃyutta Nikāya 53.1, available at https://obo.genaud.net/dhamma-vinaya/pts/sn/05_mv/sn05.53.001-012.wood.pts.htm.

12. *Vimuttimagga* (Upatissa [1961, p. 308]).

13. This extract is taken from Bhikkhu Thanissaro's (2003) translation of the *Mahā-hatthipadopama Sutta*, Majjhima Nikāya 28 (PTS: M i 184).

14. Bodhi, 1995.

15. This is described in Dennison (2020) as part of a discussion of the seventh bojjhaṅga.

BIBLIOGRAPHY

Amaravati Buddhist Monastery. *Chanting Book and Audio*. Hertfordshire: Amaravati Publications. https://amaravati.org/teachings/chanting/.

Aṅguttara Nikāya. 6 vols. London: Pali Text Society.

Bizot, François. 1992. *Le Chemin de Lanka*. Paris: l'École française d'Extrême-Orient.

Blumberg, M. S., A. J. Gall, and W. D. Todd. 2014. "The Development of Sleep-Wake Rhythms and the Search for Elemental Circuits in the Infant Brain." *Behavioural Neuroscience* 128 (3). doi: 10.1037/a0035891.

Bodhi, Bhikkhu. 1980. *Transcendent Dependent Arising: A Translation and Exposition of the Upanisa Sutta*. Kandy: Buddhist Publication Society. https://www.accesstoinsight.org/tipitaka/sn/sn12/sn12.023.bodh.html.

Bodhi, Bhikkhu. 2000. *A Comprehensive Manual of Abhidhamma: The Abhidhammattha Sangaha of Acariya Anuruddha*. Washington: BPS Pariyatti. www.saraniya.com/books/meditation/Bhikkhu_Bodhi-Comprehensive_Manual_of_Abhidhamma.pdf.

Bodhi, Bhikkhu, and Bhikkhu Ñāṇamoli. 1995. *The Bahudhātuka Sutta*. In *Majjhima Nikāya: The Middle Length Discourses of the Buddha*. Kandy: Buddhist Publication Society, p. 927.

Brahmāli, Bhikkhu. 2007. "Jhāna and Lokuttara-jhāna." *Buddhist Studies Review* 24 (1): 75–90. doi: 10.1558/bsrv.v24i1.75.

Braun, Erik. 2013. *The Birth of Insight: Meditation, Modern Buddhism, and the Burmese Monk Ledi Sayadaw*. Chicago: University of Chicago Press.

Bucknell, Roderick S., and Martin Stuart-Fox. 1986. *The Twilight Language: Explorations in Buddhist Language and Symbolism*. London: Curzon Press.

Buddhaghosa (5th cent.). 1999. *The Path of Purification: Visuddhimagga*. Translated from the Pāli by Bhikkhu Ñāṇamoli. Onalaska, WI: Pariyatti Publishing.

Chögyam Trungpa. 1995. "The Path Is the Goal." In *The Collected Works of Chögyam Trungpa*, Vol. 2. Boston: Shambhala Publications.

Cousins, L. S. 1973. "Buddhist Jhāna: Its Nature and Attainment According to Pāli Sources." *Religion* 3:115–31.

Crosby, Kate. 2000. "Tantric Theravāda: A Bibliographic Essay on the Writings of Françoise Bizot and Others on the Yogāvacara Tradition." *Contemporary Buddhism* 1 (2). doi: 10.1080/14639940008573729.

Crosby, Kate. 2013. *Traditional Theravāda Meditation and Its Modern-Era Suppression*. Hong Kong: Buddhist Dhamma Center of Hong Kong.

Crosby, Kate. 2021. *Esoteric Theravada: The Story of the Forgotten Meditation Tradition of Southeast Asia*. Boulder, CO: Shambala.

Daw Mya Tin, trans. 2019. *The Dhammapada: Verses and Stories*. Kandy: Buddhist Publication Society; first published, Rangoon: Burma Pitaka Association, 1986.

Dennison, Paul. 1997. "Language and Defence, and the Self-Representation." Essay, Regent's College School of Psychotherapy. doi: 10.13140/RG.2.1.4233.4885.

Dennison, Paul. 2012a. "Psychodynamic Staff Support Groups: Avoiding Burnout." *ResearchGate*, doi: 10.13140/RG.2.1.2954.5129.

Dennison, Paul. 2012b. *Quantum Mind: Meditation and Brain Science*. Paendim Dhamma Foundation. Bangkok: Sangsilp Press. https://osf. io/qdeyc/.

Dennison, Paul. 2019. "The Human Default Consciousness and Its Disruption: Insights from an EEG Study of Buddhist Jhāna Meditation." *Frontiers in Human Neuroscience* 13:178. doi: 10.3389/fnhum.2019.00178.

Dennison, Paul. 2020. *The Seven Bojjhaṅgās: The Buddhist Factors of Enlightenment, the Jhānas and Days of the Week Buddha Images*. London: Itipiso Publications.

Dennison, Paul, ed. 2021a. *Perspectives on Consciousness*. New York: Nova Science.

Dennison, Paul. 2021b. "The Human Default Consciousness, Jhāna Consciousness, Gaia 'Consciousness' and Some Thoughts on the Covid-19 Pandemic." In *Perspectives on Consciousness*, edited by P. Dennison. New York: Nova Science. https://doi.org/10.31219/osf.io/djsk6.

Dennison, Paul, and Jerome Carson. 2008. "The Role of Groupwork in Tackling Organizational Burnout: Two Contrasting Perspectives." *Groupwork* 18 (2): 8–25. doi: 10.1921/81122.

Dīgha Nikāya. 3 vols. London: Pali Text Society.

Freud, Sigmund. 1890. *Psychical (or Mental) Treatment*. Vol. 7 of *The Standard Edition of the Complete Psychological Works of Sigmund Freud*, edited by James Strachey, Anna Freud, Alix Strachey, and Alan Tyson. London: Hogarth Press.

Freud, Sigmund. 1895. *Project for a Scientific Psychology*. Vol. 1 of *The Standard Edition of the Complete Psychological Works of Sigmund Freud*, edited by James Strachey, Anna Freud, Alix Strachey, and Alan Tyson. London: Hogarth Press.

Friston, Karl J. 2010. "The Free-Energy Principle: A Unified Brain Theory?" *Nature Reviews Neuroscience* 11:127–39. doi: 10.1038/nrn2787.

Friston, Karl J. 2018. "Am I Self-Conscious? (Or Does Self-Organization Entail Self-Consciousness?)." *Frontiers in Psychology* 9 (579): 1–10. doi: 10.3389/fpsyg.2018.00579.

Friston, Karl J., Erik D. Fagerholm, Tahereh S. Zarghami, Thomas Parr, et al. 2020. "Parcels and Particles: Markov Blankets in the Brain." *Network Neuroscience*, doi: 10.1162/netn_a_00175.

Gethin, Rupert. 1986. "The Five Khandhās: Their Treatment in the Nikāyas and Early Abhidhamma." *Journal of Indian Philosophy* 14:35–53.

Gethin, Rupert. 1998. *The Foundations of Buddhism*. Oxford: Oxford University Press.

Govinda, Lama Anagarika 1969. *Foundations of Tibetan Mysticism*. New York: Red Wheel/Weiser.

Guevara-Erra, Ramon, Diego M. Mateos, Richard Wennberg, and Jose L. Perez Velazquez. 2016. "Statistical Mechanics of Consciousness: Maximization of Information Content of Network Is Associated with Conscious Awareness." *Physical Review E* 94, doi:10.1103/PhysRevE.94.052402.

Harvey, Peter. 1995. *The Selfless Mind: Personality, Consciousness and Nirvana in Early Buddhism*. Richmond, U.K.: Curzon Press.

Harvey, Peter. 2013. *An Introduction to Buddhism: Teachings, History and Practices*. 2nd ed. Cambridge: Cambridge University Press.

Harvey, Peter. 2021. "The Nature and Roles of Consciousness in Theravāda Buddhism." In *Perspectives on Consciousness*, edited by Paul Dennison. New York: Nova Science.

Herbet, Guillaume, Gilles Lafargue, Nicolas Menjot de Champfleur, Sylvie Moritz-Gasser, et al. 2014. "Disrupting Posterior Cingulate Connectivity Disconnects Consciousness from the External Environment." *Neuropsychologia* 56:239–44. doi: 10.1016/j.neuropsychologia.2014.01.020.

Kapur, Indrani. 1979. "Studies in Early Buddhist Symbolism and Metaphysics: Change and Continuity in Indian Religious and Philosophic Thought." PhD thesis, Australian National University (Canberra).

Khantipalo Bhikkhu. 1965. *With Robes and Bowl: Glimpses of the Thudong Bhikkhu Life.* Wheel Publications 83/84. Kandy: Buddhist Publication Society.

Kirchhoff, Michael, Thomas Parr, Ensor Palacios, Karl Friston, and Julian Kiverstein. 2018. "The Markov Blankets of Life: Autonomy, Active Inference and the Free Energy Principle." *Journal of the Royal Society Interface,* doi: 10.1098/rsif.2017.0792.

Kloetzli, W. Randolph. 1983. *Buddhist Cosmology: Science and Theology in the Images of Motion and Light.* Delhi: Motilal Banarsidass.

Kluge, Annette, and Norbert Gronau. 2018. "Intentional Forgetting in Organizations: The Importance of Eliminating Retrieval Cues for Implementing New Routines." *Frontiers in Psychology* 9 (51). doi: 10.3389/fpsyg.2018.00051.

Kornfield, Jack. 2008. *The Wise Heart.* London: Rider.

Kozhevnikov, Maria, James Elliott, Jennifer Shephard, and Klaus Grammasn. 2013. "Neurocognitive and Somatic Components of Temperature Increases during G-Tummo Meditation: Legend and Reality." *Plos One* 8 (3). doi: 10.1371/journal.pone.0058244.

Laborde, Sylvain, Emma Mosley, and Julian F. Thayer. 2017. "Heart Rate Variability and Cardiac Vagal Tone in Psychophysiological Research: Recommendations for Experiment Planning, Data Analysis, and Data Reporting." *Frontiers in Psychology* 8 (219), doi: 10.3389/fpsyg.2017.00213.

Lancaster, Brian L. 1997. "On the Stages of Perception: Towards a Synthesis of Cognitive Neuroscience and the Buddhist Abhidhamma Tradition." *Journal of Consciousness Studies* 4 (2): 122–42.

Leibniz, Gottfried Wilhelm. 1707. Reprint 1896. *New Essays Concerning Human Understanding.* Translated by Alfred G. Langley. New York: Macmillan. https://archive.org/details/cu31924032296422/page/n163/mode/2up.

Lichtenberg, Georg Christoph. (1742–99) 1990. *Aphorisms.* New York: Penguin.

Mahāsi Sayadaw. (1945) 2016. *Manual of Insight.* New York: Wisdom Publications.

Mahāsi Sayadaw. (1971) 1998. *Practical Insight Meditation.* Kandy: Buddhist Publication Society.

Majjhima Nikāya. 4 vols. London: Pāli Text Society.

Maldonato, Nelson M. 2014. "The Ascending Reticular Activating System: The Common Root of Consciousness and Attention." In *Recent Advances of Neural Network Models and Applications*. Proceedings of the 23rd Workshop, Italian Neural Networks Society. doi: 10.1007/978-3-319-04129-2_33.

McCargo, Duncan. 2012. "The Changing Politics of Thailand's Buddhist Order." *Critical Asian Studies* 44 (4): 627–42. doi: 10.1080/14672715.2012.738544.

Milner, David. 2017. "How Do the Two Visual Streams Interact with Each Other?" *Experimental Brain Research* 235 (5): 1297–1308. doi: 10.1007/s00221-017-4917-4.

Ñāṇamoli, Bhikkhu. (1952) 2010. *Mindfulness of Breathing (Ānāpānasati): Buddhist Texts from the Pāli Canon*. Kandy: Buddhist Publication Society.

Nhat Hanh, Thich. 2008. *Breathe, You Are Alive: The Sutta on the Full Awareness of Breathing*. New York: Parallax Press.

Nyanatiloka Thera. 1998. *Buddhist Dictionary: Manual of Buddhist Terms and Doctrines*. Kandy: Buddhist Publication Society.

Pascual-Marqui, Roberto D. 2002. "Standardized Low Resolution Brain Electromagnetic Tomography (sLoreta): Technical Details." *Methods and Findings in Experimental and Clinical Pharmacology* 24D:5–12.

Pascual-Marqui, Roberto D. 2007. "Discrete, 3D Distributed, Linear Imaging Methods of Electric Neuronal Activity. Part 1: Exact, Zero Error Localization." Link to PDF available at https://arxiv.org/abs/0710.3341v2.

Pearl, Judea. 1988. *Probabilistic Reasoning in Intelligent Systems: Networks of Plausible Inference*. San Mateo, CA: Morgan Kaufmann.

Petersen, Steven E., and Michael I. Posner. 2012. "The Attention System of the Brain: 20 Years After." *Annual Review of Neuroscience* 35:73–89. doi: 10.1146/annurev-neuro-062111-150-525.

Price, Cynthia J., and Carole Hooven. 2018. "Interoceptive Awareness Skills for Emotion Regulation: Theory and Approach of Mindful Awareness in Body-Oriented Therapy (MABT)." *Frontiers in Psychology* 9:798. doi: 10.3389/fpsyg.2018.00798.

Pruitt, William, ed. 2001. *The Pāṭimokkha: Sacred Books of the Buddhists* 49. Translated by K. R. Norman. London: Pāli Text Society.

Rhys Davids, Thomas W., ed. 1896. *The Yogāvacara's Manual of Indian*

Mysticism as Practiced by Buddhists [Pāli and Sinhala]. London: Pali Text Society. For an English translation, see Woodward 1916.

The Samatha Trust, UK reg. charity (CIO) no. 1179867, www.samatha. org.

Saṃyutta Nikāya. 6 vols. London: Pali Text Society.

Seth, Anil K., and Friston, Karl J. 2016. "Active Interoceptive Inference and the Emotional Brain." *Philosophical Transactions of the Royal Society: Biological Sciences* 371:20160007. doi: 10.1098/rstb.2016.0007.

Solms, Mark. 2019. "The Hard Problem of Consciousness and the Free Energy Principle." *Frontiers in Psychology* 9:2714. doi: 10.3389/fpsyg.2018.02714.

Solms, Mark, and Karl J. Friston. 2018. "How and Why Consciousness Arises: Some Considerations from Physics and Physiology." *Journal of Consciousness Studies* 25 (5–6): 202–38.

Sonnleitner, Andreas, Michael Simon, Wilhelm E. Kincses, Axel Buchner, and Michael Schrauf. 2012. "Alpha Spindles as Neurophysiological Correlates Indicating Attentional Shift in a Simulated Driving Task." *International Journal of Psychophysiology* 83:110–18. doi: 10.1016/j. ijpsycho.2011.10.013.

Stuart-Fox, Martin. 1989. "Jhāna and Buddhist Scholasticism." *Journal of the International Association of Buddhist Studies* 12 (2): 79–110.

Suppes, Patrick, Zhong-Lin Lu, and Bing Han. 1997. "Brain-Wave Representations of Words." *Proceedings of the US National Academy of Sciences* 94:14965–69.

Suvanno Mahathera. 2001. *The Thirty-One Planes of Existence.* Penang, Malaysia: Inward Path.

Thanissaro Bhikkhu, trans. 1997. *Rohitassa Sutta: To Rohitassa.* Access to Insight, https://www.accesstoinsight.org/tipitaka/an/an04/ an04.045.than.html.

Thanissaro Bhikkhu, trans. 2003. *Mahā-hatthipadopama Sutta: The Great Elephant Footprint Simile.* Available from Access to Insight, https://www.accesstoinsight.org/tipitaka/mn/mn.028.than.html.

Upatissa Thera (3rd cent.). 1961. *Path of Freedom: Vimuttimagga.* Translated from the Chinese by N. R. M. Ehara, Soma Thera, and Kheminda Thera. Maharagama, Sri Lanka: Saman Press.

Wallace, B. Alan 1999. "The Buddhist Tradition of Samatha: Methods for Refining and Examining Consciousness." *Journal of Consciousness Studies* 6 (2–3): 175–87.

Woodward, Frank L., trans. 1916. *Manual of a Mystic*. London: Pāli Text Society.

Woodward, Frank L., trans. (1930) 2015. *Gaṅgā-Peyyālo Sutta*, Saṃyutta Nikāya, Vol. 1. London: Pāli Text Society.

Pāli texts and translations of the Aṅguttara, Dīgha, Khuddikā, Majjhima, and Saṃyutta Nikāyas are available from the Pāli Text Society, www .palitext.com, and Access to Insight, www.accesstoinwsight.com.

CREDITS

TEXTUAL EXTRACTS

Extracts from *The Path of Purification: Visuddhimagga* are reprinted with permission from Pariyatti Publishing.

Some of the neuroscience data and findings in this book first appeared in "The Human Default Consciousness and Its Disruption: Insights from an EEG Study of Buddhist Jhāna Meditation," ©2019 by Paul Dennison and published in *Frontiers in Human Neuroscience*.

Some of the neuroscience material in this book appeared in a different form in *Perspectives on Consciousness: Neuroscience Research Progress*. It is reprinted here with permission from Nova Science Publishers.

IMAGES

The chapter 14 frontispiece is based on "Autumn forest landscape, colorful nature" by Diabluses. ID 233698624. Photo licensed via Shutterstock.

Figure 45 is based on "Central Organ of Human Nervous System Brain Anatomy, 3D" by Magic mine. ID 1578720724. Image licensed via Shutterstock.

Figure 49 is based on "Silhouette man with brain graphic icon" by archivector. ID 1144058780. Image licensed via Shutterstock.

The photo at p. 30 and figures 7, 30, and 34 are in the public domain.

All other images are by the author, ©2022 by Paul Dennison.

INDEX